JOAN OF ARC

JOAN OF ARC

By Herself and Her Witnesses

RÉGINE PERNOUD

Translated from the French by Edward Hyams

SCARBOROUGH HOUSE
Lanham • New York • London

1994 edition with a new cover published by
SCARBOROUGH HOUSE
Lanham, MD 20706

A SCARBOROUGH BOOK REISSUE 1982

First Stein and Day Paperback edition 1969

First published in the United States of America by
STEIN AND DAY/ *Publishers*, 1966
This translation copyright © Macdonald & Co (Publishers) Ltd., 1964
First published in the French language in 1962 as
Jeanne d'Arc par elle-même et par ses témoins
Copyright © 1962 by Editions du Seuil

Printed in the United States of America

Library of Congress Cataloging in Publication Data

Pernoud, Regine, 1909-
Joan of Arc by herself and her witnesses.

"A Scarborough book."
Translation of: Jeanne d'Arc par elle-même et par ses temoins.
Includes index.
1. Joan, of Arc, Saint, 1412-1431. 2. Christian
saints — France — Biography. I. Title.
DC103.P3783 1982   944'.026'0924 [B]   82-19312

ISBN 13: 978-0-812-81260-2

To the Reverend Daniel S. Rankin

TRANSLATOR'S NOTE

The usual practice in translation is to try to put the work in question into good English while retaining as much as possible of the style and feel of the original. This may entail some departure from the most literal translation of the foreign language. I have not felt entitled to do much in that way with the fifteenth-century documents which Mlle. Pernoud has here put together to compose an absorbing narrative. Some of her witnesses spoke or wrote smoothly enough; in others there is an awkwardness, often an expression of personality or feeling, which it was clearly my duty to retain. I offer this brief explanation in order that not all the oddities of, for example, sentence construction be attributed by indignant critics and readers to me.

E.H.

INTRODUCTION

"Tuesday, the tenth day of May, it was reported and publicly said in Paris that on the Sunday last the Dauphin's people in great number had, after several and sustained assaults in arms, entered into the fortress held by William Glasdale and other English captains and men-at-arms of the King's, with the sortie tower of the Orleans bridge across the Loire, and that on this day the other captains and men-at-arms laying siege (to Orleans) and holding the forts across the river from Orleans had departed from the said forts and raised the siege to go to the comfort of the said Glasdale and his companions and to combat the enemies who had in their company a Maid alone bearing a banner in the midst of the said enemies, if it be as they say."

This account is entered in one of the registers of the Parliament of Paris, which even now comprise one of the most impressive collections to be found in the National Archives (more than twelve thousand parchment registers forming Series X.1A, the earliest of which go back to the thirteenth century). On the date when it was written, Tuesday, May 10, 1429, the clerk to the Parliament was Clement de Fauquembergue, an exact and conscientious scribe, who had acquired the habit of setting down the principal news of the day as well as the minutes of trials, pleas and other judicial business which it was his job to record; so much is this the case that the series of registers kept by him forms a sort of official journal for his time.

In the margin of his register, beside the above note, the clerk has drawn with his pen a little sketch; no more importance should be attributed to it than to the doodles with which we decorate the margins of our telephone books while waiting for a number; he had not seen Joan and knew no more about her than what he has told us; but this little drawing has nevertheless often had the honour of being reproduced in our time; and it is worthy of it, for it is the only effigy of the heroine, drawn during her lifetime, that we possess.

The account in question is, for all its brevity, rich in meaning.

Those whom Clement de Fauquembergue refers to as "the enemies" are the French. And if he, albeit clerk to the Parliament of Paris, calls them so, it is because at the time Paris had been for ten years in the hands of the occupying power, England. A brief reminder of the principal dates will be in place here: 1415, Agincourt—the French army wiped out, with seven thousand killed as against five hundred English, and 1,500 prisoners, including an illustrious member of the French royal family, Charles, Duke of Orleans. 1418, the English enter Paris with the complicity of the Duke of Burgundy, John the Fearless; the King, Charles VI, is mad, and the Queen, the all too celebrated Isabeau of Bavaria, plotting with the enemy. Henry V of Lancaster, King of England, figures not only as victor but almost as God-sent, to chastise the French for the evil vices which reign in their midst. Speaking of the French when he visited Charles of Orleans imprisoned in the Tower of London, Henry was to say "God wished to punish them". And indeed, and especially since 1392 when the King's intermittent madness first became manifest and he handed the kingdom over to various members of his family, France's rulers had shown only the worst possible kind of selfishness, taking advantage of the King's condition to satisfy their personal ambitions and the rivalries of hatred which so soon arose among them.

The future of the dynasty was but ill-ensured by a family showing clear symptoms of degeneracy: three dauphins, Charles, Louis and Jean, had died in succession between 1401 and 1417. Of Isabeau's six sons, the dauphin referred to by Fauquembergue, the future Charles VII, born 1403, was to be the sole survivor. It was the period when, in a phrase current at the time, "there is great pity in the Kingdom of France", given over to pillage, held to ransom by armed adventurers, ravaged by wars and by the epidemics which had followed one upon another for almost a century—since the Black Death in 1348.

We come then to the Treaty of Troyes, May 21, 1420, which disinherited the Dauphin Charles in favour of England's King, Henry V. On June 2nd following, Henry married a daughter of Charles VI and Isabeau, Catherine, whose sister Michelle was thereafter married to Philip the Good, Duke of Burgundy. Under their aegis there was established in France the so-called Double Monarchy—France and England united under the English crown; henceforth the lilies of France were quartered with the leopards of England in the royal arms.

But only two years later, on August 31, 1422, Henry died suddenly in the pride of youth and victory. A few weeks later, on October 21, Charles VI, an old man at fifty-three, followed him into the grave. These deaths left the ten-month-old heir, Henry VI, who had been born to Henry V and Catherine, confronting the prince still known as the Dauphin—subsequently Charles VII. But their respective strengths were not equally balanced; under the regency of the infant King's uncle, John, Duke of Bedford, England's dominion was firmly established in the Ile-de-France and in Normandy. If the territory controlled by the English be joined to that of their ally, the Duke of Burgundy, then all the north and east of France was Bedford's, whereas Charles was derisively called "The King of Bourges". Charles had dug himself in south of the Loire, in country still loyal to him; but elsewhere only a handful of places still held out against Anglo-Burgundian pressure: Mont St. Michel, which, in the midst of its waters, held the enemy at bay for forty years; the town of Tournai; the little city of Vaucouleurs; and, above all, Orleans, which commanded the principal bridge over the Loire.

It was, indeed, because Orleans represented, as it were, the boulevard of the invasion that the English were to attach so much importance to taking it. They were to send one of the most famous of their captains, Thomas Montague, Earl of Salisbury, to besiege the town (October 12, 1428), following a campaign during which, having made sure of their grip on Normandy and la Beauce, they proposed to lay hold of those parts beyond the Loire where they could hunt down the Dauphin Charles. Orleans was the indispensable crossing-place; the taking of Orleans would, therefore, be decisive. All this was happening against a background which is only too easy for those of us who lived through 1940–45 to understand: a France divided, rent in two, in which some had taken the side of the occupying power—they were called Burgundians—and others against—the Armagnacs. The latter were so called after Bernard d'Armagnac, Charles of Orleans's father-in-law, who had, for a time, headed the resistance; the nickname also makes manifest the loyalty of Southern France to the lawful dynasty.

The siege of Orleans was maintained but not pressed by a victorious invader who felt quite sure of himself. The town, reduced to starvation, had sent delegates to treat with the Duke of Burgundy, when the news broke like a peal of thunder: Orleans had been delivered. On Sunday, May 8, 1429, the English had raised the siege. How had this come about? Everyone was attributing the victory to the "Maid bearing a banner" mentioned by the clerk Clement de Fauquembergue. Who was she? Whence came she? What had been her life and exploits?

To these questions, asked by her contemporaries as well as by us and to whom true answers were even more important, let the historic documents themselves make answer.

CONTENTS

LIST OF PLATES
Following Page 128

JOAN OF ARC

ORIGINS AND CHILDHOOD

Question: Swear to tell the truth concerning what will be asked
you touching the faith and what you shall learn.

JOAN: Of my father, of my mother, and of all that I have done
since I arrived in France, I will willingly swear. . . .

Joan, on her knees and with both hands on the book, a missal,
swears that she will speak the truth about all that is asked of
her.

Question: What are your names and surnames (*surnoms*)?

JOAN: In my town they called me Jeannette, and since I came to
France I have been called Joan. As for my surname, I know
of none.

Question: Where were you born?

JOAN: I was born in the town of Domremy which makes one
with Greux. It is in the place of Greux that the principal church
is.

Question: The names of your father and mother?

JOAN: My father was called Jacques d'Arc and my mother Isabelle.

Question: Where were you baptised?

JOAN: In the church of Domremy.

Question: Who were your godfathers and godmothers?

JOAN: One of my godmothers was called Agnes, another Jeanne,
another Sibille; one of my godfathers was called Jean Lingue,
another Jean Barre; I had many other godfathers and godmothers,
as I have heard my mother say.

Question: Who was the priest who baptised you?

JOAN: Master Jean Minet, to the best of my belief.

Question: Is he still alive?

JOAN: Yes, I think so.

Question: How old are you?

JOAN: As far as I know, about nineteen years old. And it was from my mother that I learnt Pater Noster, Ave Maria, Credo. Nobody taught me my belief, if not my mother. (C38–41)

Question: Did you learn any trade in your youth?

JOAN: Yes, to sew linen cloths and to spin; for spinning and sewing let me alone against any woman in Rouen. . . . When I was in my father's house, I busied myself with the housework.

Question: Did you confess your sins every year?

JOAN: Yes, and to my parish priest*; and when he was unable I confessed to some other priest with his permission. Once or twice or thrice, as I think it was, I confessed to begging friars; that was in the town of Neufchâteau. And I received the sacrament of the Eucharist at the feast of Easter.

Question: Did you receive this sacrament of the Eucharist at feasts other than Easter?

JOAN: Pass over that. (C46)

The evidence here given by Joan herself was confirmed by the folk of Domremy who had known her from her infancy or childhood.

Jean Moreau, farmer of Greux, seventy years of age or thereabouts: "Jeannette, whom this concerns, was born at Domremy and baptised in the Church of Saint-Remy, a parish of that place. Her father was called Jacques d'Arc and her mother Isabelette, farmers, during their lifetime, at Domremy. From what I saw and knew, they were faithful Catholics and hard workers, of good repute and decent conversation, according to their condition; for several times I spoke with them. I was myself one of Jeanne's godfathers; she had for godmothers the wife of Etienne Royer, and Beatrice, widow of Estellin dwelling in the town of Domremy, and Jeannette, wife of Tiercelin de Viteau, dwelling in the town of Neufchâteau. Jeannette, in earliest youth, was well and properly brought up in the faith and good conduct and so much so that nearly all the inhabitants of Domremy loved her. And Jeannette knew her belief, the Our Father, the Hail Mary, as little girls of her age know it.

"Jeannette was of seemly converse so far as a girl of her condition can be, for her parents were not very rich. And in her youth and until the time when she left her father's house, she went to the fields to plough and sometimes guarded the animals in the fields, and did women's work, spinning and the rest. Jeannette would go often and of her own will to the church and to the hermitage of Notre

* *curé.*

Dame de Bermont near to the town of Domremy, when her parents thought that she was ploughing or working elsewhere in the fields. When she heard the bell toll for Mass while she was out in the fields, she came away to the town and to church to hear the Mass, as I have seen her do. I have seen her confess at Paschal (Easter) time and at the other solemn feasts; she confessed to Messire Guillaume Front, at that time priest of the parish church of St. Remy de Domremy." (R.67–68)

Simonin Musnier, farm-worker, about forty-four, a childhood playmate: "I was brought up with Joan the Maid next door to her father's house. I know that she was good, simple, pious, fearing God and his saints; she went often and of her own will to church and to sacred places, caring for the sick and giving alms to the poor; this I saw myself, for when I was a child I myself was sick and Joan came to comfort me. . . ." (R.76)

Mengette or Marguerite, wife of Jean Joyart, forty-six or thereabouts, her friend: "My father's house was almost adjoining Joan's and I knew Joan the Maid, for often I span thread in her company and with her did other house tasks, day and night; she was brought up in the Christian religion and full of good ways,* as it seemed. She went of her own will and often to church and gave alms out of her father's property (biens) and was so good, simple and pious that I and the other young girls would tell her that she was too pious. She worked with a will and busied herself with a multitude of tasks; she span, did the house work, worked at the harvest and sometimes, when the time came, took her turn to guard the animals as she span. She went readily to confession; I often saw her on her knees to the priest of the town." (R.78)

Hauviette, wife of Gerard de Sionne, about forty-five years old: "From my childhood I knew Joan the Maid who was born at Domremy to Jacques d'Arc and Isabelette, husband and wife, honest and decent farmers and true Catholics of good repute. I know this because I was often in company with Joan, and being her friend I went to her father's house. I do not, however, remember her godmothers and godfathers, unless it be by what I heard said, for Joan was older than me by three or four years, or so it was said.

"Joan was a good, simple and sweet-natured girl, she went often and of her own will to church and the sacred places and often she was ashamed because of people remarking how she went so devoutly

*remplie de bonnes moeurs.

to church. I have heard the priest who was there in her time say that she came often to confession. Joan busied herself like any other girl; she did the housework and span and sometimes—I have seen her—she kept her father's flocks." (R.77)

Colin, son of Jean Colin of Greux, farmer, about fifty years old, her comrade: "Joan, from what I saw, was a good, simple, sweet-natured girl of good behaviour. She went readily to church, as I saw myself, for almost every Saturday afternoon Joan, with her sister and other women, went to the hermitage of Notre Dame de Bermont, bearing candles. She was very devout towards God and the Blessed Virgin, so much so that I myself, who was young then, and other young men, teased her. She worked with a will, watchful over feeding the animals, willingly caring for the animals of her father's house, span, and did the housework. I have heard it said by Messire Guillaume Front, formerly the parish priest, that Joan was a good Catholic, that he had never met a better and had none better in his parish." (R.75–76)

Durand Laxart or Lassois, farmer of Burey, Joan's uncle-by-marriage: "Joan was of my wife Jeanne's kinsfolk. I knew Jacques d'Arc and Isabelette well, the parents of Joan the Maid, good and true Catholics, and of good repute, and I believe that Joan was born in the town of Domremy and that she was baptised at the font of St. Remy in that town. Joan was of good behaviour, devout, patient, going readily to church, willingly to confession, and gave alms to the poor when she could, as I witnessed, both in the town of Domremy and at Burey, at my house, where Joan resided during a period of six weeks. Willingly did she work, spinning, ploughing,* keeping the cattle, and did other work suitable for women." (R.82)

Isabelette, wife of Gerardin d'Epinal, about fifty: "Willingly did she give alms and gathered in the poor and she would sleep beneath the hood of the hearth that the poor might sleep in her bed. She was not to be seen loitering about the streets, but was much in church at prayer. She did not dance, so that we, the other girls and young men, even talked about it. She was always working, spinning, cultivating the earth with her father, doing the housework and sometimes she guarded the cattle. She went readily and often to confession, as I witnessed, for Joan the Maid was my gossip, and carried Nicholas, my son, at the baptismal font. And often I went with

---

* In this and other testimony, Joan is described as "allant à la charrue". The term may not mean literally that she ploughed; it may refer to such works of cultivation as hoeing.—E.H.

her and saw her confess in church, to Messire Guillaume who was the priest at that time." (R.81)

Michel Lebuin, of Domremy, farmer at Burey, forty-four years old or thereabouts: "Joan went readily to church and very often to (other) sacred places. I know this because myself, on several occasions, when I was young, I went with her on pilgrimage to Notre Dame de Bermont, the hermitage. She went almost every Saturday to that hermitage, with her sister, and put candles there. For the love of God she gave away willingly all that she could get. She busied herself actively about women's work and helping the other girls, doing it very well and properly; she confessed frequently; I know, for I was a companion and I often saw her confess." (R.79)

Dominique Jacob, priest of a neighbouring parish (Montiers-sur-Saulx in the diocese of Toul), about thirty-five years old: "Joan was from Domremy and as far as I know she was baptised in the church of St. Remy in that town. For her parents, they were Jacques d'Arc and Isabelette, joined in wedlock, who were good Catholics and of good repute: I always heard them spoken of as such. . . . Joan was older than me. I saw and knew her three or four years before she left the house of her father and mother; she was brought up in goodly ways and decent habits and went often to church and sometimes, when the bell was tolled for Compline at the town church, she fell upon her knees and, so it seemed to me, said her prayers piously." (R.73)

Etienne de Sionne, priest of Roncessay near Neufchâteau, about fifty-four years old: "I often heard it said by Messire Guillaume Front, parish priest during his lifetime at the town of Domremy, that Joan, called the Maid, was a good and simple girl, pious, well brought up, fearing God, so much so that she had not her equal in the town. She often confessed her sins to him, and he said that had Joan had money of her own she would have given it to her priest for the saying of Masses. This priest told me that every day when he celebrated she was at the Mass." (R.73)

Perrin Drappier, churchwarden of Domremy, about sixty years old: "Joan the Maid, in the time of her youth until she left her father's house, was a good, chaste and simple girl, modest in manner, taking not the name of God nor of his saints in vain, fearing God. She went frequently to church and frequently confessed. The cause of my knowing this is that I was, in those days, churchwarden at the church of Domremy and often did I see Joan come to church, to Mass and to Compline. And when I did not ring the bells for

Compline, Joan would catch me and scold me, saying that I had not done well; and she even promised to give me some wool if I would be punctual in ringing for Compline. And Joan went often with her sister and other people to a church and hermitage of Bermont, founded in honour of the Blessed Virgin Mary. She gave much in alms; she worked with a will, spinning and doing the necessary tasks; and sometimes she went to plough and took her turn at keeping the cattle." (R.70–75)

A childhood like any other, with, like any other in this too, a few features recalling the appalling background of events which made themselves felt even in that forgotten corner at the limits of Barrois and Lorraine.

Question: Did the people of Domremy take the Burgundian side or that of their opponents?

JOAN: I knew only one Burgundian there and I could have wished his head cut off—however, only if it pleased God.

Question: In the town of Maxey, were they Burgundians or enemies of the Burgundians?

JOAN: They were Burgundians. . . .

Question: Were you ever with little children who fought for the side which is yours?

JOAN: No. I have no memory of that; but I did see that certain people of the town of Domremy had fought against those of Maxey, whence they came back sometimes much wounded and bleeding.

Question: In your extreme youth had you great wish to go out against the Burgundians?

JOAN: I had a great will and desire that my King have his kingdom. . . .

Question: Did you take the animals out to pasture?

JOAN: I answered that elsewhere. When I was quite big and had reached the years of reason, I did not generally guard the animals, but I did help to take them to the meadows and also to a fortified place which was called the Isle, for fear of men-at-arms; but I do not remember whether in my childhood I guarded them or not. (C.63–65)

The above exchange gives us something of the atmosphere of a France divided against itself, in which opinion aligned people against each other, and in which the approach of armed men alarmed the peasants and sent them and their beasts into refuge. At Domremy the place called the Isle, mentioned by Joan, was the only fortified place. And it was a refuge which sometimes turned out to be inadequate. In 1428 Antoine de Vergy, governor of Champagne for the King of England, received orders to go and besiege the city of Vaucouleurs, the only one in the whole bailiwick of Chaumont which had not yet made submission; all the others, Chaumont itself as well as Nogent-le-Roi, Coiffy, Audelot, Montigny-le-Roi, had rallied to the English crown.

JOAN: For fear of the Burgundians, I left my father's house and went to the town of Neufchâteau in Lorraine, to the house of a woman named La Rousse where I stayed for about fifteen days. (C.46)

Isabelette, wife of Gérardin d'Epinal: "Joan went to Neufchâteau with her father, her mother, her brothers and sisters who, because of the soldiers (gens de guerre), took their animals to Neufchâteau. But she did not stay there long and she came back to Domremy with her father, as I witnessed; for she did not like living there and said that she preferred to live at Domremy." (R.82)

Dominique Jacob, parish priest of Montiers-sur-Saulx: "All the inhabitants of Domremy took to flight, because of the men-at-arms, and came to Neufchâteau, and among them came also Joan with her father and mother and always in their company." (R.74)

Hauviette: "I, too, was also in Neufchâteau at the time and was seeing Joan all the time." (R.77)

Gérard Guillemette, farmer, of Greux, about forty years of age: "I who am speaking was myself at Neufchâteau with Joan, her father and her mother, and I always saw her with her father and mother, excepting that during three or four days Joan, her mother and father being present, helped the hostess with whom they lodged, called La Rousse, a worthy woman of that town. I know well that they did not stay in Neufchâteau more than four or five days, until the soldiers had gone away. Then she came back to Domremy with her father and her mother." (R.85)

Meanwhile, hard times notwithstanding, the young people of the country still managed to enjoy themselves sometimes.

JOAN: Quite close to the town of Domremy there is a tree called the Ladies' Tree, and others call it the Fairies' Tree, near which is a spring of water; and I have heard tell that those who are sick and have the fever drink the water of this spring and ask for its waters to recover their health. I have witnessed this myself but I do not know if it cures them or not. It is a big tree called beech* from which fine Maypoles are made; it belonged to Messire Pierre de Bourlemont, Knight. Sometimes I went out with the other girls and by the tree made garlands (of flowers) for the image of Our Lady of Domremy; . . . I have seen the girls put such garlands on the tree's branches and sometimes I myself put some on, with the others; sometimes we took them away with us and sometimes we left them there. . . . I do not know whether, since I reached the age of discretion (*l'âge de raison*), I ever danced about this tree; I may well have danced there with the children but I sang there more than I danced. (C.65–66)

Gerardin d'Epinal, farmer, sixty years old or thereabouts: "This tree is called the Ladies' Tree. I have seen the lords temporal and the ladies of Domremy, once or twice, in the spring, take bread and wine and go out to eat under this tree; it is then as beautiful as lilies and immense. Its leaves and its branches reach down to the ground. On Springs Sunday (*Dimanche des Fontaines*) the boys and girls of Domremy are accustomed to go out under this tree; their mothers make loaves for them and, young men and girls, off they go to celebrate Springs (*faire fontaine*) under this tree.† There they sing and dance and come back to the Spring at Rains, eat their bread and drink of its waters, as I have witnessed. Joan went there with the other girls and did all that the others did." (R.80)

Hauviette: "This tree, since ancient times, has been called the Ladies' Tree, and it used to be said that the ladies who are called fairies went there. However, I never heard it said that anyone had ever seen one. The boys and girls of the town are accustomed to go to this tree and to the Rains Spring on the Sunday of *Laetare Jerusalem* called (Sunday) of the Springs, and they take bread with them. I went with Joan the Maid, for she was my comrade, and other girls and young men to the Fairies' Tree on Springs Sunday. There we ate, we danced, we played; I have seen nuts (walnuts) taken to the tree and to the Springs." (R.77)

Jeannette, widow of Tiercelin: "The tree which is called the Ladies' Tree—it is said that in past times a lord, Messire Pierre Granier, Knight, lord of Bourlemont, and a lady called (a) fairy,

---

* *hau*, not *hêtre*.   † An old Celtic rite, apparently.—E.H.

used to meet each other under this tree and talk together; this I heard read out of a romance.* And girls and young men of the town go there every year on *Laetare* Sunday, called 'Of the Springs', for an outing. And there they eat, dance and go off to drink at the Rains Spring." (R.72)

The foregoing suffices to suggest the tales which were told on the long winter evenings, and to recall youthful revels, dances and picnics under the tree which was several centuries old. Joan was in all things "like the others" and, like the others, she had her love affair.

Question: What made you cause a certain man at the city of Toul to be summoned for (breach of promise of) marriage?

JOAN: I did not have him summoned, it was he who had me summoned. And there I swore before the judge to speak the truth and in the end he roundly said that I had made the man no promise whatever.

In the Middle Ages a promise of marriage had contractual force. It would seem that Joan had a suitor who, rejected, tried to revenge himself by haling her before the court of justice at Toul, which found against him—incidentally to the consternation of her father and mother who would have preferred to see her wed.

Question: What was the dream which your father said he had had about you before you had left his house?

JOAN: When I was still in the house of my father and mother, I was several times told by my mother that my father had told her that he had dreamt that I, Joan, his daughter, would go away with some men-at-arms. And much care did my father and mother have about it and they kept me close and in great subjection; and for my part I obeyed them in all things save only in that lawsuit I had in the city of Toul in the matter of marriage. And I have heard my mother say that my father told my brothers, "Truly, if I knew that that must happen which I fear in the matter of my daughter, I had rather you drowned her. And if you did not do it, I would drown her myself."

But why this refusal of marriage on Joan's part?

JOAN: The first time that I heard the voice, I promised to keep my

* Possibly an old ballad.—E.H.

virginity for as long as it should please God, and that was at the age of thirteen or thereabouts. (C.123–127)

For in this childhood, "like the others", something had happened concerning which Joan had said not a word to anybody.

COMMENTARY

It might at first sight seem superfluous to argue about Joan of Arc's birth and origins after reading the testimony which establishes them so clearly. The worth of the texts in question raises no doubts in the historian's mind; they emanate from eye-witnesses and bear the best sign of authenticity in that, agreeing about the real point in question, they differ sufficiently from each other to do away with any fear that one may be dealing with "faked" documents (copied from each other, for instance). The texts are taken from the trial of condemnation (C) and the trial of rehabilitation (R) and we shall see later (Chapters 7 and 9) how they were composed and in what form they still survive.

It should be noted that all the above declarations, whether made by Joan herself or by the witnesses of her childhood, were made on oath and registered as such by the clerks of the two trial courts. Joan refused to take the oath and made clear and definite reservations when making statements touching her voices or the person of the King; but in what concerned her father and mother and place of birth she did not raise even the slightest difficulty and immediately swore to speak the truth. Let us also mark, in passing, the expressions she employed (see next chapter) when the question of her leaving Domremy was raised: the idea of being a "king's daughter" was as fantastic to her as that of having "one hundred fathers and one hundred mothers".

Nevertheless the hypothesis of a "Joan of Arc bastard of Orleans" has so often been repeated that one is obliged to examine it.

Who started it?

It appeared for the first time in an article by one Pierre Caze, sub-prefect of Bergerac, who was not an historian but was under the mistaken impression that he was a dramatist. He expounded his theory in 1805, in the *Observations* which prefaced a tragedy of his composition published in Libourne and entitled *The Death of Joan of Arc* or *The Maid of Orleans*. In 1819 he returned to the subject, in two volumes: *The Truth about Joan of Arc or enlightenment on her origin.*

Since then books and articles taking up the same hypothesis have appeared periodically, so that in 1895 the learned Lefevre-Pontalis was already describing it as an "old attempt at mystification".* It should be noted that all the writers who have successively expounded this thesis of Joan's bastardy have done no more than resume the same arguments supported by the same documentation as those of P. Caze; during 150 years no new document which might reinforce the theory has come to light. All those which have been put forward as "new" have been shown on analysis to be documents already well known to historians and well studied by them.

According to this hypothesis Joan was the daughter of Isabeau of Bavaria and Louis, Duke of Orleans, brother of King Charles VI.

As Louis d'Orleans was assassinated on the night of November 23, 1407, it follows that any child of his must have been conceived before that date. Now contemporary documents (among others the *Chronique du Religieux de Saint Denis*) establish that Isabeau of Bavaria gave birth, on November 10, 1407, to a son who died within a few hours, having been hastily baptised with the name of Philippe. Since, for reasons no longer historical but gynaecological, it is impossible to suppose Isabeau again pregnant between November 10 and 23, we are obliged to suppose that the child was really a girl for whom a still-born boy was substituted. Offspring of Isabeau's and Louis' guilty passion, the child it seems was first hidden and subsequently entrusted to some peasants of the village of Domremy to whom she was taken on the night of Epiphany: for those who hold this theory, this would explain why the village cockerels, roused by the noise of the royal suite, all crowed in the middle of the night, as described in a letter written by Perceval de Boulainvilliers (see Chapter 4).

And the reason for this removal and substitution? They were because the child was illegitimate.

The liaison between Isabeau of Bavaria and her brother-in-law Louis of Orleans has never been formally established but it is a possibility; some historians consider it as probable even as early as 1404. What, on the other hand, is altogether impossible in the eyes of any historian tolerably familiar with the mores, domestic and juridical customs, and mentality of the Middle Ages is the notion of

* *Le Moyen Age*, May/June 1895.

concealing the birth of a bastard. This idea alone is sufficient to expose a profound ignorance of the period. The fact is that during the Middle Ages bastards were admitted to the family circle and acknowledged without shame; this state of mind persisted, indeed, until relatively recent times; one has only to recall Louis XIV's bastards. It was in the eighteenth and above all the nineteenth century that the distinction between legitimate and "natural" children began to be made and that some effort was made to dissimulate the latter: the reasons for this evolution in manners are too numerous to be set out here—growing influence of Roman law, fear of dispersing the family heritage by division, in a word all that characterises bourgeois civilization.

To believe that anyone could, in Joan of Arc's time, seek to conceal an illegitimate birth is simply to perpetrate an anachronism. Bastards, we repeat, were brought up as members of the family: if the family happened to be noble they bore its arms, to which was added what heraldists call a brisure, the "bar of bastardy". Examples abound: one might begin with Dunois himself, known as and called the Bastard of Orleans in Joan of Arc's day; it was thus that he signed his letters in fact: he was the son of Louis of Orleans and Yolande d'Enghien. A few years later the royal accounts carry an entry at regular intervals for the fees paid to "the wet-nurse for My Lord the Count of Maine's bastard", the child being a daughter of Charles du Maine, Queen Marie's brother and Charles VII's brother-in-law. Two chroniclers of the period, Enguerrand de Monstrelet and Jean de Wavrin, were bastards. Philippe the Good, Duke of Burgundy, had, despite his three marriages, sixteen bastards, of whom one, Antoine, was called The Great Bastard, and bore that nickname without, as we should say nowadays, developing a complex.

For any historian of the Middle Ages the hypothesis, then, at once appears in the highest degree improbable; it entails transposing the mores and state of mind of a later epoch into the past.

Furthermore, it is unacceptable from the point of view of historic method. For history—let us not forget this—is an exact science regulated by scientific method. We cannot accept a mere supposition unsupported by any document. It is, therefore, desirable that we glance at any of the documents which might support the hypothesis in question.

The birthdays of the various children born to Isabeau of Bavaria and Charles VI are established chiefly by reference to the *Chronique du Religieux de Saint Denis,* which offers to historians perfectly acceptable guarantees of authenticity. This chronicle states without prevarication that the child born on November 10, 1407, was of the male sex and was christened Philippe.

The works of an eighteenth-century historian, the Abbé Villaret, albeit suspect since he never gives his sources, also call this child Philippe in the edition which appeared during his lifetime, that is in 1764; but in two later editions, dated respectively 1770 and 1783, this same child becomes a girl called Joan. Obviously, for the modern historian, contemporary evidence is superior to the work of an eighteenth-century writer whose posthumous editions may have contained mistakes.

In default of documents—for in fact no other has ever been produced—those who favour the hypothesis of royal bastardy have recourse to various hints whose value we shall examine as they appear in the texts we shall be quoting. And to begin with those already quoted, these people evince surprise, for example, at the fact that Joan did not know her exact age (for, we must note, in order to be "bastard of Orleans" Joan would have had to be born in 1407 and consequently to have been twenty-five at the time of her trial). But, for the historian of the Middle Ages, the surprising thing would have been if Joan had known her age. For at that time nobody was much concerned to know how old he or she might be. The notions which have acquired such importance in the modern world—date and place of birth, civil status, authenticated by an identity card or a passport were utterly alien to the mediaeval world. In Joan of Arc's time historiographers and chroniclers were just beginning to record the birth dates of kings and very great noblemen; at the same period parish registers were beginning to be kept here and there, and in them christenings, weddings and deaths were noted. But they were rare, and are even rarer in surviving archives: parish registers did not begin to become numerous until the sixteenth and, above all, the seventeenth centuries.

An example of such typical uncertainties may be in place here: in 1415, one Jean Fusoris—well known to historians of the Middle Ages, for he was a famous technician in his day, a maker of astronomical instruments—was arrested on suspicion of treason in the course of the English invasion. Interrogated twice during a single year, on the first occasion, he claimed to be "fifty or thereabouts", on the other that he was "sixty or thereabouts". (L. Mirot, *Le procès de maître Jean Fusoris*, Mem. de la Soc. de l'Hist. de Paris, 1900, pp. 173 and 230.)

Thus, in all trials and inquests, the customary formula for answering the question as to one's age was: "X" years of age, *or thereabouts, vel circiter, vel circa, vel eorcirca.* In our translation of the Trial of Rehabilitation, we left out this formula, as we left out all procedural forms and repetition in general; in the present work we have restored it as it is found in the original manuscripts and in Quicherat's Latin edition.

It was, furthermore, to offset this want of precision that children were given several godparents of each sex who could at least swear that they had been baptised: proceedings were based on oral testimony, without expecting the exactitude which we expect nowadays from documentary evidence.

So we do not know Joan's age exactly; we have only what she herself said, and what was attested by the witnesses at her Trial of Rehabilitation—to wit, that at the time of her Trial of Condemnation she was nineteen or thereabouts, twenty or thereabouts.

There is a single discordant voice, Hauviette's, Joan's friend. Questioned during the Trial of Rehabilitation, January 28, 1456, she replied that she was "forty-five years old or thereabouts", which would put her birth date in the year 1411. Now in the course of her evidence she said, "Joan was older than me by three or four years, from what people said." This would advance Joan's date of birth and place it in the year 1407 or 1408—prerequisite if she is to be considered "bastard of Orleans". But one hundred and fifteen witnesses were questioned during the Trial of Rehabilitation and Hauviette's evidence cannot be allowed to outweigh that of Joan herself and the 114 other witnesses, especially since the age written down by the clerk may very well have been misheard or ill-written without anyone, at the time, bothering much about it. Moreover, note that Hauviette is not positive: "from what people said" (*à ce qu'on disait*); may not her remark have been inspired by the very feminine wish to make herself out younger than she was? At all events, it is obvious that the age question is quite inadequate to prove the supposition of bastardy.

Experience teaches us that there is a certain difference between a girl of nineteen or twenty and a girl of twenty-five. If the vast majority of witnesses and Joan herself agree that she was nineteen or twenty years old, let us admit that, in default of absolute precision, there is a strong presumption that she was born in 1412 "or thereabouts". This would, moreover, agree with other testimony, since Joan declared that she was about thirteen when she had the first of her revelations, and that these revelations persisted during four or five years.

2

VOCATION AND DEPARTURE

JOAN: When I was thirteen years old, I had a voice from God to help me govern my conduct. And the first time I was very fearful. And came this voice, about the hour of noon, in the summer-time, in my father's garden; I had not fasted on the eve preceding that day. I heard the voice on the right-hand side, towards the church; and rarely do I hear it without a brightness. This brightness comes from the same side as the voice is heard. It is usually a great light. When I came to France, often I heard this voice. . . . The voice was sent to me by God and, after I had thrice heard this voice, I knew that it was the voice of an angel. This voice has always guarded me well and I have always understood it clearly.

Question: What sort of help say you that this voice has brought you for the salvation of your soul?

JOAN: It has taught me to conduct myself well, to go habitually to church. It told me that I, Joan, should come into France. . . . This voice told me, twice or thrice a week, that I, Joan, must go away and that I must come to France and that my father must know nothing of my leaving. The voice told me that I should go to France and I could not bear to stay where I was. The voice told me that I should raise the siege laid to the city of Orleans. The voice told me also that I should make my way to Robert de Baudricourt in the fortress of Vaucouleurs, the Captain of that place, that he would give me people to go with me. And me, I answered it that I was a poor girl who knew not how to ride nor lead in war. (C.47–48)

Question: Have you some other sign that these voices are good spirits?

JOAN: Saint Michael assured me of it before the voices came.

Question: How did you know it was Saint Michael?

JOAN: I knew it by his speech and by the language of the Angels, and I believe firmly that they were Angels.

Question: How did you know that they were Angels?

JOAN: I believed it quite quickly (soon) and I had the will to believe it. Saint Michael, when he came to me, told me that Saint Catherine and Saint Margaret would come to me and that I should act by their advice, that they were bidden to lead me in what I had to do and that I should believe in what they would say to me and that it was by God's order.

Question: If the devil put himself into the form or figure of a good Angel, how would you know that it is a good or bad Angel?

JOAN: I should certainly know if it was Saint Michael or some other thing which had put itself into his resemblance. The first time I had great doubt if it was Saint Michael who came to me, and that first time I was very much afraid; and I saw him afterwards several times before knowing that it was Saint Michael.

Question: How was it that you recognized Saint Michael rather on that occasion when you did believe (it to be him), than the first time he appeared to you?

JOAN: The first time I was a child and was afraid, and afterwards Saint Michael taught me and showed me and proved to me that I must believe firmly that it was him.

Question: What doctrines did he teach you?

JOAN: Before all things he told me to be a good child and that God would help me. And, among other things he told me to come to the help of the King of France. . . . And the Angel told me the pity (pitiful state) that was in the Kingdom of France. (C.162–163)

Question: Of these visions which you say you had, did you mention them to your parish priest or to any other churchman?

JOAN: No, but to Robert de Baudricourt only, and to my King. My voices did not oblige me to hold this secret, but I feared greatly to reveal it for fear of the Burgundians, lest they prevent my journey; and above all I greatly feared my father, that he might prevent me from making my journey.

Question: Did you think you were doing well in going away without the permission of your father and your mother, since we must honour our father and our mother?

JOAN: In all other things I did obey my father and my mother, save in this leaving them, but afterwards I wrote to them about it and they gave me their forgiveness.

Question: When you left your father and your mother, did you think you were committing a sin?

JOAN: Since God commanded it, it had to be. Since God commanded it, had I had a hundred fathers and a hundred mothers, had I been a King's daughter, I should have departed.

Question: Did you ask your voices whether you could tell your father and your mother of your setting forth?

JOAN: As for my father and my mother, my voices would have been satisfied that I tell them, had it not been for the pain it would have caused them if I had announced my departure. As for me, I would not have told them for anything in the world. The voices left it to me to tell my father and my mother, or to keep silent. . . . And them within so little of going out of their senses the time I left to go to the town of Vaucouleurs. (C.124-125-127)

It was, then, in secret that Joan left Domremy. The nearest she came to giving her plans away was in allusions made to certain people who were unable to understand her.

Hauviette: "I did not know when Joan went away and because of that I wept a great deal for I loved her dearly for her sweet nature and I was her companion." (R.77)

Mengette: "On going away she bade me adieu, then passed on her way commending me to God, and went away to Vaucouleurs. (R.78)

Gerardin d'Epinal: "I know nothing (of her leaving) save that when she was wishing to go away she said to me, 'My good friend*, if you were not a Burgundian†, I should tell you something.' Me, I thought she was talking about some companion she wanted to marry." (R.81)

Michel Lebuin: "I know nothing, save that once Joan herself told me, on the eve of St. John Baptist's Day, that there lived a maid between Coussey and Vaucouleurs who, before the year was out, would have the King of France crowned. And in the year which followed, the King was crowned at Rheims; I know nothing else." (R.80)

How did Joan set about leaving Domremy without alerting her parents?

JOAN: I went to my uncle's and I told him that I wanted to stay with him for a time and there I stayed about eight days. And I then

* Or, possibly, "Godfather". E.H.
† i.e., of the "Burgundian" Party.

told my uncle that I must go to the town of Vaucouleurs and my uncle took me there. And when I came to this town of Vaucouleurs I recognized Robert de Baudricourt, whereas never before had I seen him and by my voice I knew this Robert, for the voice told me that it was him. And I told this same Robert that I must go into France. This Robert twice refused and repulsed me. (C.48–49)

Isabelette, wife of Gérardin d'Epinal: "I have heard Durand Laxart, who took her to the lord Robert de Baudricourt, say that she told him that she would tell her father that she was going to help his wife at her confinement, so that he could take her to the lord Robert" (R.82)

Durand Laxart: "I went myself to fetch Joan at her father's house and I took her to my house. And she told me that she wanted to go to France, to the Dauphin, to have him crowned, saying, 'Has it not been said that France will be lost by a woman and shall thereafter be restored by a virgin?' And she told me also that I was to go to Robert de Baudricourt that he might have her taken to the place where the lord Dauphin was to be found. This Robert several times told me that I should return her to her father's house after having cuffed her soundly."

Gérard Guillemette: "When Joan left her father's house, I saw her pass in front of the house with her uncle who was called Durand Laxart. At which time Joan said to her father, 'God be with you, I am going to Vaucouleurs.' Then I heard it said that Joan was going away into France."

One of those who were to be her companions on the "journey" from Vaucouleurs to Chinon, remembered the first encounter between Joan and de Baudricourt. Bertrand de Poulengy, esquire to the King of France, sixty-three years of age or thereabouts: "According to report, Joan was from Domremy, and her father was Jacques d'Arc of that town. I know not her mother's name, but I was several times in their house and I know that they were worthy farmers. . . . Joan the Maid came to Vaucouleurs at the time of the Ascension of Our Lord, as I recall it, and there I saw her speak with Robert de Baudricourt who was then captain of the town. She told him that she was come to him, Robert, sent by her Lord to bring word to the Dauphin that he hold himself prepared but make no war on his enemies, for the Lord would aid him before mid-Lent. Joan said that the kingdom did not belong to the Dauphin but to

her Lord, and that the Lord wanted the Dauphin to be made King
and he was to place his kingdom at her command, saying that
despite his enemies the Dauphin would be made King and that she
would lead him to his coronation. Robert asked her who was her
Lord. She answered: 'The King of Heaven'. That done, she returned
to her father's house with her uncle called Durand Laxart of Burey-
le-Petit. And thereafter, towards the end of Lent, Joan came again
to Vaucouleurs, asking for a company to go to the lord Dauphin.
Which perceiving, myself and Jean de Metz together offered to lead
her to the King, at that time Dauphin." (R.98)

The chronological hints here given by Bertrand de Poulengy
allow us to place Joan's first attempt in the month of May 1428:
it took place, therefore, about one month before the Sire de Vergy's
attack on Vaucouleurs. The second attempt took place at the
beginning of the year 1429. Lent began very early that year since
Ash Wednesday fell on February 9. This second residence in
Vaucouleurs was, as we shall see, longer than the first, and we know
more about it, Robert de Baudricourt first refusing to yield to Joan's
demand, then letting himself be convinced.

JOAN: Robert twice refused and repulsed me, and the third time
he received me and gave me men. The voice had told me that
it would so happen.

Durand Laxart: "When the Maid saw that Robert did not want to
send her to the place where the Dauphin was, she herself handed
me my cloak and told me that she wished to withdraw. And, withdrawing, I took her to Saint-Nicholas, and when she was there she
went with a safe-conduct to the lord Charles, Duke of Lorraine,
and when the lord Charles saw her, he spoke with her and gave her
four francs, which she showed me. Then Joan went back to
Vaucouleurs, and the inhabitants of the town of Vaucouleurs bought
for her men's clothes, hose, leggings, and all that she needed.
And myself and Jacques Alain of Vaucouleurs, bought her a horse
for the price of twelve francs at our own expense. However,
thereafter the lord Robert de Baudricourt caused us to be reim-
bursed. And that done, Jean de Metz, Bertrand de Poulengy, Colet
de Vienne and Richard Larcher, with the two servants of Jean de
Metz and Bertrand, took Joan to the place where the Dauphin was."
(R.83)

It was thus that Durand Laxart, in curt phrases proper to a far from garrulous peasant, summed up the events. Other witnesses gave more details.

Jean de Novellompont or de Metz, esquire, ennobled by Charles VII in 1448, fifty-seven years old or thereabouts: "When Joan the Maid came to the place and town of Vaucouleurs, in the diocese of Toul, I saw her, dressed in poor clothes, women's clothes, red; she lodged at the house of one Henri Le Royer of Vaucouleurs. I spoke to her, saying, 'My dear girl, what are you doing here? Must it not be that the King be cast out of the kingdom and we become English?' And the Maid answered me, 'I am come here to a King's Chamber' (i.e., to a royalist place) 'to talk with Robert de Baudricourt that he may be willing to lead me or send me to the King, but he pays no attention to me nor to my words. And yet, before we are in mid-Lent, I must be at the King's side, though I wear my feet to the knees. For indeed there is nobody in all the world, neither king nor duke, nor daughter of the King of Scotland, nor any other who can recover the kingdom for France. And there will be no help (for the kingdom) if not from me. Although I would rather have remained spinning at my mother's side, for it is not my condition, yet must I go and must I do this thing, for my Lord wills that I do so.' I asked her who was her Lord. And she told me that it was God. Whereupon I, Jean, who bear witness here, promised the Maid, putting my hand in hers in a gesture of good faith, that, God helping, I would lead her to the King. And I asked her when she wished to set out. She said to me, 'Rather today than tomorrow and tomorrow than later.' Then I asked her if she wanted to go in her own clothes. She replied that she would rather have men's clothes. Then I gave her clothes and hose of my servants that she might don them. And that done, the inhabitants of Vaucouleurs had men's clothes made for her and shoes and all things necessary to her and they delivered to her a horse which cost about sixteen francs. When she was dressed and had a horse, with a safe conduct from the lord Charles, Duke of Lorraine, the Maid went to speak with that lord and I went with her to the city of Toul. And when she returned to Vaucouleurs, it being about Bures Sunday*—twenty-seven years ago come next Bures Sunday, that would be—myself and Bertrand de Poulengy and two of his servants and Colet de Vienne, King's Messenger, and one Richard, an archer, we conducted the Maid to the King who was at Chinon, at my expense and Bertrand's." (R.91–92)

* Dimanche des Bures. First Sunday in Lent. In 1429 this fell on February 12th.

It was thus that Joan won over to her cause not only the two squires who led the escort, but a whole group of inhabitants of Vaucouleurs, beginning with the Le Royer couple with whom she lodged.

Catherine Le Royer of Vaucouleurs: "At the time when Joan sought to leave the town she had been in my house for a period of three weeks. And it was then that she sent to have speech with the lord Robert de Baudricourt that he take her to that place where the Dauphin was. But the lord Robert would not. And when Joan saw that Robert would not take her, she said—I heard her—that she must go to the place where the Dauphin was: 'Have you not heard it said that it has been prophesied that France shall be lost by a woman and restored by a virgin from the Lorraine marches?' I remembered having heard that and I was stupefied. Joan ardently desired this and the time lagged for her as for a woman pregnant of a child until (the time) when she would be taken to the Dauphin. And after that I believed in her words and with me many others, so much so that Jacques Alain and Durand Laxart were willing to take her and did take her as far as Saint-Nicholas, but thereafter came back to Vaucouleurs, for Joan said that it was not thus that it suited her to go away. When they came back, certain inhabitants of the town caused a tunic to be made for her, hose, leggings, spurs, a sword and other such things, and bought her a horse, and Jean de Metz, Bertrand de Poulengy, Colet de Vienne with three others, took her to the place where the Dauphin was. I saw them mount their horses to set off."

Henri Le Royer, her husband: "Joan said that she must make her way to the noble Dauphin, for her Lord, the King of Heaven, wished her to go there and that the King of Heaven was thus her sponser; that though she be obliged to make her way there on her knees, go she would. Joan came into my house. She was dressed in a woman's garment, red. Later she was dressed in a vest, hose and other clothes proper to a man, and rode on a horse to the place where the Dauphin was. I saw them set out all together. When she sought to go, she was asked how she would do it, when there were so many men-at-arms everywhere. She answered that she feared not men-at-arms for her way was open, and if there were men-at-arms on her road, she had God, her Lord, who would clear the way for her to go to the lord Dauphin, and that she had been born to do this." (R.94-96)

At the time of the rehabilitation, several witnesses remembered Joan as they had seen her at Vaucouleurs twenty-seven years before.

Jean le Fumeux, parish priest of Ugny, canon of Vaucouleurs, thirty-eight years of age or thereabouts: "Joan came to Vaucouleurs and said that she wanted to go to the Dauphin. Me, I was young at that time and I was churchwarden of the chapel Notre-Dame of Vaucouleurs. I often saw Joan the Maid come to that church very piously. She heard mass in the morning and remained long at prayer. I have seen her beneath the vault of that church on her knees before the Holy Virgin, sometimes with bowed head, sometimes with her head raised. I believe her to have been a good and holy girl." (R.86)

Geoffrey Dufay, knight, of de Baudricourt's suite, fifty years of age or thereabouts: "I often heard the Maid talked of. She was saying that she wanted to go to France. I saw that Jean de Metz, Bertrand de Poulengy, and Julien, who was a squire, took the Maid to the King. I did not see her at that time, but it was they who told me that she was to go with them."

Albert d'Ourches, another of Baudricourt's people sixty years of age or therabouts: "I saw Joan at Vaucouleurs when she wanted to be taken to the King. I heard the Maid several times say that she wanted to go to the King and that she only wished she could be taken to him for the great advantage of the Dauphin. This Maid, as it seems to me, was full of goodness in her conduct (*remplie de bonnes meurs*). I should have liked to have so well-behaved a daughter. I saw her later in the company of soldiers. I saw the Maid confess to Brother Richard before Senlis and receive the Body of Christ, with the Dukes of Clermont and Alençon, during two days. And I believe that she was a perfectly good Christian—I said above, she demanded to be taken to the King. This Maid spoke very well. She was taken there by Bertrand de Poulengy, Jean de Metz and their servants." (R.96–97)

Noble as well as simple must have been talking about her in Vaucouleurs at that time. The fame of the young peasant girl who wanted to go to the King's aid, and whose mission was in fact heralded in a prophecy which was going the rounds in that part of the country and here and there all over the kingdom, will have come to the ears of the Duke Charles of Lorraine who must have wanted to see her for himself. The old duke was sick, and it was as a thaumaturge from whom a miracle might be hoped that he sent for her, rather than as the instrument of a victory and a coronation which he did not much care about.

JOAN: The Duke of Lorraine required that I be taken to him. I went and I told him that I wanted to go to France, and the duke questioned me about the restoration of his health and I told him that of that I knew nothing; I said little to him about my journey, but I said to the duke that he (should) give me his son and some men to take me into France and that I would pray to God for his health; I went to him by means of a safe-conduct and I returned afterwards to the town of Vaucouleurs. (C.49)

Another witness, Marguerite de Touroulde, widow of the King's counsellor Regnier de Bouligny, with whom Joan stayed in Bourges for some time on her return from the coronation and in whom she had confided, had a few words to say about the above encounter: "I have heard Joan say that the Duke of Lorraine, who was sick, wanted to see her. And Joan had been to speak with him and had told him that he was behaving badly and that never would he recover his health if he did not mend his ways, and she exhorted him to take back his good spouse." (R.120)

In fact Charles of Lorraine had for some time been neglecting his "good spouse" Marguerite of Bavaria for a girl named Alison Dumay by whom he had had five bastards: the son Joan mentioned was in reality his son-in-law, René of Anjou, husband of Charles's daughter Isabelle and future heir to Lorraine, of which he was to take possession when the duke died on January 25, 1431.

It was on her return from Nancy (Nancy is about fifty kilometres from Vaucouleurs, say a day on horseback) that Joan found the atmosphere somewhat changed in her favour and Baudricourt himself, perhaps prompted by Jean de Metz, whom Joan, as we have seen, had succeeded in winning over by the ardour of her pleading, disposed to help her. But he was to take one preliminary precaution: he was to have Joan exorcised.

Catherine Le Royer: "I saw Robert de Baudricourt, then captain of the town of Vaucouleurs, and Messire Jean Fournier, come into my house. I heard it from Joan that the latter, a priest, had brought a stole and that he had conjured her before the captain, saying that if there was any bad thing in her that she go hence from them, and that if there was a good thing then let her approach them. And Joan approached this priest and went down on her knees; and she said that this priest had not done well, since he had heard her confession." (R.94)

Then came her departure.

Joan, on leaving the city of Vaucouleurs: "I was in man's clothes, holding in my hand a sword which Robert de Baudricourt had given me and without other arms, with a knight, an esquire and four servants. I came to the town of Saint Urbain and there I spent the night in the abbey.

"Robert de Baudricourt caused those who escorted me to swear that they would lead me truly and surely, and Robert said to me, 'Go' as I set off, 'Go and let what is to be come to pass.' On the way I passed the town of Auxerre and there I heard mass in the great church. Often, at that time, I had my voices." (C.49–50)

Astonishing, surely, this undertaking on which Jean de Metz and Bertrand de Poulengy were embarking. Later, they gave some account, notably to Marguerite la Touroulde, of the somewhat contradictory feelings which animated them on the subject of Joan.

Marguerite la Touroulde: "Afterwards I heard those who took her to the King speak of it and heard them say that, to begin with, they thought her presumptuous and their intention was to put her to the proof. But when they had set out to take her, they were ready to do whatever Joan pleased and were as eager to present her to the King as herself, and that they could not have resisted Joan's will. They said that in the beginning they wanted to require her to lie with them carnally. But when the moment came to speak to her of this they were so much ashamed that they dared not speak of it to her nor say a word of it." (R.119)

And they themselves summoned to bear witness at the trial of rehabilitation, swore to the astonishing influence which the girl had gained over them in the course of a ride which, at all events for her companions, constituted in itself an almost decisive ordeal: the ordeal of daily life and the ordeal of chastity.

Bertrand de Poulengy: "Upon leaving the town, on the first day, we were afraid because of the Burgundian and English soldiers who were masters of the roads, and we made our way during the night. Joan the Maid said to me, as to Jean de Metz and those who travelled with us, that it would be a good thing to hear mass, but because of the wars in the countryside we could not, for we had to pass unperceived. Every night she lay down with Jean de Metz and me, keeping upon her her surcoat and hose, tied and tight. I was young then and yet I had neither desire nor carnal movement to touch woman, and I should not have dared to ask such a thing of Joan, because of the abundance of goodness which I saw in her. We were eleven days on the road going to the King, then Dauphin. But on the way we had many anxieties. But Joan repeatedly told us not to be afraid, and that once we came to the town of Chinon the noble Dauphin would give us good countenance. She never swore, and I myself was much stimulated by her voices, for it seemed to me that she was sent by God, and I never saw in her any evil, but always was she so virtuous a girl that she seemed a saint. And thus all together, without great difficulties, we made our way to the place of Chinon where the King, then Dauphin, lay." (R.99)

Jean de Novellompont or de Metz: "Leaving the town of Vaucouleurs, for fear of the English and the Burgundians who were everywhere across our road to the King, we sometimes moved at night. And we kept on the road for a period of eleven days, riding towards the town of Chinon; and making my way beside her, I asked her if she would do what she said, and the Maid always told us to have no fear and that she had a mandate to do this thing, for her brothers in Paradise told her what she had to do; that for four or five years already her brothers in Paradise and her Lord, to wit God, had been telling her that she must go to the war to recover the Kingdom of France. On our way, Bertrand and I, we lay down with her, and the Maid lay beside me, keeping on her doublet and hose; and I, I feared (respected) her so that I would never have dared make advances to her, and I say upon oath that neither did I have for her desire nor carnal motion. . . . On her way she would have liked to hear mass, for she often said to us, 'If we could hear mass, we should do well.' But, to my knowledge, we only heard mass twice upon our way. I had great confidence in the Maid's sayings, and I was fired by her sayings and with love for her, divine as I believe. I believe that she was sent by God; never did she swear, she liked to hear mass and she crossed herself with the sign of the Cross. And thus we took her to the King, to the place of Chinon, as secretly as we could."

COMMENTARY

In the matter of Joan's residence at Vaucouleurs and of her departure from it, a question of dates arises. Traditionally, the date of departure was placed between February 20 and 25, 1429, and the arrival at Chinon on March 6. The learned Pierre Boissonade had corrected these dates and his conclusions are now accepted by the majority of historians. (See his article: *Une etape capitale de la mission de Jeanne d'Arc*, Revue des Questions Historiques, 3rd Series, Vol. XVII, 1930, pp. 12–67.) He bases his argument principally on the *Journal du greffier de La Rochelle* (published by Quicherat in the *Revue Historique*, Vol. IV, 1877, pp. 327–344). This clerk wrote up his journal in September 1429 on the basis of notes taken from day to day. He was in a position to be well-informed for La Rochelle was at that time the only port which the King of France disposed of; the town was, therefore, in continual touch with the other towns which had remained loyal to Charles VII, the more so in that La Rochelle was the port of disembarkation for the Scottish troops which arrived from time to time to reinforce those serving with the King. His account is very exact; and this is what he wrote: "The 23rd February there came to the King our lord who was at Chinon a maid aged sixteen or seventeen years."

The evidence given by Jean de Metz indicates, as we have seen, that the date of their departure was "about Bures Sunday", that is to say the first Sunday in Lent, which in 1429 fell on February 12th. The two dates agree very well since, also according to his evidence, the journey lasted eleven days. Moreover Joan herself had declared, "Before it be mid-Lent, I must be with the King." Mid-Lent that year (Shrove Thursday) fell on March 1st.

Other evidence, including that of the *Journal of the Siege of Orleans*, points to February as the month.

It may, therefore, be taken that Joan and her escort left Vaucouleurs on the 12th to arrive at Chinon on the 23rd. In that case it was on the evening of February 23rd that Joan was received by the King himself in the great hall of the chateau of Chinon.

Thus set forth, the chronology of events leaves room for the Poitiers interrogatories which, according to witnesses, lasted six weeks, which would mean that Joan was in that town from March 1st to April 10th or thereabouts. From Poitiers Joan returned to Chinon where she spent only a short time. She resided at Tours where her equipment was got ready for her between April the 12th and 21st, and thence, on April 22, she went to Blois, the royal army's GHQ.

Diverse questions of varying importance have been raised touching the events described in this chapter.

Surprise has been expressed at the fact that Joan was "sufficiently

well-informed" to speak of the project of a marriage between the
Dauphin and King of Scotland's daughter. In point of fact this project was in no sense a state secret.
The year before, in April 1428, Charles VII had sent an embassy to James I
of Scotland, an embassy which included among others the famous
poet Alain Chartier, to ask the hand of Margaret of Scotland for his
son, the young Dauphin Louis: this had been promised him, and
the promise became part of the treaty of alliance made at that time
between France and Scotland. This treaty did, in any case, no more
than renew the numerous treaties of alliance concluded between
France and traditionally friendly Scotland, expressions of a policy
going back more than a century and which the French hastened to
reaffirm upon the renewal of hostilities with England. Scottish
battalions had always fought shoulder to shoulder with the armies of
the "King of Bourges". At the time of the first offensive operation
undertaken by Charles VII as King (in 1423, against Cravant), the
commanding officer was a Scot, John Stuart; the King's gratitude
was expressed by a licence to quarter the arms of France with his
own.

There can be no doubt that the marriage project was at once
communicated to the King's good towns, for Charles was punctual
in informing them of all diplomatic and military events: Joan, like
everybody else, was *au courant.*

Then there has been an attempt—once again it is the old business
of getting the bastardy theory accepted—to inflate the part played
by the two gentlemen who agreed to escort Joan, Jean de Metz and
Bertrand de Poulengy. They are supposed to have known Joan
before her arrival in Vaucouleurs, to have instructed her in her
mission, taught her the part she was expected to play, etc. etc. On
what are these suppositions founded? Solely on Bertrand de Poulengy's declaration, reported above: "I was *often* in their house"
(Joan's parents' house). (More precisely, *pluries,* i.e., "several
times".) The reader can judge for himself the disingenuousness of
such an interpretation. At no time did Bertrand say that he had ever
been there *before* he met Joan in Vaucouleurs; and there is nothing
extraordinary in the fact that after his astonishing eleven-day ride
with Joan he should, upon returning to his own town, have called
several times on her parents.

As for Jean de Metz or de Novellompont, it emerges quite clearly
from his deposition that, on the day when he addressed himself to
Joan in a tone of irony, that was the first time he had ever seen her.

Finally, Colet de Vienne, another member of the escort, has been cast in the role of messenger sent especially by the King to fetch Joan, the moment being come to reveal to the world that he had a bastard sister from whom he expected marvels. (Why, one wonders?)

Now, on the subject of Colet de Vienne we have absolutely no documentary evidence excepting in the depositions set down above. And understandably, for he was a King's messenger, indeed, but only one among many, *nuntius regis*, whose function it was to carry letters and dispatches addressed by the King to his captains and his good towns, an office very little superior to that of any procurator (*procureur*) or royal sergeant. His presence in Vaucouleurs was perfectly natural since the town's commanding officer had remained loyal to the King of France and, despite the disturbed times, messengers had never ceased to move freely about whether to Vaucouleurs or even as far as Tournai which had also remained loyal. (On this subject see Charles Samaran's *Pour la défence de Jeanne d'Arc*, in the *Annuaire-Bulletin de la Société de l'Histoire; de France*, Vol. LXXXV, 1953, pp. 50–63.)

Yet another theory: Jean de Metz and Bertrand de Poulengy according to this one, had been members of "the Queen of Sicily's entourage". The bastardy idea has been dropped, at this point, and in default of making Joan out to be a royal bastard, an attempt is made to turn her into somebody's "instrument". Note that even in her own day a Burgundian chronicler had tried to discredit her by representing her as Baudricourt's tool. (Jean de Wavrin, Q IV, 407.) The idea now—for the theory is quite recent—is to represent her as the instrument of the Queen of Sicily, Yolande of Aragon, who became Yolande of Anjou when she married Louis of Anjou, and so mother-in-law to Charles VII who married her daughter, Marie of Anjou. For the purposes of the theory here in question she is called Yolande of Bar, a name she never bore but which had been her mother's before she married the King of Aragon. Yolande had received the Duchy of Bar as a legacy from her mother, and in 1419 she succeeded in marrying her son René (the future King René) to the heiress of Lorraine, Isabelle, daughter of Duke Charles—the same Charles as had sent for Joan, hoping for a miracle which would restore his health. Their wedding was celebrated in 1420.

That Joan was, in fact, a native of the Lorraine-Barrois region might have made Yolande of Aragon—who, however, had never been to Lorraine in her life—regard her with benevolent interest.

But to represent Jean de Metz and Bertrand de Poulengy as being "of the Queen of Sicily's entourage" is to assert what no document justifies. Jean de Metz was a native of Novellompont, in the Messin country, which was never part of the Duchy of Lorraine; it is well known that Metz and its district were independent, and owed allegiance to the Empire. A simple gentleman of Baudricourt's suite, Jean de Metz was only very belatedly enobled by Charles VII (see the *lettre d'anoblisement* in QV363) in 1448, that is nearly twenty years after the famous ride which ought, however, to have drawn the King's attention to him. As for Bertrand de Poulengy, who, at the Trial of Rehabilitation was still a mere esquire, he makes no other appearance in history whatsoever.

We repeat, history is not made of suppositions but of documents. No document establishes any kind of action, direct or indirect, on the part of either Charles VII or Yolande of Aragon, designed to "bring" Joan to Chinon. As for Baudricourt, all we have touching his personal action in the matter are the documents we have quoted, and these show him twice sending Joan away before he—like everybody else—lets himself be won over by her.

Joan, to convince her own entourage, was not afraid to invoke the prophecies which were going the rounds. It was widely claimed that the kingdom lost by a woman (identified, of course, as the calamitous Isabeau of Bavaria) would be saved by a virgin; a prophecy of Merlin's was commonly invoked—it told of a virgin who would ride on the back of Sagittarius, etc. In all such times of troubles prophetic sayings are invoked; we do not have to seek far back for an example; it suffices to remind ourselves of a certain "prophecy of Saint Odile" which everybody heard about between 1940 and 1945.... That Joan should have made use of it to convince her following proves nothing but that she was clever and knew how to turn everything to account to gain her point; it is worth noting that when dealing with Jean de Metz, or with the King, her language was of a very different order.

One final point: many have wondered how she came to be able to ride a horse. The question becomes pointless to anyone who, even in our own time, has watched Lorraine farm-girls, perched on the backs of the massive horses of that horse-and-cattle-breeding country, taking the cattle to water. At a time when the horse was the only means of locomotion it is obvious that Joan must have been riding her father's, and riding them astride, since her childhood. When she protested against the summons of her voices, saying that

she did not know how to ride, it is important to note that she used
a term translated into Latin as *equitare*, which means to ride a war-
horse, a very different matter from knowing how to sit an ordinary
horse. That, indeed, she did not know how to do, but it does not
seem very extraordinary that she should subsequently have learnt
the art; easier, surely, and at all events, than delivering the City of
Orleans!

3

JOAN BEFORE THE DAUPHIN

Question: The said Joan then says that she reached him whom she calls her King without obstacle. [Thus the record of the Trial of Condemnation.]

JOAN: When I came to the town of Sainte-Catherine de Fierbois, then I sent (wrote) to my King; then I went to the town of Château-Chinon where my King is.* I reached there at about noon and took lodging at an inn (*hotellerie*). And after a meal I went to my King who was in the castle. When I entered my King's room, I knew him among the others by the counsel of my voice which revealed him to me. I told my King that I wanted to go and make war against the English.

Question: When the voice showed you him you call the King, was there any light in that place?

JOAN: Pass that question.

Question: Did you see an angel over your King?

JOAN: Spare me that and pass the question. Before my King put me to work, he himself had had many apparitions and some beautiful revelations.

Question: What revelations and apparitions did your King have?

JOAN: I shall not tell you that. I shall not answer you, but send to my King and he will tell you. The voice had promised me that, as soon as I came to the King, he himself would receive me. (C.51–52)

To appreciate exactly the value of Joan's evidence at the Trial of Condemnation concerning her revelations and in general her acts touching the King of France, it is necessary, in the first place, to glance at the court's opening session when Bishop Cauchon tried to get her to swear to speak the truth: "Swear to speak the truth on all that will be asked of you concerning matters of the faith and that which you know."

* The text of the record repeats, each time she speaks of "her" King, the form "him whom she calls her King".

JOAN: Of my father, of my mother and of all that I have done since I came to France I will willingly swear, but of the revelations which have been made to me by God's means, never have I said or revealed anything to anyone whatsoever, excepting it be to Charles only, my King, and I will not reveal them though it cost me my head. I have orders from my visions and my secret counsel to reveal them to nobody.

To this prohibition she was to return more than once.

JOAN: I will willingly tell you whatsoever I have received permission from God to reveal: but as to that touching the revelations concerning the King of France, I will not tell it without the permission of my voices. (C.70)

And again:

JOAN: There are some revelations which go to* the King of France and not to those who are questioning me. (C.72)

It is very obvious that it was precisely on this point that the Rouen judges would have liked to receive exact answers; they were conducting a trial which, over and beyond Joan herself, was aimed at belittling the King of France. We shall see below, in the detail of her examination during the trial, how Joan evaded such questions. For the time being it will be enough simply to note that in anything concerning her relations with the King and the manner of her reception by him, nothing decisive can be gathered from the evidence at the Trial of Condemnation.

Question: Was there an angel above the King's head when you saw him for the first time?
JOAN: By Saint Mary! if there was I know nothing of it and did not see him.
Question: Was there any light there?
JOAN: There were present more than three hundred knights and some fifty torches, not to mention the spiritual light. And rarely had I revelation but there was light.
Question: How came the King to have faith in what you said?

* i.e., Are proper to.

JOAN: He himself had good countersigns,* and through the clergy.

Question: What revelations did your King have?

JOAN: You will not have that out of me this year. I was questioned for three weeks by the clergy of the towns of Chinon and of Poitiers. And the King had a sign of my matters before he would believe me, and the clerics of my party were of this opinion, that it seemed to them that in my matter was nothing but good.

Question: Have you been to Sainte-Catherine de Fierbois?

JOAN: Yes. There I heard three masses in one day and thereafter I went to the town of Chinon. I sent letters to my King in which it was contained that I sent them to know if I could enter the town where my King was, and that I had made my way one hundred and fifty leagues to come to him and bring him succour, and that I knew many things (to the) good touching him, and I believe that in the same letters it was contained that I should know the King well (from) among all others. (C.65)

Eye-witnesses of the scene at Chinon testified to what they remembered at the Trial of Rehabilitation. Raoul de Gaucourt, grand master of the King's household, eighty-five years of age or thereabouts: "I was present in the castle and town of Chinon when the Maid arrived, and I saw her when she presented herself before the royal majesty, with much humility and great simplicity, the poor little shepherdess, and I heard the following words which she spoke to the King: 'Very noble Lord Dauphin, I am come and am sent by God, to bring succour to you and your kingdom.' The King, having seen and heard her, to be better informed of her matter, ordered that she be placed in the keeping of Guillaume Bellier, Master of his house (major domo), bailiff of Troyes, and his Lieutenant at Chinon, whose wife was a most devout woman and of most excellent good fame." (R.11)

Simon Charles, President of the Chamber of Accounts: "The year when Joan went to seek the King, I had been sent by him with an embassy to Venice and I returned about the month of March. At the time I heard Jean de Metz, who had escorted Joan, say that she was with the King. I know that, when Joan arrived in Chinon, there was deliberation in counsel to decide whether the King should hear her or not. To start with they sent to ask her why she was come and what she was asking for. She was unwilling to say anything

---

* Actually *"intersignes"*.—E.H.

without having spoken to the King, yet was she constrained by the King to say the reasons for her mission. She said that she had two (reasons) for which she had a mandate from the King of Heaven; one, to raise the siege of Orleans, the other to lead the King to Rheims for his sacring. Which being heard, some of the King's counsellors said that the King should on no account have faith in Joan (believe her), and the others that since she said that she was sent by God, and that she had something to say to the King, the King should at least hear her.

"However, it was the King's will that she be first examined by clerks and churchmen, which was done. And at last, albeit with difficulties, it was decided that the King would listen to her. When she entered the castle of Chinon to come into his presence, the King, on the advice of the principal courtiers, hesitated to speak to her until the moment when it was reported that Robert de Baudricourt had written to him that he was sending him a woman and that she had been conducted through the territory of the King's enemies; and that, in a manner quasi-miraculous, she had crossed many rivers by their fords, to reach the King. Because of this the King was pressed to hear her and Joan was granted an audience. When the King knew that she was coming, he withdrew apart from the others. Joan, however, knew him at once and made him a reverence and spoke to him for some time. After having heard her, the King appeared radiant. Thereafter, still not wishing to do anything without having the advice of churchmen, he sent Joan to Poitiers that she be examined by the clerks of the University of Poitiers. When he knew that she had been examined and it was reported to him that they had found nothing but what was good in her, the King had arms (armour) made for her and entrusted her to his men of war, and she was given command in the matter of the war." (R.102–104)

Louis de Coutes, Joan's page: "The year when Joan came to the King in the town of Chinon, I was fourteen or fifteen years old and served and dwelt with the lord of Gaucourt who was captain of the place of Chinon. At that time Joan arrived at the place of Chinon with two men and she was taken to the King. I often saw Joan going in to the King and returning thence.

A lodging was assigned to her in a tower of the castle of Couldray, and I lived in that tower with Joan. And all the time she was there I was continuously with her during the day. At night, she had women with her. And well do I remember that at the time she dwelt in Couldray tower, several times men of high rank came to converse with Joan. What they did or said I know not, for always, when I saw these men arrive, I went away and I do not know who they were. At that time, when I was with Joan in that tower, I often saw Joan on bended knees and engaged in prayer, as it seemed to me. However, I was never able to hear what she said, although sometimes she wept. Then, Joan was taken to the town of Poitiers, then came back (and) to Tours, in the house of a person named Lapau."

Jean, Duke of Alençon—a prince of the blood royal, in 1429 he was twenty-five years old, and just returned from five years' captivity, having been taken prisoner at the battle of Verneuil in 1424. He had been released upon payment of a very heavy ransom. His great-grandfather, who was killed at Crécy, was the grandson of Philippe the Bold, King of France: "When Joan came seeking the King, the latter was in the town of Chinon and I in the town of Saint-Florent (Saint Florent-les-Saumur). I was out shooting quail when a messenger came to tell me that there was come to the King a maid who affirmed that she was sent by God to drive out the English, and to raise the siege which was laid by the English to Orleans. That was why, on the morrow, I went to the King who was in the town of Chinon and I found Joan talking with the King. When I drew near, Joan asked who I was and the King replied that I was the Duke of Alençon. Thereupon, Joan said: 'You, be very welcome. The more they shall be together (who are) of the blood royal of France, the better will it be.' And on the morrow Joan came to the King's mass, and as she saw the Kings he bowed and the King took Joan into a chamber and I was with him and the Lord of la Tremoïlle whom the King kept with him, telling the others to withdraw. Then Joan made several requests of the King,* among others that he give his Kingdom to the King of Heaven, and that the King of Heaven after that gift would do unto him as He had done unto his predecessors and would restore him to his original estate; and many other things which I do not remember were said until the time of the meal. And after the meal the King went out to walk in the meadows and Joan galloped a-tilt with a lance, and I seeing her behave in this manner, bearing a lance, and tilting, I gave her a horse. Thereafter, the King came to the conclusion that Joan should be examined by some churchmen. To this end were deputed the bishop of Castres, confessor to the King (Gérard Machet), the bishop of Senlis (Simon Bonnet, bishop of Senlis in

---

* Or it could be "required certain things of the King".—E.H.

1456), those of Maguellone and Poitiers (Hugues de Combarel) Master Pierre of Versailles, thereafter bishop of Meaux, and Master Jean Morin and several others whose names I do not recall. They questioned Joan in my presence: why she was come and who had made her come to the King. She answered that she was come on the King of Heaven's behalf and that she had voices and a counsel that told her what she was to do, but of that I remember no more. But afterwards Joan, who took her meal with me, told me that she had been very closely examined but that she knew and could do more than she had said to those who questioned her. Once he had heard the report of those delegated to examine her, it was the King's will that Joan go to the town of Poitiers and that there she be examined again. But I was not present at the examination in the town of Poitiers. I only know that thereafter in the King's council it was reported that those who had examined her had said that they had found nothing in her contrary to the Catholic faith and that, considering his necessity, the King could make use of her to help him." (R.102–148)

Jean d'Aulon, Knight, King's Counsellor and Seneschal of Beaucaire: "It was about twenty-eight years ago, the King our sire being in the town of Poitiers, I was told that the Maid, who had set out from Lorraine, had been brought to the said lord by two gentlemen calling themselves Messire Robert de Baudricourt's men, one called Bertrand and the other Jean of Metz. And to see her I went to the place of Poitiers.

"After the presentation, spake the Maid with the King, our sire, secretly and told him certain secret things, the which I know not, but that, a little later, that Lord sent to fetch some who were of his council, among whom I was, to whom he said that the Maid had told him that she was sent by God to help him to receive his kingdom which at that time and for the most part was occupied by the English, his ancient enemies.

"After these words announced by the King to the people of his Council, it was decided to interrogate the Maid, who was then aged about sixteen or thereabouts, on certain points touching the faith. To do this the King sent for certain masters of theology, jurists and other expert men who examined and questioned her on these points well and diligently. I was present in Council when these masters made their report of what they had found about the Maid and (it) was by one of them publicly said that they saw, knew nor were aware of anything in this Maid soever but only all

that can be in a good Christian and true Catholic and that as such
they held her (to be), and it was their opinion that she was a very
good person." (R.155-156)

Thus the order of events, if not their exact chronology (we shall
see in the commentary on this chapter how that can be established),
can easily be reconstructed on the basis of the testimonies which are
in agreement. Passing through Sainte-Catherine de Fierbois, Joan
sends a member of her escort to announce her coming to the King
and ask for an audience. She, herself, arrived at Chinon, asks to be
received by the King, who hesitates and, eventually, receives her.
The meeting takes place at evening. "It was high hour" (late in the
day), said Joan, during her interrogation (C.135), in the great hall of
the castle of which nothing today remains but a fragment of wall
and a fireplace hanging in a void. The scene in which Joan re-
cognizes the King and makes unerringly for him has been developed
in our minds and in anecdotal history to an extent which it does not,
perhaps, deserve.

It had already undergone this inflation as it appears in Jean
Chartier's *Chronique*: "Then, Joan, who was come before the King,
made the bows and reverences customary to make to the King,
as if she had been nurtured at court, and this greeting done said,
addressing her speech to the King: 'God give you life, gentle
King,' whereas she knew him not and had never seen him. And
there were (present) several lords, dressed with pomp and richly
and more so than was the King. Wherefore he answered the said
Joan, 'Not I am the King, Joan.' And, pointing to one of his lords,
said, 'There is the King.' To which she replied, 'By God, gentle
prince, it is you and none other.' "

The writer who gives us the interview in greatest detail was not
an eye-witness of it but was unquestionably well-informed: this
was Jean Pasquerel, a hermit of Saint-Augustin, formerly of the
monastery at Bayeux and subsequently Joan's confessor and her
companion on all her campaigns until the moment of her capture at
Compiègne. "The Count of Vendome conducted Joan to the King
and led her into the King's chamber. When he saw her he asked
Joan her name and she replied: 'Gentle Dauphin, Joan the Maid is
my name, and to you is sent word by me from the King of Heaven
that you will be anointed (*sacré*) and crowned in the town of
Rheims and you will be Lieutenant to the King of Heaven who is
King of France.' And after other questions put by the King, Joan

said to him again: 'I tell thee, on behalf of Messire, that thou art
true heir of France and King's son, and He has sent me to thee to
lead thee to Rheims, that thou mayst receive thy coronation and
thy consecration, if thou wilt.' That heard, the King told those who
were present that Joan had told him certain secrets that none knew or
could know, excepting only God; that is why he had great confidence
in her. All this I heard from Joan's mouth, for I was not present."
(R.176)

What was this secret? We shall probably never know any more
about this than did the Rouen judges themselves. The only testimony touching this subject which exists is to be found in a very
late and somewhat anecdotal chronicle, that of Pierre Sala, who, after
having served successively Louis XI and Charles VIII, in his old
age wrote, at Lyons, a work entitled *Hardiesse des grands rois et
empereurs.* He claims to have had what follows directly from
Guillaume Gouffier, lord of Boissy, chamberlain and intimate of
Charles VII: "He told me, among other things, the secret which
had been between the King and the Maid; and well might he know it,
for in his youth he had been greatly loved by that King, so much so
that he would never allow any gentleman to be his bedfellow but
him. In that great privacy of which I tell you was he told by the
King the words which the Maid had said to him. . . . In the time of
the great adversity of this King Charles VII, he found himself
(brought) so low that he no longer knew what to do. . . . The King,
being in this extremity, entered one morning alone into his oratory
and there he made a humble petition and prayer to Our Lord in his
heart, without utterance of words, in which he petitioned devoutly
that if so it was that he was true heir descended from the noble
House of France and that the kingdom should rightly belong to
him, that it please Him to keep and defend him, or, at worst, to
grant him the mercy of escaping death or prison, and that he might
fly to Spain or to Scotland which were from time immemorial
brothers in arms and allies of the Kings of France, wherefore had he
there chosen his last refuge. A little time afterwards, it came about
that the Maid was brought to him, who, while watching her ewes
in the fields, had received divine inspiration to go and comfort the
good King. She did not fail, for she had herself taken and conducted by her own parents even before the King and there she gave
her message at the sign aforesaid (*dessusdit*) which the King knew
to be true. And thenceforth he took counsel of her and great good it
did him."

What appears to be certain is that the King, having consented to receive Joan, was convinced by her that he was face to face with something extraordinary and worthy of closer study. It should, moreover, be remembered that for this anxiety-ridden man, tortured by doubts of his legitimacy planted by his mother herself, the mere fact that this girl claiming to be sent by the King of Heaven and from so great a distance, had reached him and hailed him, "Thou art true heir of France and King's son," must have had something comforting about it and even quasi-miraculous.

At all events, a few days later he decides to take Joan to Poitiers, to which town most of the University masters had retreated. The English had filled the places at the University of Paris with their own paid creatures, which was, as we shall see, to have consequences for Joan herself. It was with the professors, prelates and theologians who had remained loyal to the French cause that, in 1432, the University of Poitiers was founded. François Garivel, King's Counsellor (in the matter of taxes*): "I remember that at the time of Joan the Maid's arrival, the King sent her to Poitiers where she was lodged at the house of the late Master Jean Rabateau, at that time King's advocate in the Parliament. Deputed in this city of Poitiers, by order of the King, were certain solemn doctors and masters, to wit, Master Pierre of Versailles, at that time Abbot of Talmont, later Bishop of Meaux; Jean Lambert, Guillaume Aimeri of the Order of Preaching Friars; Pierre Seguin of the Order of Carmelite Friars, Doctor of Holy Scripture; Mathieu Mesuage; Guillaume Lemaire, Bachelor of Theology, with several other King's counsellors, licenciates in Civil Law and Canon Law, who, on several occasions, during a period of about three weeks, examined Joan."

Joan, several times during the Trial of Condemnation, referred her questioners to the "book of Poitiers".

JOAN: That is in writing at Poitiers.
Question: The masters who examined you there, some over a month, others over three weeks, did they question you about the change in your apparel?
JOAN: I do not remember. (C.93)

One of the Poitiers examiners survived to be present at the Trial

* "sur le fait des aides": *taxes* is perhaps too formal: "in the matter of raising subsidies" might be better.

of Rehabilitation, Brother Seguin Seguin of the Order of Preaching Friars, professor of theology and, by this time, at about seventy years of age, Dean of the Faculty at Poitiers University: "I saw Joan for the first time at Poitiers. The King's Council had met there in the house of one La Macée, and among them was the Lord Archbishop of Rheims, then Chancellor of France (Regnault de Chartres). Summoned, apart from myself, were Master Jean Lombard, professor of theology at the University of Paris, Guillaume Lemaire, Canon of Poitiers, Bachelor of theology, Guillaume Aimeri, professor of theology of the Order of Preaching Friars, Brother Pierre Turelure, Master Jacques Madelon and several others whom I no longer remember. We were told that we had been summoned by the King to interrogate Joan, and to report what we made of her (*ce qu' il nous semblait d'elle*) to the King's Council, and we were sent to the house of Master Jean Rabateau at Poitiers, where Joan was lodging, to examine her. When we arrived we put several questions to Joan and, among other questions, Master Jean Lombard asked her why she was come and that the King wanted to know what had impelled her to come to him. And she answered boldly and gravely that while she was guarding the beasts, a voice had manifested itself to her which told her that God had great pity on the people of France and that she, Joan, must go to France. Upon hearing that, she had begun to weep; then the voice told her that she should go to Vaucouleurs and that there she would find a captain who would take her safely into France and to the King, and that she should doubt not; and she had done accordingly and had come to the King without any obstacle.

"Master Guillaume Aimeri interrogated her: 'Thou hast said that the voice told thee that God wishes to deliver the people of France from the calamities which afflict it. If he wishes to deliver it, it is not necessary to have men-at-arms.' Then Joan answered him: 'By God the men-at-arms will do battle and God will give victory.' With this answer Master Guillaume held himself satisfied. I asked her what language the voice spoke. She answered me: 'Better than yours.' Me, I spoke Limousin. And again I asked her if she believed in God; she answered me, 'Yes, better than you.' And then I told Joan that it was not God's will that she be believed if nothing appeared by which it should seem that she ought to be believed, and that the King could not be advised, on her mere assertion, to entrust her with soldiers that they be placed in peril, unless she had something else to say. She answered: 'In God's name, I am not come to

Poitiers to make signs; but take me to Orleans, I will show you the signs for which I have been sent,' adding that men be given her in such number as should seem good to her and that she would go to Orleans. Then she told me, me and others present, four things which were then to come and which thereafter happened. First, she said that the English would be defeated and that the siege which was laid to the town of Orleans would be raised and that the town of Orleans would be liberated of the English, but that first she would send them summonses.* She said next that the King would be crowned at Rheims. Thirdly, that the town of Paris would return to its obedience to the King; and that the Duke of Orleans would return from England. All that I have seen accomplished.

"We reported all that to the King's Council, and were of opinion that, given the imminent necessity and the peril in which the town of Orleans stood, the King could well use her help and send her to Orleans.

"We enquired, I and the others designated, into Joan's life and morals (mores) and we found that she was a good Christian and lived as a Catholic and was never known to be lazy. And the better to understand how she comported herself, women were sent to her who reported all she did and said to the Council. I believe that Joan was sent by God, considering that the King and the people who were his lieges (*en son obeissance*) had no hope, but that all believed in beating a retreat." (R.107-109)

That the case was, indeed, desperate is attested by all the writings of the times. In Joan's own circle, a woman who was well qualified to speak since her husband was in charge of the royal finances, the Marguerite la Touroulde whose evidence has already been quoted, conveys this impression for us: "When Joan came to the king at Chinon," she declares, "I was at Bourges where the Queen was. At that time there was in his kingdom and in those parts obedient (loyal) to the King, such calamity and such penury of money that it was piteous, and indeed those true to their allegiance to the King were in despair. I know it because my husband was at the time Receiver General and, both of the King's money and his own, he had not four crowns. And the city of Orleans was besieged by the English and there was no means of going to his aid. And it was in the midst of this calamity that Joan came, and, I believe it firmly, she came from God and was sent to raise up the King and the people still

---

* i.e., she would summon them to go or to surrender.—E.H.

within his allegiance, for at that time there was no hope but in God." (R.118)

The impression made by the contemporary texts is that things had come to such a pass that in the general opinion Joan might just as well be tried: things might, perhaps, go better in consequence, but could not go worse.

Jean Barbin, advocate in the Parliament: "Finally, it was concluded by the clerks after the interrogations and examinations by them accomplished, that there was in her nothing evil nor anything contrary to the Catholic faith, and that, given the King's necessity and the kingdom's, since the King and the inhabitants who were faithful to him were then in despair and could not hope for aid of any sort if it came not from God, that the King might as well take her in aid." (R.109–110)

Joan, meanwhile, was bearing all these delays impatiently.

Jean Pasquerel: "I have heard her say that she was not pleased with all these interrogations and that they were preventing her from accomplishing the work for which she was sent and that the need and time were come to act." (R.176)

Her first care, when at last permission was given her to take action, was to send the English a letter of summons.

Gobert Thibault, King's esquire: "I was at Chinon when Joan came seeking the King who was then residing at Chinon, but I did not have much acquaintance with her at that place. I knew her better thereafter, for, as the King wished to go to Poitiers, Joan was taken there. . . . She was lodged in the house of one Rabateau, and it was in that house that Pierre de Versailles and Jean Erault, in my presence, talked to Joan. As we were arriving there, Joan came to meet us and she clapped me on the shoulder, saying that she would like well to have many men of my sort. Then Pierre de Versailles told Joan that they were sent to her by the King. She answered, 'I think that you are sent to question me,' saying (adding), 'Me, I know neither A nor B.' Then we asked her why she was come. She answered, 'I come on behalf of the King of Heaven to raise the siege of Orleans and to conduct the King to Rheims for his coronation and sacring.' She asked us if we had paper and ink, saying to Master Jean Erault: 'Write what I shall tell you: "You Suffort, Classidas and La Poule, I summon you, in the name (de par, by) of the King of Heaven, that you go away to England."' And on that occasion, Versailles and Erault did nothing else, that I remember, and Joan remained in Poitiers for as long a time as did the King."

The "book of Poitiers", the Minute-book in which the questions put to Joan, and her answers, were recorded in writing, has not, unfortunately, been preserved for us; were it ever to be found it would be a source-document of the very highest value, for it would give us what the Trial of Condemnation does not: Joan freely answering questions put to her in good faith, whereas what the Trial of Condemnation shows us is a prisoner being questioned by people bent upon convicting her, under the control of a judge whom she knows perfectly well to be "her capital enemy", as indeed she was to tell him, since he had revealed himself to be an agent of the English.

Nothing remains to us of the Poitiers interrogatories but a few lines, the conclusions which were passed on by the doctors to the King and used again at the Trial of Rehabilitation: "That in her is found no evil, but only good, humility, virginity, devotion (devoutness), honesty, simplicity."

And the fact is that this conclusion convinced the King that she could perfectly well be allowed to take action and undertake that trial which, she declared, would be the "sign" of her mission: the attempt to deliver Orleans. Another examination had, however, taken place, which was, as it were, a double-check to the first: the girl was calling herself Joan the Maid; but was she, or was she not, a virgin? If she was not then she was clearly guilty of a flagrant imposture; if she was, that might be proof that she had, as she claimed, indeed "vowed her virginity to God", virginity being the sign of one who dedicates himself or herself wholly to God.

Jean Pasquerel: "I have heard it said that Joan, when she came to the King, was examined by women to know how it was with her, whether she was a man or a woman and whether she was corrupt or virgin. She was found to be woman and virgin and maid. Those who visited her (person) were, as I have heard say, the lady de Gaucourt (Jeanne de Preuilly) and the lady de Treves (Jeanne de Mortemer)." (R.175)

Both these ladies were in the suite of Yolande of Aragon, Queen of Sicily, the King's mother-in-law and one of the notabilities utterly devoted to his cause. It was under her influence it is said that Charles VII, albeit himself vacillating and timorous, had made up his mind, some years previously, to take the title of King of France.

Jean d'Aulon: "The Master's report having been made to the King, this Maid was put into the hands of the Queen of Sicily, mother of the Queen our sovereign lady, and to [sic] certain ladies being with her, by whom this maid was seen, visited and secretly regarded and examined in the secret parts of her body. But after they had seen and looked at all there was to look at in this case, the lady said and related to the King that she and her ladies found with certainty that she was a true and entire maid in whom appeared no corruption or violence. I was present when the lady made her report.

"After having heard these things, the King, considering the great goodness which was in this maid and what she had said to him, that by God was she sent to him, concluded in his Council that, henceforth, he would use her aid for the war, given that to do so was she sent to him. It was, therefore, deliberated that she should be sent into the City of Orleans which was then besieged by the English. For this were given to her people for the service of her person, and others to take her there. For the ward and conducting of her, I was ordered by the King, our lord.*

"For the safety of her body, the lord King had made for the Maid harness (armour) proper to her body and, that done, ordered her a certain quantity of men-at-arms to lead and conduct her safely, she and those of her company, to the place of Orleans." (R.156-157)

Joan was taken first to Tours where, while the King was making an effort to raise a fresh army, her armour and banner were made. It was in Tours that Jean Pasquerel made her acquaintance.

Jean Pasquerel: "The first time I heard Joan spoken of and heard tell how she was come to the King, I was at Puy. In that town were Joan's mother and some of those who had brought Joan to the King.† As they knew me slightly, they told me that I ought to go with them to Joan and that they would not let me go until they had taken me to her. And I went with them to the town of Chinon and beyond to the town of Tours in whose convent (monastery) I was Lector.

"In this town of Tours, Joan was lodged at the house of Jean Dupuy, a burgess of Tours. I found Joan at his house and those who had brought me spoke, saying, 'Joan, we have brought you this good Father, if you knew him well you would love him much.'

"Joan answered that she was well pleased and that she had already heard tell of me and that on the morrow she would like

* Jean d'Aulon became Joan's intendant, sharing her fate throughout the wars and even into prison.
† 1429 was one of the years in which the famous pilgrimage to Puy takes place—years in which Good Friday falls on March 25, day of the Annunciation.

to confess to me. The next day I heard her confession and sang mass before her, and from that hour I followed her always and remained with her unto the town of Compiègne where she was seized. . . .

"Joan had her standard made on which was painted the image of Our Saviour seated in judgment in the clouds of the sky, and there was an angel painted holding in his hand a *fleur-de-lys* which the image was blessing. I was in Tours, there where this standard was painted. . . .

"When Joan left Tours to go to Orleans, she asked me not to leave her, but to remain always with her as her confessor, which I promised her to do. We were at Blois, about two or three days, waiting for the victuals which were there being loaded into boats, and it was there that she bade me have made a banner to rally the priests, and on this banner to have painted the image of Our Lord crucified, which I did. This banner completed, Joan twice a day, morning and evening, caused all the priests to assemble and, when they were met together, they sang anthems and hymns to Saint Mary, and Joan was with them and she would not have the soldiers mingle with the priests if they had not confessed. And she exhorted all the soldiers to confess that they might come to this assembly. And at the assembly itself all the priests were ready to hear those who wished to confess. When Joan set out from Blois to go to Orleans, she caused all the priests to rally about this banner, and the priests marched ahead of the army. They went out by the Sologne way thus assembled, singing the *Veni Creator Spiritus* and many other anthems, and camped that night in the fields and the same on the day following."

This banner differed from the standard which Joan bore into battle as her "ensign", carried by a standard-bearer who preceded her. It was the custom at the time, a time when, since one was completely encased in iron when leading an attack, a distinctive sign was necessary to rally the men of one's "battle", a "battle" being a captain's company. The account book of Master Hemon Raguier, King's treasurer, contains the following entry: "And to Hauves Poulnoir, painter, living at Tours, for painting and providing the stuff for a great standard and a small for the Maid, 25 pounds* *tournois*."

She had not only an intendant, Jean d'Aulon, but two pages: one called Raymond who was to be killed during the assault on Paris, and Louis de Coutes. In addition, two heralds named, respectively,

---

* The *livre tournois* was probably about one silver shilling.– -E.H.

Ambleville and Guyenne. In other words, she was equipped and treated exactly the same as any other captain.

"It was at Tours," declares Louis de Coutes, "that I was told and ordered that I was to be Joan's page, with one named Raymond. From that hour I was always with Joan and I always went with her, serving her in my office of page at Blois as at Orleans, until we arrived before Paris. At the time when she was at Tours, a suit of armour was given to her and Joan received her condition (commission, rank) from the King. And from Tours she went to the town of Blois in company with some men-at-arms of the King, and that company, from that very time, had great confidence in Joan, and Joan kept with the soldiers in the town of Blois during some time, I no longer remember how much, and then it was decided to withdraw from Blois and to go to Orleans on the Sologne side. And Joan withdrew with her troops of men-at-arms, continually exhorting the soldiers that they trust altogether in God and confess their sins. And in her company I often saw Joan receive the sacrament of the Eucharist." (R.169)

Certain details of her equipment are known to us. Thus, and again in Hemon Raguier's accounts, we find, for May 10, 1429, a payment: "To the Master Armourer, for a complete harness for the Maid, 100 pounds *tournois*."

In addition to the armour there was the sword itself, of which we know that she had caused it to be taken from the church of Sainte-Catherine at Fierbois.

JOAN: When I was at Tours or at Chinon I sent to seek a sword which was in the church of Sainte-Catherine of Fierbois, behind the altar, and it was found at once all covered with rust.

Question: How did you know that this sword was there?

JOAN: This sword was in the earth, all rusty, and there were upon it five crosses and I knew it by my voices and I had never seen the man who went to seek this sword. I wrote to the prelates of the place that if they please I should have the sword and they sent it to me. It was not very deep under ground behind the altar, as it seems to me, but I do not know exactly whether it was before or behind the altar. I think that I wrote at the time that it was behind the altar. After this sword had been found, the prelates of the place had it rubbed, and at once the rust fell from it without difficulty. There was an arms merchant of Tours who went to seek it, and the prelates of that place gave me a sheath, and those of Tours also, with them, had two sheaths made for me: one of red velvet and the other of cloth-of-gold, and I myself had another made of right strong leather. But when I was captured, it was not that sword which I had. I always wore that sword until I had withdrawn from Saint-Denis after the assault against Paris. (C.76–77)

Question: Had you, when you went to Orleans, a standard, and of what colour?

JOAN: I had a standard whose field was sewn with fleurs-de-lys and there was the world figured and two angels at the sides and its colour was white, (and) of *boucassin* canvas. And there, it seems to me, were written the names of Jesus and of Mary, and they were embroidered in silk. . . .

Question: Which did you like the better, your standard or your sword?

JOAN: I liked better, even forty times, my standard than my sword.

Question: Who caused you to have this painting on the standard done?

JOAN: I have told you often enough that I did nothing but by God's commandment. I bore this standard when we went forward against the enemy to avoid killing anyone. I have never killed anyone. (C.78)

What impression did this girl—whose company, given to her by the King, were obliged to obey her as they had to obey any other military commander—make on her soldiers? Several of them have told us.

Thiband d'Armagnac or de Termes, Knight, bailiff of Chartres: "Apart from the matter of the war, she was simple and ignorant. But in the conduct and disposition of armies and in the matter of warfare, in drawing-up the army in battle (order) and heartening the soldiers, she behaved as if she had been the shrewdest captain in the world and had all her life been learning (the art of) war."

Louis de Coutes: "As far as I was in a position to know, Joan was a good and honest woman, living in Catholic fashion. She very readily heard mass and never missed going to hear it if that was possible for her. She waxed very wrath when she heard the name of God blasphemed, or if she heard someone swear. Several times, I heard, when the lord Duke of Alençon swore or spoke some blasphemy, that she reprimanded him, and in general nobody in the army dared, before her, swear or blaspheme for fear of being by her reprimanded. She would not have any women with the army. Once, near to the town of Château-Thierry, having seen the mistress of one of the soldiers, a Knight, she pursued her with drawn sword. She did not, however, strike the woman, but warned her gently and charitably that she be no longer found in the company of the soldiers, otherwise she would do something to her which would not please her." (R.176)

This testimony is confirmed by the Duke of Alençon himself: "Joan was chaste and she detested the women who follow soldiers. I saw her once at Saint-Denis, returning from the King's coronation, pursue with drawn sword a girl who was with the soldiers, and in such manner that in chasing* her she broke her sword. She became very incensed when she heard the soldiers swear, and scolded them much and especially me who swore from time to time. So that when I saw her, I refrained from my swearing. Sometimes in the army I lay down to sleep with Joan and the soldiers, all in the straw together (a la paillade), and sometimes I saw Joan prepare for the night and sometimes I looked at her breasts which were beautiful, and yet I never had carnal desire for her. . . .

"Joan, in these matters, apart from the matter of war, was simple and young, but in the matter of war she was very expert, in the management of the lance as in the drawing up of the army in battle order and in preparing the artillery. And at that all marvelled, that she could act in so prudent and well-advised a fashion in the matter of war as might a captain of twenty or thirty years experience have done, above all in the preparation of the artillery, for it was in that that she comported herself very well." (R.153–154)

Simon Beaucroix, esquire: "Joan was a good Catholic, fearing God . . . I remember very well that from the moment I was with her never did I have the will to do evil. Joan slept always with young girls, she did not like to sleep with old women. She detested swearing and blasphemy, she apostrophised those who swore and blasphemed. In the army she would never have had those of her company pillage anything. Never would she eat victuals when she knew them to have been looted. Once, a Scot gave her to understand that she had eaten of a calf which had been looted. She was very angry and for that made to strike the Scotsman.

"She would never have women of evil life in the army with the soldiers. That is why none such would have dared be found in company with Joan. When she found any of them, she obliged them

* The word is *poursuivant*; it could possibly mean *chastising*.—E.H.

to go away, unless the soldiers were willing to take them as wives. I believe that she was a true Catholic, fearing God and keeping his precepts, obedient according to her capacity to the Church's commandments. She showed pity not only for the French, but also for the enemies. I know this for during a long time I was with her and often I helped her put on her armour." (R.115–116)

We have in her page Louis de Coutes another witness to that pity shown to the enemy: "Joan was pious and she felt great pity at such massacres. Once, when a Frenchman was leading away some English prisoners, he struck one of the Englishmen on the head so hard that he left him for dead. Joan, seeing this, dismounted from her horse. She had the Englishman make his confession, supporting his head and consoling him with all her power." (R.172)

But it was above all Joan's purity which seems to have struck the men-at-arms.

Gobert Thibault: "Joan was a good Christian. She willingly heard mass every day and often received the sacrament of the Eucharist. She was much vexed when she heard swearing, and that was a good sign according to what was said by the lord confessor of the King, who took great pains to inform himself concerning her life and all things about her.

"In the army she was always with the soldiers, and I have heard it said by several of Joan's familiar acquaintances, that they had never felt desire for her, that is to say that sometimes they had the carnal desire for her (*ils en avaient volonté charnel*), however never dared give way to it, and they believed that it was not possible to try it (or "to want to"). And often, when they were talking among themselves about the sin of the flesh and spoke words which might excite lust, when they saw her and drew nigh her they could no longer talk of such things and abruptly ceased their carnal transports. On this subject I questioned several of those who sometimes lay down to sleep at night in Joan's company, and they answered me as I have said, adding that they had never felt carnal desire at the moment of seeing her."

We will, by way of summing up these impressions, conclude with the evidence of Marguerite la Touroulde, of particular value because it is the judgment of a woman who lived intimately with Joan and must have known her in all her diverse aspects. Marguerite la Touroulde: "I did not see Joan until the time when the King returned from Rheims where he had been crowned. He came to the town of Bourges where the Queen was and me with her . . . Joan was then brought to Bourges and, by command of the lord d'Albret, she was lodged in my house. . . . She was in my house for a period of three weeks, sleeping, drinking and eating, and almost every day I slept with Joan and I neither saw in her nor perceived anything of any kind of unquietness*, but she behaved herself as an honest and Catholic woman, for she went very often to confession, willingly heard mass and often asked me to go to Matins. And at her instance I went, and took her with me several times.

"Sometimes we talked together and some said to Joan that doubtless she was not afraid to go into battle because she knew well that she would not be killed. She answered that she was no safer than any other combatant. And sometimes Joan told how she had been examined by the clerks and that she had answered them: 'In Our Lord's books there is more than in yours. . . .' Joan was very simple and ignorant and knew absolutely nothing, it seems to me, excepting in the matter of war. I remember that several women came to my house while Joan was staying there, and brought paternosters (chaplets) and other objects of piety that she might touch them, which made her laugh and say to me, 'Touch them yourself, they will be as good from your touch as from mine.' She was open-handed (large) in almsgiving and most willingly gave to the indigent and to the poor, saying that she had been sent for the consolation of the poor and the indigent.

"And several times I saw her at the bath and in the bath-houses (étuves), and so far as I was able to see, she was a virgin, and from all that I know she was all innocence, excepting in arms, for I saw her riding on horseback and bearing a lance as the best of soldiers would have done it, and at that the men-at-arms marvelled."
(R.119-120)

COMMENTARY

Poitiers was, indeed, what Boissonade called it, a "stage of capital import in Joan of Arc's mission". When she arrived there she was as yet no more than a strange young girl whose words people wondered whether to take seriously. The King was manifestly shaken by some revelation which she made to him, but was not yet sure whether it had been made by a witch, a woman possessed, or simply by an *illuminata*.

* "*quoi que ce soit de trouble*": the witness means, I think, any troubling, any want of clear purity of Joan's mind and spirit.—E.H.

What did the "royal sign" consist of? We have already given all that we have by way of documents touching this subject, and are bound to conclude only that we do not know, that our ignorance is as total as that of the Rouen doctors. Some have insisted on believing that there must have been a material "sign", legendary sayings which went the rounds in the Middle Ages are recalled; legends of a crimson cross or fleur-de-lys on the right shoulder, which Kings (of France) were supposed to have been born with. (See, in this connection, *Le signe royal et le secret de Jeanne d'Arc*, Antoine Thomas, Rev. List. CIII. p. 278.)

In fact, given the almost total want of documentation, any hypothesis whatsoever is permissible—on condition that it be offered as an hypothesis and not as a certainty.

After Poitiers, Joan had permission to take action. She was not really "War Chief" (*chef de guerre*) as it was put in the letter-of-summons sent by her to the English (see next chapter); she herself denied or deprecated the epithet which was probably added by the clerk to whom she dictated the letter. Some such proceeding was common enough at the time: you dictated your letter to a clerk who "cast it into correct form", not infrequently adding something of his own devising. The conduct of the military operations at Orleans was entrusted to the Bastard of Orleans, subsequently count of Dunois, the town being a fief of his half-brother Charles, at that time a prisoner-of-war. As to the Loire campaign, the expeditionary force was commanded by the Duke d'Alençon. But Joan was nevertheless treated as a captain on an equality with the other captains, a La Hire, for example, or a Xaintrailles, with her own military household, her own "battle", her own men-at-arms.

Her Poitiers examination was studied in detail by Boissonade (*op. cit.* above). It included a theological enquiry: during three weeks Joan was questioned at the house of Master Jean Rabateau, Counsellor in the Parliament of Poitiers who lived "in the hotel of the Rose" (on the site of the rue de la Cathedrale). During this time two mendicant friars were sent to Domremy to enquire into Joan's origins and morals (Jean Barbin's deposition). Subsequently came the verification of Joan's virginity under the control of Yolande of Sicily, the King's mother-in-law. That, it should be noted, was the only occasion when we find her interfering directly in any matter concerning Joan. She financed, in part at least, the Orleans expedition, but that was neither the first nor the last time she did something of the kind, having energetically espoused her son-in-law's cause and played the part of a mother to him whose own mother, Isabeau of Bavaria, was neither inclined nor able to do so. Impossible to infer from this, as some however have done, that Joan was the Queen of Sicily's "tool"; for in that case we should also have to see her as Bedford's "tool" since, on the occasion of the second verification of Joan's virginity which was to take place at Rouen, control of the examination was entrusted to Anne of Burgundy, Duchess of Bedford. The most we can say is that on both occasions choice was made of the woman best placed to inspire complete confidence.

The Poitiers "trial" was conducted, as were to be the two others—those of condemnation and rehabilitation—by a series of interrogatories recorded by clerks. Theologians were, as far as possible, also called into consultation, and it is to this that we owe two treatises: Jean Gerson's*—he was ex-Chancellor of the University of Paris but had taken refuge in Lyon at the time of the English invasion—and Jacques Gelu's, Archbishop of Embrun and loyal partisan of the French cause. And once conclusions had been reached, the King's council, having deliberated, adopted them.

What happened to the *Book of Poitiers?* The only part we find recorded in the Minutes of the Rehabilitation Trial is the text of the doctors' conclusions (Q.111, 391-392). It has been supposed that Regnault de Chartres, Archbishop of Rheims, who had been chairman of the Poitiers Commission of Prelates and theologians, destroyed it in 1431: given the man's character—he was the very type of the opportunist—it may well have been so; he may have been afraid that he had protected a heretic.

But there is no reason why a copy should never have been made. There are so many documents, bundles of papers and registers in our archives still unidentified or inadequately studied that we may legitimately hope to recover the whole text one of these days; and it will surely be the greatest historical discovery of the times. Some surprise, even, may be felt at the fact that methodical research into so captivating a subject has never been undertaken.

On the other hand, there has of recent years been a rumour going the rounds that this Poitiers record exists—and is to be found "in a secret cupboard at the Vatican". Let us first make it clear that the Vatican's secret cupboards must be of monstrous dimensions to contain all the documents on all kinds of subjects which are attributed to them; but that is not the point. According to the tittle-tattle we

---

* See the study of this treatise by Wayman, Dorothy G., *The Chancellor & Jeanne d'Arc*, Vol. 17, Nos. 2-3, 1 957. *Franciscan Studies*, St. Bonaventure University, New York.

are alluding to, the text of the Poitiers trial is kept hidden "by order of the Church" because, it seems, in it is to be found the proof of Joan's "bastardy".

History has nothing to do with such allegations. If we really have a "secret" cupboard to deal with, who is supposed to have been able to get a sight of the document? And if someone has seen it, why on earth did he not bring away a classification mark, reference, an indication of some sort, capable of persuading us to believe in its existence? A document devoid of reference and which nobody can consult, and whose existence is unverifiable, does not exist for the historian. It is really altogether too easy to "prove" an imaginary fact by announcing it to be based on a "secret" document.

(i) It would be necessary to prove, then: That the record of the Poitiers trial is still actually in existence; where; and in what form.

(ii) That it does indeed contain proof of Joan of Arc's "bastardy".

And it is by no means clear why "the Church" should be so bent on keeping it hidden. the Church never showed any great enthusiasm in the matter of Joan's sainthood. One might rather reproach it for want of enthusiasm, since it waited 500 years to canonise her. If, less than forty years after that canonisation, a new fact compromising the heroine's sanctity came to light, it may safely be assumed that the Church would not be unduly disturbed: the Church did not hesitate to demote St. Philomena when archaeological research revealed a mistaken identity.

Furthermore, since when has bastardy been a bar to canonisation? The Church's most recently made saint, Martin de Porres, beatified in 1837 and canonised 6 May 1962, was the bastard son of a Negro mother and a Spanish father. In the eyes of the Church, at least, bastardy is not an obstacle to perfection.

We will add a word or two which will give some idea of the methods, methods incompatible with historical method to say the least of it, which are used by partisans of the bastardy hypothesis. During her trial, Joan stated that the sword which she had sent for from the church of Sainte-Catherine of Fierbois was marked with five crosses. Cauchon, trying to confound her by proving that she had made use of crosses as magical signs in her military activities, asked: "Of what use were the five crosses which were on the sword?" And Joan answered: "I do not know." The bastardy-theorists consider this question and answer "singular"; they consider that for "crosses" we should read "fleurs-de-lys" and that this would prove that Joan was of royal birth; and that the words "fleurs-de-lys" were scratched out and "crosses" substituted in order to preserve the secret.

Refutation of such stuff would serve no purpose here: one must resign oneself to the fact that texts are texts, legends—legends.

4

ORLEANS

"Jhesus-Maria, King of England, and you, Duke of Bedford, who call yourself regent of the Kingdom of France, you, Guillaume de la Poule, count of Suffort*, Jean, sire of Talbot, and you, Thomas, sire of Scales, who call yourselves lieutenants of the Duke of Bedford, acknowledge the summons of the King of Heaven. Render to the Maid here sent by God the King of Heaven, the keys of all the good towns which you have taken and violated in France. She is here come by God's will to reclaim the blood royal†. She is very ready to make peace, if you will acknowledge her to be right, provided that France you render, and pay for having held it. And you, archers, companions of war, men-at-arms and others who are before the town of Orleans, go away into your country, by God. And if so be not done, expect news of the Maid who will come to see you shortly, to your very great injury. King of England, if (you) do not so, I am chief-of-war and in whatever place I attain your people in France, I will make them quit it willy nilly‡. And if they will not obey, I will have them all slain; I am here sent by God, the King of Heaven, body for body, to drive you out of all France. And if they will obey I will be merciful to them. And be not of another opinion, for you will not hold the Kingdom of France from God, the King of Heaven, Son of St. Mary, but will hold it for King Charles, the rightful heir, for God, the King of Heaven so wills it, and that is revealed to him by the Maid who will enter into Paris with a goodly company. If you will not believe the news (conveyed) by God and the Maid, in what place soever we find you, we shall strike into it and there make such great *babay*, that none so great has been in France for a thousand years, if you yield not to right. And believe firmly that the King of Heaven will send greater strength (more forces) to the Maid than you will be able to bring up

---

* William de la Pole, Earl of Suffolk.
† i.e., "rightful heir."
‡ *veuillent on ne veuillent.*

against her and her good men-at-arms; and when it comes to blows will it be seen who has the better right of the God of Heaven. You, Duke of Bedford, the Maid prays and requires of you that you cause no more destruction to be done. If you grant her right, still may you come into her company there where the French shall do the greatest feat of arms which ever was done for Christianity. And make answer if you wish to make peace in the city of Orleans. And if you make it not, you shall shortly remember it, to your very great injury. Written this Tuesday of Holy Week (March 22, 1429)." (C.221–222)

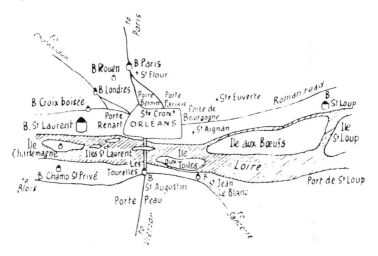

THE SIEGE OF ORLEANS

The capital B preceding certain names means Blockhouse.

It was in these terms that the letter of summons sent by Joan to the English was written, the moment she was made free to act, after the Poitiers examination. And it seems likely that it was from this letter that the enemy first heard of her existence. Until then nothing but vague rumours had gone the rounds, rumours which must have been eagerly seized upon wherever the people were for the French king, but which the English, sure of themselves, had probably made fun of as a lot of old wives' tales. Up until the moment when Orleans had been delivered, as we shall see in the following quotations, Joan was treated by them as nothing but an adventuress on whom insults should be heaped; thereafter, in the stupefaction caused by her unexpected victory, she was, for them, nothing but a witch and magician.

Orleans was the essential feat of arms, the very sign of her mission, as she herself had expressly stated (see Seguin Seguin's evidence in the previous chapter). It is therefore necessary to go back a little in time again, in order to follow events in Orleans before Joan arrived.

"The Count de Salebris (John, Earl of Salisbury), who was a very great lord and the most renowned for feats of arms of all the English and who, for Henry, King of England, whose kinsman he was and as his lieutenant and chief of his army in his kingdom, had been present in several battles and diverse encounters and conquests against the French, in which he had always borne himself valliantly, thinking to take by force the city of Orleans which was held by the party of the King its sovereign and lord, Charles, Seventh of that name, had besieged it Tuesday the twelfth day of October 1428 with great power and army which he encamped on the Sologne side and near to one of the villages which is called the Portereau. In this army were with him Messire Guillaume de la Poule, count of Suffort and Messire Jean de la Poule (John de la Pole), his brother, the Lord of Scales—Classidas, of great renown (William Glasdale)—and several other lords and soldiers* both English and others false Frenchmen on their side. But the soldiers who were there (i.e., in Orleans) by way of garrison, had that same day, before the coming of the English, with the aid and council of the citizens of Orleans, pulled down the church and monastery of the Augustins of Orleans and all the houses which were at the Portereau, in order that their enemies could not use them as billets nor there construct fortification against the City."

The *Journal of the Siege of Orleans*, from which these details are taken,† was composed, at least as to the part which concerns us (touching the beleaguering and deliverance of the City) from notes written down day by day, some of which can be checked by still extant documents in the town's archives. It gives the detail of what took place beginning on Tuesday, October 12, 1428.

"The Sunday following (October 17th) hurled the English into the City six score and four stones from bombards and great canon, of which there was one such stone weighed 116 pounds. Among the others, they had installed near Saint-Jean-le-Blanc . . . a great

---

* Literally "war people".
† Page 96 of the Quicherat edition.

canon which they called Passe-volant. This one hurled stones weighing 80 pounds which did great damage to the houses and buildings of Orleans albeit it killed not nor wounded any unless one woman, named Belle, living near to the Chesnau postern.*

"This same week did the English canon damage or destroy twelve mills which were on the river Loire between the city and the Tourneuve. Accordingly those of the town had made eleven horse-mills which much consoled them. And meanwhile the canons and engines of the English made, against the French within Orleans, several sorties and raids between the Tourelles† of the bridge and Saint-Jean-le-Blanc since that Sunday until Thursday one -and-twentieth day of the same month.‡

"On this day of Thursday, the English assailed a boulevard (rampart) which was made of faggots and earth, before the Tourelles, against which the assault lasted four hours without ceasing, for they began at ten o'clock in the forenoon and did not leave off until two o'clock in the afternoon. There were done several great feats of arms on one side as on the other. The women of Orleans were of great succour, for they ceased not to carry very diligently to them that defended the boulevard, several things neces-sary, as water, boiling oil and fat, lime, ashes and caltrops. At the end of the assault there were some wounded on both sides but especially the English of whom died more than twelve score. It came to pass that during the assault (there) rode about Orleans the lord de Gaucourt of which he was governor, but in passing before Saint-Pierre-au-Pont, he fell from his horse peradventure, so that he broke his arm. He was at once taken to the baths to have it dressed.

"The Friday following, twenty-second of the month of October, tolled the belfry bell, for the French thought that the English were attacking the Tourelles boulevard from the end of the bridge by way of the mine which they had dug; but they brought themselves not to it in that hour . . . The Saturday following, twenty-third day of this month, those of Orleans burnt and threw down the Tourelles boulevard and abandoned it because it was all mined and was no longer tenable from what the soldiers said.

"The Sunday following twenty-fourth day of October the Eng-lish attacked and took the Tourelles from the end of the bridge

---

* A low door in the ramparts opening on to the Loire bank.
† Watch or guard turrets.
‡ At the east point of the town on the Loire.

because they were all demolished and broken by the canon and
heavy artillery which they had hurled against (them). Thus there
was no defence because none dared any longer stay in them."
(J.S.O.07-100)

The information contained in this shows how the English, with
great strategic shrewdness, had from the beginning of the siege cut
Orleans itself off by severing its only communicating link with
what we should now call the "free zone". This bridge, defended
by the Tourelles fortification, and taken on October 24th, was in
fact the bridge over the Loire which linked Orleans with the left
bank—the part of France which, as we have seen, was still in the
French King's hands. The two fortifications named above, Saint-
Jean-le-Blanc and the Augustins were, likewise, on the left bank of
the Loire, on the river bank, and they were immediately occupied. Having made themselves masters of this vitally important
point, the English settled down to besiege at their leisure a town
which was now sure to fall into their hands sooner or later. For
the preceding months had witnessed a brilliant advance along the
whole front; and in August the Earl of Salisbury had made sure of
all the country between Dreux and Chartres, then the towns and
countryside of Toury, Le Puiset, Jauville, Meung and Beaugency.
However, this same day of October 24th ended with a serious
loss for the whole English Army:
"This day, Sunday, in the evening, the Earl of Salisbury, having
with him the Captain Glasdale and several others, went into the
Tourelles after they had been taken, the better to look over the site
(*assiette*) of Orleans. But while he was there, looking at the town
through the windows of the Tourelles, he was struck by a canon
that was said to have been fired from a tower called the Tour
Notre-Dame (situated at the west of the town). . . . The canon-
shot struck him so in the face that it beat in one half of the cheek
and put out one of his eyes. Which was a very great good to this
kingdom, for he was chief of the army, the most feared and renowned in arms of all the English.
"The Monday following there arrived in Orleans, to comfort,
succour and aid the city, several noble lords, knights, captains and
esquires very renowned in warfare in which they were the princi-
pals. Jean, Bastard of Orleans, the lord of Saint-Sévère, marshal of
France, the lord Du Bueil, messire Jacques de Chabannes, seneschal
of the Bourbonnais, and a valiant Gascon captain called Etienne of

Vignolles, called La Hire, who was of most great renown, and the valiant men of war who were in his company.

"The Wednesday following, twenty-seventh day of October, departed this life during the night the Earl of Salisbury, in the town of Meung-sur-Loire, where he had been carried from the siege after he had received the canon-shot of which he died. At his death were right dumbfounded and doleful the English maintaining the siege and they made great mourning albeit they did so as secretly as they might for fear lest those of Orleans should perceive it. . . . The earl's death did great injury to the English and, on the other hand, great profit to the French. Some have said since that the Earl of Salisbury came to that end by the divine judgment of God and they believe it as much because he failed of his promise to the Duke of Orleans, prisoner in England, to whom he had promised to injure none of his lands, as because he spared neither monasteries nor churches but looted them and had them looted as soon as he could enter. . . . Especially there was looted by him the church of Notre-Dame de Clery and its village (bourg)." (J.S.O.100–102)

However, this loss was to be rapidly made good:

"The first day of December following, arrived at the Tourelles of the bridge several English lords of whom among the rest him of greatest renown was messire Jean Talbot, premier baron of England, and the lord of Scales, accompanied by three hundred combatants who brought victuals, canons, bombards and other gear of war by which they have since been hurling against the walls and into Orleans continually and more powerfully than before they had done in the lifetime of the Earl of Salisbury, for they cast such stones as weighed eight score four pounds which wrought much evil and injury against the city and many houses and fine buildings." (J.S.O.103)

The siege continued during several months without any notable event; at the time the English counted mainly on famine and exhaustion to reduce the town. However, the diarist of the *Journal of the Siege* did preserve for us some notes worth recording here, for they help us to recapture the atmosphere of the time and place.

There were, for example, the exploits of master Jean, the "culverineer", a native of Lorraine . . .

". . . Who was said to be the best master there was in that trade. And well he showed it, for he had a great culverin from which he often hurled . . . so much so that he wounded and killed many English. And to mock them he let himself sometimes fall to the ground, feigning to be dead or wounded, and had himself borne into the town. But he returned at once to the fray and so wrought that the English knew him yet living to their great injury and displeasure." (J.S.O.105)

Or, again, there is the episode of the Christmas truce:

"Christmas Day were given and granted truces on one side as on the other from nine o'clock in the morning until three o'clock in the afternoon. And during this time, Glasdale and other lords of England requested of the Bastard of Orleans and of the lord of Saint-Sévère, Marshal of France, that they might have a note of high minstrelry (*haut menetriers*), trumpets and clarions, which was granted them. And they played the instruments quite a long time, making great melody. But as soon as the truces were broken (i.e. over), each fell again on guard." (J.S.O.105)

And the days succeeded each other and brought the people none but bad news: their reserves of victuals were diminishing and they began to feel the pinch of famine. Thus, every arrival of fresh victuals was noted in the *Journal of the Siege*:

"The 3rd January arrived before Orleans one hundred and fifty-four swine large and fat, and four hundred sheep, and passed these cattle in by the Saint-Loup gate at which the people were right joyful, for they came at need." (J.S.O.108)

The sorties which were attempted did not succeed:

"Saturday fifteenth day of January, about eight o'clock at night, sallied out of the city the Bastard of Orleans, the lord of Saint-Severe and messire Jacques de Chabannes, accompanied by many knights, esquires, captains and citizens of Orleans, and thought to charge upon a part of the army at Saint-Laurent...." (A fortified islet in the Loire off Orleans.) "... But the English perceived it and cried the alarm among their troops whereby they were armed, so that there was a great and hard affray. At last the French retired for the English were coming out in full strength." (J.S.O.110)

And above all there was the disastrous February 12, 1429, the "day of the herrings". The English were bringing into their camp a convoy of victuals composed chiefly of barrels of salt herring, since it was Lent, the day being the eve of *Brandons*, first Sunday in Lent. Moreover, salt herring was, at that time, a staple food. The Bastard of Orleans, the Constable John Stuart, and other knights, joined by the count of Clermont and his troops, decided to attempt an assault against the convoy:

"Many knights and esquires of the lands of England and France, accompanied by fifteen hundred combatants, as English, Picards, Normans and people of diverse other countries, were bringing about three hundred carts and small carts" (possibly hand barrows), "laden with victuals, and with much war gear as canons, bows, bundles, arrows and other things, taking them to the other English who were maintaining the siege of Orleans. But when they knew by their spies the countenance of the French and learned that their intention was to attack them, they enclosed themselves (by) making a park [sic] with their carts and pointed stakes by way of barriers . . . and put themselves in good order of battle, there waiting to live or die; for to escape they had scarcely hope, considering their small number against the multitude of French who were all come together by a common accord, and concluded that none would dismount except the archers and baggage bearers* . . ."

However, the French Captains and the Constable of Scotland, who had joined forces with them, were unable to agree as to strategy. The battle opened in a tentative manner while they waited for the Count of Clermont, who kept sending messages asking that the enemy should not be engaged until he had brought up his reinforcements.

"So that, between two and three o'clock in the afternoon, the French archers drew near to their adversaries, of whom some had already come out of their park" [sic: say, laager] ". . . whom they forced to withdraw hastily. . . . Those who were able to escape went back inside their fortification with the rest. Now, when the Constable of Scotland saw that they had held themselves thus shoulder to shoulder in their ranks, without showing any wish to come out, was he too wishful to attempt to assail them, so much so that he disobeyed the order which had been given to all that none should dismount, for he began to assault without waiting for the others and, at his example, to help him, dismounted likewise the Bastard of Orleans . . . and many other knights and esquires with about four hundred combatants. . . . But little did it avail them, for, when the English saw that the great battle" (i.e., the main body) "which were quite far off, came on timidly (or slowly), and joined not with the Constable, they charged out swiftly from their park and struck among the French who were on foot, and put them to rout and flight. . . . More than that, the English, not sated with the slaughter that they had done on the place, before their park, spread themselves swiftly over the fields, chasing the foot soldiers, so much

* gens de trait—E.H.

so that at least twelve of their standards were to be seen far from each other in diverse places. Therefore, La Hire, Poton* and several other valiant men who were making off so shamefully, rallied to the number of sixty or eighty combatants and struck at the English who were thus scattered, so that they killed many. And certainly had all the other French turned about as they did, the honour and profit of the day would have been with them. . . . From this battle escaped among others the Bastard of Orleans, albeit at the beginning he was wounded by an arrow in the foot: two of his archers dragged him with great difficulty out of the press, put him on a horse and thus saved him. The Count of Clermont, who that day had been dubbed knight, and all his great army, never even pretended to succour their companions, as much because they had dismounted (to fight) on foot against the general agreement, as because they saw them almost all killed before their eyes. But when they saw that the English were the masters, they set out towards Orleans; in which they did not honourably, but shamefully." (J.S.O.120–124)

This inglorious day was also the last attempt to deliver the town before Joan's arrival. The count of Clermont hastened to withdraw his troops (18 February). After which only Jean, the Bastard, later Count of Dunois, and the Marshal Saint-Sévère, with their men, were left to defend the town. It was at this point that the citizens of Orleans, feeling themselves abandoned, sent an embassy to the Duke of Burgundy imploring him, in the name of his kinsman Charles, Duke of Orleans, still a prisoner in England, to do something for them. According to chroniclers, Philippe the Good is supposed to have asked the regent Bedford that Orleans be given into his keeping, and neutralised. Bedford refused, saying—still according to the chroniclers—"That he would be very angry to have beaten the bushes that others might take the birds." Philippe the Good, discontented with this answer, withdrew his troops from the force besieging Orleans.

Nevertheless the siege continued and the Journal now mentions none but insignificant supplies reaching the town:

"Friday 4 March, twelve horses laden with wheat, herrings and other victuals.
Sunday the 6th, seven horses laden with herrings and other victuals.
The Tuesday following, nine horses laden with victuals"—

* Poton de Xaitrailles.

etc., showing to what extremities the inhabitants were reduced. The town was, in fact, so closely invested that only a single issue remained open: the Bourgoyne gate opening on to the old Roman road on the right bank of the Loire, that is in the direction of the zone controlled by the English.

Numerous, subsequently, were those citizens of Orleans who bore witness to their anguish during those interminable days: thirty-six of them were to give evidence on the single day of March 16, 1456, during the Trial of Rehabilitation; and what they said may be summed up as follows:

"The inhabitants and citizens found themselves squeezed in such necessity by the besieging enemies that they knew not whom to have recourse to for a remedy, excepting (or, unless it be) to God." (R.139)

It was at this point that news reached these same inhabitants and citizens that a young girl had gone to the King of France, saying that she was sent by the King of Heaven to recover his kingdom for him. Obviously if we are to get some idea of the effect produced, we must enter into the general mentality of the period. Everybody at that time—or let us say almost everybody, for who will ever be able to estimate individual adherences to the general beliefs?—believed in God, and in a God who was master of all eventualities and could, therefore, intervene at will to make the unexpected happen: in other words, everyone believed in miracles. Furthermore, in the kingdom's state of disorganisation, and in view of the Orleanais' feeling that they had been abandoned, there could be no hope excepting in a miracle.

The Bastard of Orleans—that same brilliant captain who, two years before, had forced the enemy to raise the siege of Montargis —although his honour as a soldier was engaged, since he was in command of the defence of Orleans, was, when giving his evidence, foremost in declaring that all Joan's acts seemed to him, in the event, "divinely inspired". In any case, as soon as he heard of her, he sent to seek more information about her.

Jean, Bastard of Orleans: "I was in Orleans, at that time besieged by the English, when certain rumours circulated according to which had passed through the town of Gien a young girl, the Maid so-called, assuring that she was on her way to the noble Dauphin to raise the siege of Orleans and to take the Dauphin to Rheims that he might be crowned. As the city was in my keeping, being Lieutenant-General in the matter of warfare, for more ample infor-

mation in the matter of this maid, I sent to the King the Sire de
Villars, Seneschal of Beaucaire, and Jamet du Tillay who later became bailiff of Vermandois. Returned from their mission to the
King they told me, and said in public, in the presence of all the people
of Orleans who much desired to know the truth concerning the
coming of this Maid, that they themselves had seen the said maid
arrive to find the King in Chinon. They said also that the King,
in the first instance, was not willing to receive her, but that she
remained during two days, waiting to be allowed to enter the royal
presence. And this although she said and repeated that she was come
to raise the siege of Orleans and to conduct the noble Dauphin to
Rheims that he be there consecrated, and although she demanded
immediately a company of men, horses and arms.

"A space of three weeks or a month being passed, time during
which the King had commanded that the Maid be examined by
certain clerks, prelates and doctors of theology on her doings and
sayings in order to know if he could in all surety receive her, the
King called together a multitude of men to force some victuals into
the city of Orleans. But, having gathered the opinion of the prelates and doctors—to wit, that there was no evil in this Maid—he
sent her, in company with the lord archbishop of Rheims, then
Chancellor of France (Regnault de Chartres), and of the lord de
Gaucourt, now grand master of the king's household, to the town
of Blois wherein were come together those who led the convoy of
victuals, to wit the lords de Rais and de Boussac, Marshal of France,
with whom were the lords de Culant, Admiral of France, La Hire,
and the lord Ambroise de Loré, since become Provost of Paris,
who all together with the soldiers escorting the convoy of victuals
and Joan the Maid, came by way of the Sologne in good military
order (en armée rangée) to the river Loire directly and as far as
the church called Saint Loup in which were numerous English
forces." (R.127–129)

It was, in fact, at Blois that the army which the Dauphin had, at
Joan's instance, decided to raise, was concentrated. The Duke of
Alençon told how he had been entrusted with the preparation of
this expeditionary force:

Jean d'Alençon: "The King sent me to the Queen of Sicily"
(Yolande of Aragon, Charles VII's mother-in-law) "to get together
the victuals to be taken to Orleans for moving the army there. And
there I found the lord Ambroise de Loré and a lord Louis whose
other name I no longer recall who had prepared the provisions.

But there was need of money, and to have money for these victuals I returned to the King and notified him that the victuals were ready and that it remained only to give the money for these victuals and for the soldiers. Then the King sent someone to deliberate of the money needful to conclude all this, so that the supplies and the soldiers were ready to go to Orleans to attempt to raise the siege if that was possible." (R.148)

This was confirmed by the man whom Charles VII was to appoint as his official chronicler, Jean Chartier, a monk of Saint-Denis:

"Were laden in the town of Blois many carts and small carts (chars et charettes) of wheat and were taken great plenty of beeves, sheep, cows, swine and other victuals, and Joan the Maid set out as also the captains straight towards Orleans by the Sologne way. And lay one night in the open and on the morrow came Joan the Maid and the captains with the supplies before the town of Orleans."

Properly to understand the order of march and route adopted it is necessary to consider the English strategic positions before Orleans (see map, p. 71). As they had concentrated on fortifying the approaches to the bridge and had surrounded the west of the town with a series of forts, only the Bourgogne* Gate remained, as we have seen already, open to the east. Consequently the captains made a detour so as to reach Orleans on its eastern side, the side least exposed to danger. But this was hardly likely to satisfy Joan, anxious as she was to fight.

The Bastard of Orleans: "As the King's army and the soldiers escorting the convoy did not seem to me, any more than to the other lords-captains, sufficient to defend and conduct the supplies into the city, the more so in that there was need of boats and rafts which it would have been difficult to procure to fetch the supplies, for it was necessary to go upstream against the current and the wind was absolutely contrary, then Joan spoke to me these words which follow: 'Are you the Bastard of Orleans?' I answered her: 'Yes, I am so and I rejoice at your coming.' Then she said to me: 'Did you give the counsel that I should come here, to this side of the river, and that I go not straight there where are Talbot and the English?' I answered that myself and others wiser had given this counsel, thinking to do what was best and safest. Then Joan said to me: 'In God's name, the counsel of the Lord your God is wiser and safer than yours. You thought to deceive me and it is yourself above all whom you deceive, for I bring you better succour than has

* or Bourgoyne

reached you from any soldier or any city: it is succour from the King of Heaven. It comes not from love of me but from God himself who, at the request of Saint Louis and Saint Charlemagne, has taken pity on the town of Orleans, and will not suffer that the enemies have the bodies of the lord of Orleans and his town.' Forthwith and as in the same moment, the wind which was contrary and absolutely prevented the boats from moving upstream, in which were laden the victuals for Orleans, changed and became favourable. Forthwith I had the sails hoisted, and sent in the rafts and vessels. . . . And we passed beyond the Church of Saint-Loup despite the English. From that moment I had good hope in her, more than before; and I then implored her to consent to cross the river of Loire and to enter into the town of Orleans where she was greatly wished for." (R.129)

After having hesitated a little to leave the main body of the expeditionary force, Joan agreed to enter Orleans with him.

"Then Joan came with me, bearing in her hand her standard which was white and upon which was the image of Our Lord holding a fleur-de-lys in his hand. And she crossed with me and La Hire the river of Loire, and we entered together into the town of Orleans."

He added: "For all that" (i.e., for these reasons), "it seems to me that Joan and also what she did in warfare and in battle was rather of God than of men; the change which suddenly happened in the wind, after she had spoken, gave hope of succour, and the introduction of supplies, despite the English, who were in much greater strength than the royal army." (R.131)

Jean d'Aulon: "After it came to the knowledge of my lord de Dunois, whom then was called my lord Bastard of Orleans, who was in the city to preserve and keep it from the enemies, that the Maid was coming, he rallied together a number of soldiers to go out to meet her, as La Hire and others, and to this end and the more safely to bring and conduct her into the city, this lord and his men got into a boat and by the river of Loire went to meet her about quarter of a league and there found her." (R.157)

The *Journal of the Siege* recounts in detail Joan's entry into the town on the Friday evening, April 29, 1429: "The Friday following twenty-ninth of the same month, came into Orleans certain news that the King was sending by the Sologne way victuals, powder, canon and other equipments of war under the guidance of the Maid, who came from Our Lord to re-victual and comfort the town and raise the siege—by which were those of Orleans much comforted. And because it was said that the English would take pains to prevent the victuals, it was ordered that all take up arms throughout the city. Which was done.

"This day also arrived fifty foot soldiers equipped with *guisarmes* and other war gear. They came from the country of Gatinais where they had been in garrison.

"This same day there was a great skirmish because the French wished to give place and time for the victuals to enter, which were brought to them. And to keep the English busy elsewhere, they went out in great strength, and went running and skirmishing before Saint Loup d'Orleans and engaged them so closely that there were many dead, wounded and taken on both sides, and so that the French bore into the city one of the English standards. While this skirmish was making, entered into the town the victuals and the artillery which the Maid had brought as far as Checy. To meet her went out to that village the Bastard of Orleans and other knights, esquires and men of war from Orleans and elsewhere, right joyful at her coming, who all made her great reverence and handsome cheer (i.e., right welcome) and so did she to them; and they concluded all together that she should not enter into Orleans before nightfall, to avoid the tumult of the people. . . . At eight o'clock, despite all the English who never attempted to prevent it, she entered, armed at all points, riding upon a white horse; and she caused her standard to be borne before her, which was likewise white, on which were two angels, holding each a fleut-de-lys in their hands; and on the pennon was painted an annunciation (this is the image of Our Lady having before her an angel giving her a lily).

She entered thus into Orleans, having on her left hand the Bastard of Orleans very richly armed and mounted, and after came many other noble and valiant lords, esquires, captains and men of war, and several from the garrison, and likewise some burgesses of Orleans who had gone out to meet her. On the other hand came to receive her the other men of war, burgesses and matrons of Orleans, bearing great plenty of torches and making such rejoicing as if they had seen God descend in their midst; and not without cause, for they had many cares, travails and difficulties and great fear lest they be not succoured and lose all, body and goods. But they felt themselves already comforted and as if no longer besieged, by the divine virtue* which they were told was in this simple maid, who looked upon them all right affectionately, whether men, women, or little

* In the sense "by virtue of"; i.e., not her goodness but the spirit of God in her.— E.H.

children. And there was marvellous crowd and press to touch her
or the horse upon which she was. So much so that one of those
bearing a torch drew so near to her standard that the pennon took
fire. Wherefore she struck spurs to her horse and turned him right
gently towards the pennon and extinguished the fire of it as if she
had long served in the wars; which thing the men-at-arms held a
great marvel and the burgesses of Orleans likewise who bore her
company the whole length of their town and city, manifesting great
joy, and by way of a very great honour, led her all to the near
neighbourhood of the Regnard Gate, into Jacques Boucher's great
house (*hotel*), who was then Treasurer to the Duke of Orleans,
where she was received with great joy, with her two brothers and
two gentlemen and their body-servants who were come with them
from the country of Barrois.''

Both in the *Journal of the Siege* and in the depositions of the
Rehabilitation Trial, we can follow, day by day, the events which
followed in Orleans during a week which was to be decisive.

Saturday, April 10th. No notable event. Much against her will
Joan had to resign herself to wait, the other captains-at-war being
of opinion that the enemy should not be engaged until the rest of
the army, which had remained at Blois, had reached Orleans.

Louis de Coutes: "Joan went to see the Bastard of Orleans and
spoke to him, and on her return she was in great anger; for, said she,
he had decided that on that day they would not go out against the
enemy. However, Joan went to a boulevard which the King's
soldiers were holding against the English boulevard, and there she
spoke with the English who were in the other boulevard, telling
them in God's name to withdraw that otherwise she would drive
them out. And one called the Bastard of Granville spoke many
insults to Joan, asking her if she expected them to surrender to a
woman, calling the French who were with Joan miscreant pimps."
(R.170)

"When evening fell, Joan went to the boulevard of the Belle
Croix on the bridge and thence spoke to Classidas (Glasdale) and
to the other English who were in the Tourelles and told them
that if they would yield themselves at God's command (*de par Dieu*)
their lives were safe. But Glasdale and those of his company answered
basely, insulting her and calling her 'cow-girl', shouting very loudly
that they would have her burned if they could lay hands on her.
At which she was much enraged and answered them that they lied,
and that said, withdrew into the city." (J.S.O.155)

Sunday, May 1st. Still nothing happened. The Sunday truce was generally observed. On that day, in any case, the Bastard of Orleans left the town to go and fetch the reinforcements massed at Blois.

"That day rode about the city Joan the Maid, accompanied by many knights and esquires because those of Orleans wanted so greatly to see her that they almost broke down the door of the mansion where she was lodged, to see her; there was such a press of townspeople in the streets she passed through that with great difficulty did she pass, for the people could not weary of seeing her, and it seemed to all a great marvel how she could sit her horse with such ease and grace (*si gentiment*) as she did. And in sooth, she bore herself as highly in all ways as a man of arms who had followed the wars since his youth would have been able to." (J.S.O.155)

Monday, May 2nd: Still nothing. It is self-evident that in the absence of the Bastard of Orleans, charged with the city's defence, Joan could not and would not undertake any operations.

Tuesday, May 3rd: Still nothing, unless it be what the town's account books reveal. "For those who bore the torches in the procession of May 3rd last, being present Joan the Maid and other war chiefs, to implore Our Lord for the deliverance of the town of Orleans, 2 *sous parisis*."

And again, these details, at once typical and touching: "To Raoulet de Recourt, for a shad presented to the Maid the 3rd May—20 *sous parisis*. To Jean le Camus, for a gift to three companions (friends) who had come to see Joan and had not the means to eat—4 *sous parisis*." (q.v. 259)

Wednesday, May 4th. Dunois' return with the reinforcements is heralded.

Jean d'Aulon: "As soon as she knew they were come and that they were bringing the others that they went to seek for the reinforcement of the city, hastily the Maid sprang to horse and, with some of her men, went out to meet them and to strengthen and succour them if need there should be.

"Within sight and knowledge of the enemies, entered the Maid, Dunois, the marshal (Boussac) La Hire, I who speak and our men, without any impediment whatsoever.

"That same day, after dinner came my lord of Dunois to the Maid's lodging where she and I had dined together. And speaking to her his lord of Dunois told her that he knew it for true by trustworthy men, that one Falstaff (John Falstaff, captain of freebooters), an enemy captain, would soon be coming to the besieger enemies, both to bring them succour and reinforce the army and to revictual them, and that he was already at Janville. At these words the Maid was right rejoiced, as it appeared to me, and she spoke to my lord of Dunois these words, or similar ones: 'Bastard, Bastard, in God's name I command thee that, as soon as thou knowest that Falstaff is come, thou shalt make it known to me, for if he pass without my knowing of it, I promise thee I will have thy head taken off!' To which answered the lord of Dunois that she doubt not, for he would indeed make it known to her.

"After these exchanges, I who was weary and fatigued cast myself down on a mattress in the Maid's chamber, to rest a little. And likewise did she, with her hostess, on another bed, to sleep and rest. But while I was beginning to take my rest, suddenly the Maid rose from the bed, and making a great noise, roused me. At that I asked her what she wanted. She answered me: 'In God's name my counsel has told me to go out against the English and I know not whether I must go against their fortification (*bastide*) or against Falstaff who is to revictual them.' Upon which I arose at once and, as swiftly as I could, put the Maid into her armour." (R.159)

Louis de Coutes also tells how Joan, after having slept a little, "Came down again and said to me these words: 'Ah, bleeding boy, you told me not that the blood of France was spilling!' while urging me to go fetch her horse. In the interval she had her armour put on by the lady of the house and her daughter, and when I came back from saddling and bridling her horse, I found her ready armed; she told me to go and fetch her standard which was upstairs and I handed it to her through the window. After having taken her standard, Joan hastened, racing towards the Burgundy Gate. Then the hostess told me to go after her, which I did. There was at that time an attack or a skirmish over towards Saint-Loup. It was in this attack that the boulevard was taken, and on her way Joan encountered many French wounded, which saddened her. The English were preparing their defence when Joan came in haste at them, and as soon as the French saw Joan, they began to shout (? cheer) and the bastion and fortress of Saint-Loup were taken."

Jean Pasquerel: "I recall that it was on the eve of Ascension of Our Lord, and there were many English killed. Joan lamented much, saying that they had been killed without confession, and she wept much upon them and at once confessed herself to me, and she told me publicly to exhort all the soldiers to confess their sins and to give thanks to God for the victory won; if not she would stay not with them but would leave them. And she said also, on that vigil of the Ascension of the Lord, that within five days the siege of Orleans would be raised and that there would linger no more English before the city. . . . That day, at evening, being returned to her lodging, she told me that on the morrow, which was the day of the Feast of the Ascension of the Lord, she would make no war nor take up arms, out of respect for the Feast. And that day she wished to confess and to receive the sacrament of the Eucharist, which she did. And that day she commanded that no man should dare on the morrow go out of the city to assault or attack if he had not first been to confession. And let them take care that women of ill-fame follow not the army, for it was for those sins that God allowed the war to be lost. And it was done as Joan had commanded." (R.80)

Thursday, May 5th. Joan sent to the English the third and last letter of summons. We do not have the text of the second unless it did no more than repeat the letter already quoted.

"You, Englishmen, who have no right in this Kingdom of France, the King of Heaven orders and commands you through me, Joan the Maid, that you quit your fortresses and return into your own country, or if not I shall make you such *babay* that the memory of it will be perpetual. That is what I write to you for the third and last time, and shall write no more. Signed: Jhesus-Maria, Joan the Maid." "For my part I shall have sent you my letters honourably, but for yours you detain my messengers, for you have held my herald named Guyenne. Be so good as to send him back (*veuillez le renvoyer*) and I will send you some of your people taken in the fortress of Saint-Loup, for not all were dead there."

Jean Pasquerel: "She took an arrow, tied the letter with a thread to the end of the arrow and ordered an archer to shoot the arrow to the English, crying 'Read, it is news!' The English received the arrow with the letter and read it. And having read it they began to utter great shouts, saying, 'News of the Armagnacs' whore!' At these words Joan began to sigh and to weep copious tears, calling the King of Heaven to her aid. And thereafter was she consoled, as she said, for she had had news of her Lord. And that evening, after dinner, she ordered me to rise on the morrow earlier than I had done on Ascension Day, and that she would confess herself to me very early in the morning, which she did."

Friday, May 6th. Jean Pasquerel: "That day, Friday, the morrow of the Feast of the Ascension, I rose early in the morning and heard Joan's confession and sang mass before her and her men in Orleans. Then they went out to the assault which lasted from morning until evening. And that day was taken the fortress of the Augustins, by grand assault; and Joan, who was accustomed to fast on Fridays, could not fast that day, for she had been too much fatigued and she dined." (R.181)

Yet this assault seems to have been a surprise (not a meditated) attack, if we are to believe the testimony given by Simon Charles: "Of what was done at Orleans I know nought but by hearsay, for I was not present there, but there is one thing which I heard said by the lord de Gaucourt when he was at Orleans: it had been decided by those who had charge of the King's men that it was not advisable to make assault nor attack on the day when the bastion of the Augustins was taken, and this lord de Gaucourt was charged to guard the gates so that none should go out. Joan, however, was ill-content with that. She was of opinion that the soldiers should go out with the townsmen and attack the bastion. Many of the men of war and townsmen were of the same opinion. Joan said to this sire de Gaucourt that he was a bad man. 'Whether you will or not, the fighting men will come and will obtain what they have elsewhere obtained.' And against the will of the lord de Gaucourt, the soldiers who were in the town went out and made an attack to invade the Augustins bastion which they took by storm. And from what I have heard tell by the sire de Gaucourt, he was himself in great peril." (R.104)

Jean d'Aulon: "The Maid and her men went out of the city in good order to go and assail a certain bastion before the city, called the bastion of Saint-Jean-le-Blanc. To do this, as they saw that they could not goodly (well) reach this bastion by land given that the enemy had built another and very strong at the foot of the city bridge, so that it was impossible for them to pass that way, it was resolved between them to cross to a certain isle in the river Loire and that there they would assemble to go out and make their attack on the bastion of Saint-Jean-le-Blanc. And, to cross the other arm of the river Loire, they sent for two boats of which they made a bridge to go to the bastion.

"That done, they went towards the bastion which they found all disordered because the English who were in it no sooner saw the French coming than they went away and withdrew into another stronger and bigger bastion called the bastion of the Augustins. The French, seeing that they were not strong enough to take this bastion, it was resolved that they would return from it without doing anything.

"While the French were retreating from the bastion of Saint-Jean-le-Blanc to return to the island, the Maid and La Hire both crossed, each with a horse in a boat, from the other side of this island, and mounted these horses as soon as they were across, each with lance in hand, and when they perceived that the enemies were coming out of the bastion to charge their men, at once the Maid and La Hire, who were always before them to guard them, couched their lances and were the first to strike among the enemies. Thereupon the others all followed them and began to strike at the enemy in such fashion that by force they drove them to retire and enter again into the bastion of the Augustins. . . . Very bitterly and with much diligence they assailed it from every side so that in a little while they gained and took it by storm; and there were killed or taken the greater part of the enemies, and those who could escape retired into the bastion of the Tourelles at the foot of the bridge. And thus won the Maid, and those who were with her, victory over the enemies upon that day and was the great bastion taken, and there remained the lords and their men with the Maid, all that night." (R.161-163)

The taking of this bastion of the Augustins was an important feat of arms; the bastion was the most considerable of those which covered the Tourelles, the fortification commanding the approach to the bridge. The Orleanais were quick to realise the value of the achievement, a fact confirmed by the *Journal of the Siege*: "Those of Orleans were most diligent in bearing all night long bread, wine and other victuals to the men of war maintaining the siege."* (J.S.O.159)

Jean Pasquerel: "After dinner came to Joan a valiant and notable knight whose name I no longer recall. He told Joan that the King's captains and soldiers had held counsel together and that they saw they were but few by comparison with the English and that God had shown them great mercies in the satisfactions already obtained, adding: 'Considering that the town is well provided with victuals, we might well keep the city while awaiting help from the King, and it does not seem advisable to the council that the soldiers go out tomorrow!' Joan answered him: 'You have been at your counsel

* Of the Tourelles bastion.—E.H.

and I at mine; and know that my Lord's counsel will be accomplished and will prevail and that that (other) counsel will perish.' And addressing herself to me who stood at her side: 'Rise tomorrow early in the morning and earlier than you did to-day and do the best that you can; be always at my side, for tomorrow I shall have much to do, and more than I ever had, and tomorrow the blood will flow out of my body above my breast.'" (R.181–182)

Saturday, May 7th. Jean Pasquerel: "On the morrow, Saturday, I rose early and celebrated mass. And Joan went out against the fortress of the bridge where was the Englishman Classidas. And the assault lasted there from the morning until sunset. In this assault, after the morning meal, Joan, as she had predicted, was struck by an arrow above the breast, and when she felt herself wounded she was afraid and wept, and was consoled as she said. And some soldiers, seeing her so wounded, wanted to apply a charm to her wound, but she would not have it, saying: 'I would rather die than do a thing which I know to be a sin or against the will of God.' And that she knew well that she must die one day, but knew not when or how or at what time of the day. But if to her wound could be applied a remedy without sin, she was very willing to be cured. And they put on to her wound olive oil and lard. And after that had been applied, Joan made her confession to me, weeping and lamenting." (R.182)

The Bastard of Orleans: "The assault lasted from the morning until eight o'clock of vespers, so that there was hardly hope of victory that day. So that I was going to break off and wanted the army to withdraw towards the city. Then the Maid came to me and required me to wait yet a while. She herself, at that time, mounted her horse and retired alone into a vineyard, some distance from the crowd of men. And in this vineyard she remained at prayer during one half of a quarter of an hour. Then she came back from that place, at once seized her standard in hand and placed herself on the parapet of the trench, and the moment she was there the English trembled and were terrified. And the king's soldiers regained courage and began to go up, charging against the boulevard without meeting the least resistance." (R.132)

Jean d'Aulon: "They were before that boulevard from morning until sunset without being able to take nor win it. And the lords and captains being with her, seeing that they could not well win it that day, considering the time, that it was very late, and also that all were very weary and tired, it was concluded between them to sound the retreat of the army, which was done, and as the clamour of the trumpets sounded each would retire for that day. In beating this retreat, he who bore the Maid's standard and held it still erect before the boulevard, being weary and tired, passed the standard to one named Le Basque, who was the lord de Villard's man. And because I knew this Basque to be a valiant man and that I feared lest because of this retreat the worst befall . . . it occurred to me that if the standard was driven forward by reason of the great ardour which I knew to be among the men of war who were there, they might by this means win the boulevard. So I asked Le Basque, if I entered and went to the foot of the boulevard, if he would follow me. He told me and promised me that he would do so. Then I went into the trench and as far as the foot of the boulevard ditch (moat, trench), covering myself with my shield for fear of stones, and left my comrade on the other side, for I thought he would be following close in my footsteps. But when the Maid saw her standard in the hands of Le Basque and thought that she had lost it, for he who bore it had gone down into the trench, she went and seized the end of the standard in such manner that he could not carry it away, crying 'My standard, my standard!' and waved the standard in such fashion that I imagined that so doing the others would think that she was making them a sign. Thereupon I shouted, 'Ah! Basque, what didst thou promise me?' Then Le Basque tugged so at the standard that he tore it from the Maid's hands and so doing came to me and raised the standard. This occasioned all who were of the Maid's army to come together and to rally again, and with such bitterness assail the boulevard that a little time thereafter this boulevard and the bastion were taken by them and by the enemy abandoned; and thus went in the French to the city of Orleans by way of the bridge." (R.163–164)

"No sooner had the attack recommenced than the English lost all power to resist longer and thought to make their way from the boulevard into the Tourelles, but few among them could escape, for the four or five hundred soldiers they numbered were all killed or drowned, excepting some few whom were taken prisoners, and these not great lords. And thinking to save themselves the bridge broke under them, which was great disorder to the English forces and great pity for the valiant French, who for their ransom might have had much money (*grand finance*)." (J.S.O.162)

Jean Pasquerel: "Joan returned to the charge, crying and saying: 'Classidas, Classidas, yield thee, yield thee to the King of Heaven;

thou hast called me "whore", me; I take great pity on thy soul
and thy people's!' Then Classidas, armed (as he was) from head to
foot, fell into the river of Loire and was drowned. And Joan,
moved by pity, began to weep much for the soul of Classidas and
the others who were there drowned in great numbers. And that
day all the English who were beyond the bridge were taken or
killed." (R.182)

Jean d'Aulon: "The same day I had heard the Maid say, 'In God's
name, we shall this day enter the town by the bridge.' And that done,
withdrew the Maid and her men into the town of Orleans where I had
her cared for, for she had been wounded by an arrow in the charge.

"They (the army and people of Orleans) made great rejoicing
and praised Our Lord for this great victory which He had given
them; and right was it that they should do so, for it is said that
this assault, which lasted from morning until sunset, was so greatly
fought in both attack and defence, that it was one of the grandest
feats of arms that there had been for a long time before. . . . And
the clergy and people of Orleans sang devoutly *Te deum laudamus*
and caused all the bells of the city to be pealed, most humbly
thanking Our Lord for that glorious divine consolation. And made
great joy on all sides, giving marvellous praises to their valiant
defenders, and above all others to Joan the Maid. She remained
that night, and the lords, captains and men-at-arms with her, in the
field, both to guard the Tourelles thus valiantly captured, as to watch
lest the English, over by Saint-Laurent, came out, trying to succour
or avenge their companions. But they had not the heart for it."
(J.S.O.163)

The Bastard of Orleans: "Thus the bastion was taken, and I
came in again, as also the Maid, with the other French, into the city
of Orleans, in which we were received with great transports of joy
and piety. And Joan was taken to her lodgings that her wound
might be dressed. When the dressing had been done by the sur-
geon, she took her meal, eating four or five toasts washed down with
wine mixed with much water, and took no other nourishment or
drink during all that day." (R.133)

Sunday, May 8th: "The following morning, Sunday and eighth
day of May, this same year 1429, the English demolished their
bastion . . . and raising their siege ranged themselves in battle. . . .
Whereupon the Maid . . . and many other valiant men of war and
citizens went out of Orleans in great strength and placed and ranged
themselves before them in ordered battle. And at some points were

very near to each other for the space of an hour without touching each other. Which thing the French submitted to with a very ill grace, obeying the will of the Maid, who commanded and forbade that for love and honour of the holy Sunday, they begin not the battle nor make assault on the English; but if the English attacked them let them defend themselves strongly and boldly and let them have no fear, and they would be the masters. The hour being passed, the English set off and marched away, well ordered in their ranks, into Meung-sur-Loire, and raised and utterly abandoned the siege which they had maintained before Orleans since the twelfth day of October 1428 until that day. Nonetheless, they went not away nor got safely off with their baggage, for some from the city garrison pursued them and struck at the tail of their army in diverse assaults, so that they won from them great bombards, and canon, bows, arbalests (cross-bows) and other artillery . . . Meanwhile, entered to great rejoicing the Maid into the City of Orleans, and the other lords and men of war, in (the midst of) the very great exultation of all the clergy and people who all together gave humble thanks to Our Lord and well-deserved praises for the very great succours and victories which He had given them and against the English, ancient enemies of this kingdom. . . . That same day and on the morrow also, made very grand and solemn procession the Church-men, lords, captains, men-at-arms and burgesses being and residing in Orleans, and visited the churches in great devoutness. And in all truth, although the burgesses had not been willing at first and before the siege began that any men of war enter their city, fearing lest they come to pillage them or be too hard masters, nonetheless did they afterwards allow in as many as would come, once they knew (realised) that they came only for their defence and bore themselves so valiantly in the face of their enemies; and they were with them very united for the defence of the city, and shared them out among themselves in their mansions (*hotels*) and fed them with all good things which God gave them, as familiarly as if they had been their own sons." (J.S.O.164–167)

As for Joan herself, she was not really given a chance during the Trial of Condemnation to recall memories of Orleans. Quite obviously, her judge was anxious to avoid any mention of it. Her exploit had been altogether too resounding. She did, however, manage to tell, in a single phrase, what her conduct had been in the course of that exploit: "I was the first to place a scaling ladder on the bastion of the bridge." (C.79)

Year fourteen hundred and twenty-nine
Came out again the sun.
Good times anew came with its shine
As long they had not done.
Long time did many who were apine
Live through: I was one,
But no more at aught now do I pine
When I see my want is won.*

L'an mil quatre cent vingt et neuf
Reprit a luire le soleil
Il ramène le bon temps neuf
Que l'on n'avait vu du droit œil
De longtemps, dont plusieurs en deuil
En vécurent: je suis de ceux
Mais plus de rien je ne me deuil
Quand ores vois ce que je veux.

These lines are probably the last which were written by the poetess Christine de Pisan, in 1429. She had withdrawn into a nunnery eleven years before—at the time of the English entry into Paris—and had written nothing since. If, in her old age, she now took up her pen again, it was to celebrate the incredible event which was changing the course of history and restoring confidence to the people of France.

Qui vit donc chose advenir
Plus hors de toute opinion
Que France, de qui mention
On faisait qu'à terre est tombée,
Soit par divine mission
De mal en si grand bien mué,

Et par tel miracle vraiment
Que, si chose n'était notoire
Et évident quoi et comment,
Il n'est homme qui le pût croire!
Chose est bien digne de mémoire
Que Dieu, par une vierge tendre
Ait ainsi voulu [chose voire (vraie)]
Sur France si grand grâce étendre. (Q. v, 3 and s.)

---

* The translation is not good but gives the sense, the simplicity and the tolling effect of repeating not only rhyme but the same words.—E.H.

It is a fact that the extraordinary nature of the event had been fully realised. Even as late as the Trial of Rehabilitation the ordinary people of Orleans could hardly contain their enthusiasm as the victory was recalled. In a manuscript which was discovered in Quicherat's time, in the Vatican library (Fonds de la reine de Suède No. 891), are to be found some details on the establishment of the famous feast and procession of May 8th which was to be celebrated every year thereafter in Orleans, and was not even dropped during the Terror; these details seem to have been given by an eye-witness of the raising of the siege who must have written down what he remembered in about 1460:

"My lord bishop of Orleans, with all the clergy and also by order of my lord of Dunois, brother of my lord the Duke of Orleans and with his counsel, and also the burgesses, labourers (churls) and inhabitants of Orleans, ordered to be formed a procession on May 8th and that each bear in it a torch and that they were to go as far as the Augustins and everywhere there had been fighting and that they should make station and propitious service, and prayers. And the twelve procurators of the town would each bear a candle in his hands, on which would be the town's arms. . . . Thus should we be very devout in this procession especially such as are of Orleans, since they of Bourges-en-Berry (also) make a solemnity of it—but they take the Sunday after Ascension. And also several other towns make a solemnity of it, for if Orleans had fallen into the hands of the English, the rest of the kingdom would have been much harmed. . . . Everyone is required to go to the procession and to carry a burning torch in hand. The return is about the town by way of the church of Our Lady of Saint-Paul and there is given great praise to Our Lady and thence to Sainte-Croix, and there is the sermon and the Mass thereafter and also the vigils at Saint-Aignan: and on the morrow Mass is said for the dead." (Q.v, 296–298)

The Orleans account books several times make mention of the expenses incurred by the town for this procession from as early as 1435:

"To Jacquet Lepretre, servant of the town of Orleans, for the purchase of twenty-three pounds of new wax, bought to remake the town's torches and put with twenty-six pounds of old wax left from the said torches, for the solemnity of the procession of the Tourelles, held on the eighth day of May 1435, at a price of two sous ten deniers the pound . . . 62 sous four deniers. . . .

"To Jean Moynet, candle-maker, for the fashioning of the torches and candles and for the sticks* and for a torch (*flambeau*) given on the morrow of the said procession at a mass sung for the dead in the the church Monseigneur Saint-Aignan . . . 26 sous." (Q.v, 308)

As for the prince whom Joan called the Dauphin, we know very precisely how he received the news of the event, by means of a circular letter which he was engaged in dictating to the "good towns" of the kingdom and of which the text was, fortunately for us, preserved by at least one of the recipient cities, to wit Narbonne. Other towns, like La Rochelle, only have a note of its receipt in their registers. It was dictated in three parts, between the evening of May 9th and dawn on the 10th when the messenger bringing the news of victory reached Chinon:

"From the King, dear and well-beloved, we believe that you have been informed of the continual diligence by us exercised to bring all succour possible to the town of Orleans long besieged by the English, ancient enemies of our kingdom, and the endeavours into which we have entered on diverse times, having always good hope in Our Lord that at length he would extend to it His mercy and would not permit that so notable a city and so loyal a people perish or fall into subjection to the said enemies. And for as much as we know that greater joy and consolation you, as loyal subjects, could not have than to hear announced good news, we make known to you that, by our Lord's grace from which all proceeds, we have again caused to be revictualled in strength the town of Orleans twice in a single week, well and greatly, in the sight and knowledge of the enemies, without their being able to resist.

"And since then, to wit, last Wednesday, our people sent with the victuals, together with the men of the town, have assailed one of the enemy's strongest bastions, that of Saint-Loup, the which, God aiding, they have taken and won by great assault which lasted four or five hours, and all the English having been killed who were inside it without any being dead of our people but two men only, although the English who were in the other bastions had come out in battle, seeming to offer combat, nevertheless when they saw our people come to meet them, they turned about hastily without daring to wait for them. . . . Since these letters written, there has come to us a herald about one hour after midnight, who has reported to us on his life that last Friday our aforesaid people crossed the river by boat at Orleans and besieged, on the Sologne side, the bastion at the end of the bridge and the same day won the fort of the Augustins.

* *Batons*—E.H.

And on the Saturday likewise assailed the rest of the said bastion which was the boulevard of the bridge, where there were at least six hundred English fighting men under two banners and the standard of Chandos. And finally, by great prowess and valiance in arms, yet still by means of Our Lord's grace, won all the said bastion and of it were all the English therein killed or taken. For that more than ever before must praise and thank our Creator, that in His divine clemency He has not forgotten us. And cannot sufficiently honour the virtuous acts and things marvellous which this herald who was present has reported to us and likewise the Maid who was always present in person at the doing of all these things. . . .

"And since then again, before the completion of these letters, have arrived with us two gentlemen who were at this work, who certify and confirm all, more amply than the herald, and from thence have brought us letters from the hand of the sire de Gaucourt. After that our men had last Saturday taken and demolished the bastion of the bridge end, on the morrow at dawn, the English who were in it, decamped and fled so hastily that they left their bombards, canons and artilleries, and the best part of their provisions and baggage.

"Given at Chinon, the tenth day of May. Signed: Charles." (Q. v, 101–104)

Note here—as we shall have occasion to note again—that Charles VII showed himself very discreet touching the matter of Joan's exploits. Among the people of his suite, however, were some who were more enthusiastic; among other evidence there is the famous letter of Alain Chartier, the poet, written to a foreign prince whom it has proved impossible to identify, at the end of July 1429, a copy of which is preserved in the Bibliothèque Nationale.

Chartier gives a swift résumé of what was known of the Maid's origins, and tells how she came to the King's court, and gives an account of the events which followed, up to the deliverance of Orleans. He concludes:

"Here is she who seems not to issue from any place on earth, but rather sent by Heaven to sustain with head and shoulders a France fallen to the ground. O astonishing virgin! worthy of all fame, of all praise, worthy of all the divine honours! Thou art the honour of the reign, thou art the light of the lily, thou art the splendour, the glory, not only of Gaul but of all Christians. Let Troy celebrate her Hector, let Greece pride herself upon Alexander,

Africa upon Hannibal, Italy upon Caesar and all the Roman generals. France, though she count many of these, may well content herself with this Maid only. She (France) can pride herself and compare herself with these other nations for the honour of the ladies, and can even, if she so wish, set herself above them." (Latin text in Q. v, 131-136)

Whereas Alain Chartier, full of enthusiasm though he was, kept strictly to the facts in his account of the essential event, that is the raising of the siege of Orleans in the extraordinary circumstances we have described, we cannot say as much for another personage, Perceval de Boulainvilliers, King's Councillor and Seneschal of Berry. One of his letters has survived, addressed to the Duke of Milan, Philippe Maria Visconti, with whom he was in touch, having married the governor of Asti's daughter. This letter implies in its author a taste for the anecdotal which drives him to seek the marvellous where it is not to be found. One can sense, as one reads it, that already there must have been old wives' tales about Joan in circulation. It was natural enough: there is hardly a hero in history whom legend has not seized upon even in his lifetime. Boulainvilliers tells of her birth in Domremy, and it is he who gives us an exact date, which may be the true one, saying that she was born on the night of Epiphany, January 6th, adding that that night the cocks crowed at an unusual time, "Like heralds of a new joy" . . . which caused the people of the town to wake and wonder. A little later we have Joan, put in charge of the ewes, never losing a single one. When she played in the meadows with the other little girls her feet did not touch the ground, and she ran with such swiftness that one of her playmates cried, "Joan, I can see you flying above the ground" etc. etc. The writer then has a great deal to say about her apparitions, then gives an account of the succeeding episodes: Vaucouleurs, Chinon, Orleans—his letter being dated June 21st. Of more value to us are the details which Boulainvilliers gives on Joan's physical appearance; for despite the exaggerated tone of the whole letter, these may be more or less true since he did probably see Joan. "This Maid," he says, "has a certain elegance. She has a virile bearing, speaks little, shows an admirable prudence in all her words. She has a pretty, woman's voice, eats little, drinks very little wine; she enjoys riding a horse and takes pleasure in fine arms, greatly likes the company of noble fighting men, detests numerous assemblies and meetings, readily sheds copious tears, has a cheerful face; she bears the weight and burden of armour incredibly well, to such a point that she has remained fully armed during six days and nights." (Latin text in Q. v, 114-121)

The terms of this letter were to be recapitulated in a poem written some time later by a poet of Asti named Antonio.

It is, on the other hand, surprising that Charles, Duke of Orleans, himself a poet, whose town Joan had saved for him, never makes the slightest allusion to her in his poetry. But warfare, and in general the fortunes and misfortunes of the kingdom, do not in any case receive much attention from him. Reading his works, it is difficult to believe that they were composed by a man who was a prisoner-of-war for twenty-five years. His gratitude was expressed in the traditional way, that is by having made for Joan a "livery" bearing his arms. By an assignation bearing the date September 30, 1429, he approves and undertakes the cost of making this suit of clothes, the work having been put in hand in June by his treasurer at Orleans, Jacques Boucher:

"To the people of our accounts (exchequer) . . . we authorise (*mander*) you that the sum of thirteen golden crowns . . . which by our beloved and loyal treasurer general, Jacques Boucher, was paid and delivered in the month of June last to Jean Luillier, merchant, and Jean Bourgeois, tailor, residing at Orleans, for a robe and cloak which the men of our council had made and delivered to Joan the Maid in our town of Orleans, having consideration to the good and agreeable services which the Maid did for us at the encounter with the English, ancient enemies of my lord the king and of ourselves (this sum to be allowed in the accounts of our treasurer and deducted from his revenue). That is to say, to the said Jean Luillier, for two ells of fine Brussels vermillion cloth of which the said robe was made, eight crowns of gold; . . . and for one ell of deep green for the making of the *huque*, two crowns of gold; and to the said Jean Bourgeois for the making of the robe and *huque*, and for white satin, *cendal* (a silk material) and other stuffs, for the whole, one crown of gold." (Q. v, 113)

So resounding was the exploit at Orleans that it rallied to Charles VII's cause certain notabilities who had hitherto been hesitating to embrace it. For example, the Duke of Brittany sent a religious, his confessor, and a herald to congratulate him upon his victory; this fact is known to us by means of a register of accounts which was formerly preserved in the Nantes Archives of the Chamber of Accounts; and also from a German chronicle of the times, composed by the Emperor Sigismund's treasurer, Eberhard of Windecken;

this official had all the emperor's official correspondence through his hands, and he made good use of it. It is he who tells how "the Duke of Brittany sent his confessor to the girl to question her whether it was by God that she was come to succour the King. The girl answered 'Yes'. Then the confessor said: 'If it be so, my lord the duke of Brittany is disposed to come to the King's aid with his service', and he called the duke her right lord. 'He cannot come in his proper person', he added, 'for he is in a great state of infirmity, but he can send his eldest son with a great army.' Then the girl said to the confessor that the duke of Brittany was not her right lord, for it was the King who was her right lord, and that the duke should not reasonably have waited so long to send his men to help the King with their services." (German text and translation in Q. v, 498)

Nor was a note of comedy missing from the concert of praise: the *capitouls*, municipal councillors, of the city of Toulouse, then very embarrassed by the state of the city's finances, decided, in the course of their meeting of June 2nd, to write to the Maid, "explaining to her the inconveniences of money changing and asking her what remedy to apply". . . . Joan seemed to them to be a sort of magician whose abilities must be universal! In the same spirit, Bonne de Visconti, Duchess of Milan, wrote asking her to restore her to the possession of her duchy. And then there was the case of the Duke of Armagnac who wrote her a letter which was to be exploited by the judges at her Trial of Condemnation, asking her which of the three popes at that time claiming to be the rightful sovereign pontiff ought to be considered the true head of Christianity. The duke had an axe to grind; he had supported two antipopes in succession and had been placed under an interdict by the legitimate pope, Martin V.

Furthermore, while the deliverance of Orleans had a tremendous importance for the French, its effect was no less great on the English and Burgundian side. Its extent can be measured by the fact that in the course of the following year, on May 3rd and December 12, 1430, two mandates were published "against the captains and soldiers, deserters terrified by the Maid's enchantments". These mandates were proclaimed in the name of the infant King of England by his uncle the Duke of Gloucester.

As for the Regent himself, John, Duke of Bedford, his feelings are known to us from a letter which he wrote in 1434, summing up events in France for his nephew the King of England:

"And alle thing there prospered for you, til thety me of the siege of Orleans taken in hand, God knoweth by what advis. At the whiche tyme, after the adventure fallen to the persone of my cousin of Salysbury, whom God assoille, there felle, by the hand of God, as it seemeth, a greet strook upon your peuple that was assembled there in grete nombre, caused in grete partie, as y trowe, of lakke of sadde beleve, and of unlevefulle doubte that thei hadde of a disciple and lyme of the Feende, called the Pucelle, that used fals enchauntements and sorcerie. The which strooke and discomfiture nought oonly lessed in grete partie the nombre of youre people, there, but as well withdrowe the courage of the remenant in merveillous wyse, and couraiged youre adverse partie and ennemys to assemble hem forthwith in grete nombre."

Clearly from the beginning of these events the English were desirous of attributing Joan's victories to "enchantments and sorceries". Which is what the judges at her trial tried to establish, though without success as we shall see.

As for the "foresworn Frenchmen" . . . or, as we should say nowadays, collaborators, their feelings are known to us by those of, among others, a man who can be taken as being thoroughly representative, to wit that "Bourgeois of Paris", who was, in reality, a clerk of the University of Paris which Bedford had taken good care to pack with his creatures, and who wrote a *Journal* kept from day to day throughout the whole course of events. In 1429 he wrote as follows:

"There was then on the Loire a Maid, as she was called, who claimed to be a prophet and who said: 'Such-and-such a thing will surely happen'. She was against the regent of France and his allies. It is said that despite the siege she entered into Orleans at the head of a host of Armagnacs with a great quantity of victuals, and that the English made no move, although she was at a bow-shot or two and despite so great a want of sustenance that one man had eaten three silver coins' worth of bread at least at his meal. And those who preferred the Armagnacs to the Burgundians and to the regent of France said of her many other things: they affirmed that as a little child she kept the sheep and that the birds of the woods and fields came to her call to eat bread from her lap, as if tamed.

"In that time the Armagnacs raised the siege of Orleans from which they drove the English, then marched on Vendome which they took, it was said. This Maid in arms accompanied them everywhere, bearing her standard on which was inscribed only 'Jesus'.

It was said that she had told an English captain to abandon the siege with his troop otherwise would happen to them only ill and shame. And this captain had much insulted her, calling her, for example, a ribald woman and a whore. She answered that they would all depart swiftly despite themselves, but that he would no longer be there to see it and that a great part of his troop would likewise be killed. It was so for he drowned himself on the day of battle." (The allusion is to William Glasdale.) (*Journal d'un bourgeois de Paris de 1405 à 1449*, Ed. J. Megret, p. 90)

The Burgundian chroniclers give a correct account of the facts touching the siege of Orleans, but do their best to run down Joan herself. We quote, as representative, Enguerrand de Monstrelet, a bastard of good family in the personal service of Philippe the Good, Duke of Burgundy, from 1430:

"In the year (1429) came to the King Charles of France at Chinon, where he dwelt a great part of the time, a Maid aged twenty years or thereabouts, named Joan, she being attired and dressed as a man and was born in a part between Burgundy and Lorraine, in a town called Domremy quite close to Vaucouleurs; the which Joan was long serving-maid in a hostelry and was bold in riding horses and taking them to water and also in other skills which young girls are not accustomed to do. She was put on the road and sent towards the King by a knight called messire Robert of Baudricourt, a captain of the King, at Vaucouleurs, which knight gave her horses and four or five companions. She said that she was a maid inspired by divine grace and that she was sent to the King to restore him to the possession of his kingdom. . . ." (Q. iv, 361 et seq., after the MS in the Bibliothèque Nationale, Fr. No. 8. 346)

And here is a piece of evidence all the more valuable in that it comes from foreigners not directly involved or interested in the strife but who, owing to their situation, were particularly well informed. Our witness is the agent of a great Venetian commercial house, the Morosini—a square in Venice still bears their name. In the fifteenth century their house of business was one of the most important of the Republic, with branches all over Europe. The branch in Bruges, at the time a principal centre for West European trade, was directed by Pancrazio Giustiniani, himself a member of another great Venetian family. It happens that the head of the central office, Antonio Morosini, preserved letters and news from his agents in a *Journal*: the firm dealt, among other things, in arms, and it was important for him to be kept in touch with the political situation in a Europe in which the armourers had good reason to be flourishing.

On June 18, 1429, he transcribed into his *Journal* a letter which had been written to him from Bruges during May, probably about May 20th, since couriers took from twenty to twenty-five days to travel from Flanders to Venice. The letter was from Giustiniani: "Fifteen days ago, and since then also, there has been much talk of prophecies found in Paris and other things touching the dauphin . . . especially in the matter of a maid, a shepherdess, born near the confines of Lorraine. A month and a half ago she went to the dauphin; she wished to speak to him alone, to the exclusion of anyone else. She told him . . . that he should make a military effort, throw victuals into Orleans, and give battle to the English; that he would certainly be victorious and the siege of the town would be raised. . . . An Englishman called Lawrence Trent, whom Marino knew well, honest and discreet, wrote of all this, seeing what so many men, albeit honourable and in all good faith, were writing in their letters: 'This is driving me mad.' He adds, as an eye-witness, that many barons hold her in esteem as well as many of the common people. . . . Her incontestable victory in the argument with the masters of theology makes her like another Saint Catherine come down to earth. Many knights, hearing her argue and say every day so many admirable things, say that here is a great miracle." (See R. Herval, *Jeanne d'Arc et ses témoins vénitiens*, in *Revue des sociétés savantes de Haute Normandie*, No. 19, 1960, p. 7.)

A little later, on June 23rd, Antonio Morosini copied another letter into his *Journal*, this time from his Avignon correspondent: "This damsel told messire the dauphin that she would go to Rheims to cause him to assume the crown of all France; and we know that all she has said has always come to pass, that her words are always confirmed by the event. She is in truth come to accomplish magnificent things in this world."

It should be noted here, while on the subject of the resounding impression made by the exploit of Orleans, that already pro- and anti-Joan parties were appearing clearly in France. And that already the "renegade Frenchmen", those who had espoused the enemy's cause, were giving expression to their hostility by the mouth of the University of Paris. In May a memorandum drawn up by a clerk of the university, but which has not been preserved, was accusing Joan of heresy; and it may have been in defence of her and in reply to this *libelle* that Jean Gerson, former Chancellor of the University but still loyal to the French King, composed the work we have already referred to; or it may be that this work was called for by the Poitiers doctors themselves. At all events Gerson's work—his last since he was to die on July 12, 1429—was very soon in circulation, as indeed were all the writings of that eminent man. Thus it was that, at the end of the year 1429, Giustiniani was writing:

"I have recently had occasion to be talking of this affair with certain religious. As I understand it, the University of Paris, or rather the enemies of the King, have had her accused—I mean, this maid—of heresy at Rome before the pope. Likewise for those who believe in her. They accuse her of sinning against the faith because she insists on being believed and can foresee the future. But the chancellor of the university, who is a most learned man and a doctor of theology, has composed in honour, in the defence and in praise of the said maid, a very fine work which I send you with the present letter. I think that messire the Doge, as well as many others, will take great pleasure in it." (*Op. cit.* p. 12)

Finally, we will quote Jean Pasquerel, who sums up the impressions made by Joan's victory:

"It was said to her: Never have been seen such things as you have been seen to do; in no book are to be read of deeds like them." (R. 183)

COMMENTARY

Why was Joan always called the Maid of Orleans, unless because she did indeed belong to the House of Orleans of which she was a bastard daughter?

The fact is, however, that there is another reason why Joan could rightfully be called "the Maid of Orleans"; or that, at least, is what emerges from a study of contemporary texts. For, after all, the deliverance of the city did not seem an ordinary or easy thing to the people of that time; and the merit of it is universally attributed to Joan. We have quoted only the principal texts and facts which, immediately following the victory of May 8, 1429, demonstrate the gratitude felt by the people of Orleans, a gratitude which has remained a living feeling even into our own times. But examples could be multiplied: for one, there was the composition of a *Mystery of the Siege of Orleans* in twenty-five thousand lines of verse, a

manuscript copy of which is to be found in the Vatican Library.
(See Q. iv, 79)

Again, as early as the fifteenth century, probably in the reign of
Louis XI, a monument was erected on the Orleans bridge itself,
cast in bronze and showing Charles VII and Joan kneeling at the
foot of a Calvary. A Dutchman who passed through Orleans while
travelling in France in 1560 described it (Q. iv, 448) before it was
destroyed, for the first time, by the Huguenots in 1567. We still
have the accounts of the cost of restoring it in 1571 (Q. v, 222–225);
likewise, the banner which was brought out to be carried in the
May 8th procession, and which also shows Joan kneeling at the foot
of a crucifix, is preserved at the Musée Historique of the Orléanais.

There were, then, many reasons why Joan should have been
called "the Maid of Orleans". But as a matter of fact she was *never*
so called in her lifetime. On this subject, the detailed study made
by the historian Edouard Bruley should be read. (*Sur l'expression
Pucelle d'Orleans*, Bul. de la Soc. Arch. et Hist. de l'Orléanais, Vol.
XXIII, 1939, No. 237.) This author took the trouble to examine
every manuscript cited as a basis for justifying this epithet: every
time the term "Maid of Orleans" appears, it is only as a title added
subsequently, in a different and later hand, whereas in the original
account Joan is referred to simply and only as "The Maid". That
was the only epithet by which she was known to her contemporaries.
This piece of research wipes out all the deductions which had been
based on an epithet which did not, in fact, become current until the
sixteenth or seventeenth centuries. Edouard Bruley has shown that
the oldest work in which the epithet is used is "an allegorical work
written in about 1552 and published in 1555: *Le Fort inexpugnable de
l'honneur du sexe féminin construit par François de Billon secrétaire*"
(*op. cit.*). In that work, on folio 47, the author refers to "the very
courageous maid, Joan, called of Orleans".

Attempts have also been made to draw inferences from the fact
that Joan received a livery bearing the Orleans arms as a gift. They
overlook the fact that gifts of such livery, bearing the arms of the
lord for whom they had fought, were common form during the
Middle Ages; moreover, at the time a gift of clothes was a common
practice quite apart from any question of rewarding a military
exploit; from the time of Charlemagne there are innumerable cases
of princes making a present of robes, mantles, cloaks or other such
gear. It will suffice here if we quote a few examples from Joan's
own epoch: for the New Year in 1400, Charles VI ordered three

hundred and fifty surcoats in his colours and bearing his arms, as gifts for his courtiers; we can hardly infer that all three hundred and fifty recipients were his bastards. (See M. Defourneaux, *La Vie quotidienne au temps de Jeanne d'Arc*.) Louis d'Orleans did the same thing in 1404. And in the very complete accounts which we possess of the Duke of Burgundy's household expenses (Philippe the Bold), similar gifts appear repeatedly: 1378, gift of clothes to all the knights of his suite for the emperor's visit; in 1390 the Dukes of Burgundy and of Nevers (John the Fearless) gave green taffeta tunics bearing the Burgundian arms to eight knights and fifty esquires for their appearance in the jousting tournament organised by the King at St. Denis. (See E. Petit, *Itineraire de Philippe le Hardi*, notably on pp. 480, 506, 521, 529, 531, 536, 542, 546, 549, 552 . . . which show gifts of clothes specifying whether or not they are to bear the donor's arms.)

So that, here again, the mistake of giving the gift of clothes to Joan a special significance derives from ignorance of the customs of her time.

A word should also be said here touching the lease of a house in the rue des Petits-Souliers, at Orleans, long supposed to have been taken by Joan. The mistake derives here from a simple misreading; the word which was taken to be *Pucelle* is, in fact, *Pinelle*, the wife of the Jean Pinel named later in the document. The correction was made by Eugene Jarry as early as 1908. (See the 1908 *Bulletin de la Soc. Arch. et Hist. de l'Orleanais*.)

Of more validity in the eyes of historians than all this supposed evidence for Joan's "bastardy" are the arguments about the numbers of fighting men and weapons confronting each other in the two armies at Orleans. But although floods of ink have been consumed over this question, there can be no certain conclusion. It will have been clear from the texts we have quoted that inexactitude was the rule in the matter of figures as of dates. We must repeat that what we have here is a radical difference between the civilization of the Middle Ages and our own. We are accustomed to see even the time taken to run a race, the motions of factory workers, exactly measured; and to see the humblest domestic chores converted into statistics. In Joan's day, on the other hand, the actions of daily life were regulated, whether hourly or yearly, by the course of the sun. There was a beginning—for example, after Agincourt, at least on the English side—of the practice of taking some account of numbers, after battle; but it was rarely done and the figures were far from exact. In the case of Orleans we are even short of basic facts and figures; moreover, in order to strike a balance we should have to take into account factors which we have no means of evaluating; for example, the means of defence were, at the time, very superior to the means of attack (again, contrary to the state of affairs in our own time). That, indeed, is why sieges lasted so long and why the taking of a "bastion" did not depend solely upon the numbers attacking and defending respectively.

A theory has also been put forward to the effect that the Orleans victory might have been a feat of arms carefully prepared in advance by Charles VII to raise his prestige in the eyes of his contemporaries. According to this opinion, he is supposed to have sent for a "shepherdess" who was carefully tutored and prepared for the part she must play, and thereafter contrived a victory for her, actually won by his usual captains, simply in order to have everyone crying out that it was a miracle. It must be confessed that if this be true then Charles VII must have had an imagination without equal before or since; must have solved a military problem in a manner quite unprecedented; and must have been gifted with miraculous foresight since he would have had to foresee the siege of Orleans: eight months would hardly have been time enough in which to train a girl for so difficult a role and to arrange, at a distance too, all the necessary complicities. And it is surely rather surprising to find him, after all this, making hardly any use of his idea at all: the slight mention which he makes of the Maid, in the circular letter announcing the good news to his loyal towns, seems rather pitiful after all the Machiavellic devices which must have been required.

Moreover, before the hypothesis in question is received, it would be necessary to show that all the texts and documents in which the manner of Joan's advent is so clearly revealed, as well as her origins, are false and perhaps forged; and that all the historians and learned men, deeply read in the relevant fifteenth-century texts, have been mistaken.

5

THE ROAD TO RHEIMS

The Bastard of Orleans: "After the deliverance of Orleans, the Maid, with me and the other captains of war, went to seek the King who was at the castle of Loches, to ask him for armed forces in order to recover the castles and towns situated on the river Loire, that is to say Meung, Beaugency, Jargeau, so as to clear the way and make it safe for him to go to Rheims for his coronation. She urged the King eagerly and often to hasten and not to delay any longer. From that time he used all possible diligence, and he sent me, as likewise the Duke of Alençon and the other captains, with Joan, to recover the said towns and castles. . . . After the liberation of the town of Orleans the English gathered a great army to defend the towns and castles in question and those which they held. . . ."
(R. 133–134)

The German chronicle which we have already quoted gives some details about the meeting between Joan and the King at Loches: "She took her banner in her hand and rode to the King and they encountered. Then the young girl bowed her head before the King as much as she could and the King at once bade her raise it. And it was thought that he would readily have kissed her in his joy. This came to pass the Wednesday before Pentecost (May 11, 1429) and she remained with him until after the twenty-third day of May. Then the King held council on what he should do, for the young girl still wanted to take him to Rheims and crown him and proclaim him King. The King came round to her opinion. He set out hoping to win Meung and Jargeau. God willed it so and it came to pass."
(Q. iv, 497)

It was, of course, obvious that they ought to take advantage of the effects, both moral and material, produced by their victory, and to continue the campaign with the army which had been gathered. But what should be their objective? From the strategic point of view, it would have seemed natural to attempt the reconquest of Normandy and La Beauce, in order to make an effort to regain Paris.

The Bastard of Orleans: "I remember that after the victories of which I have spoken, the lords of the blood royal, and the captains, wanted the King to go into Normandy and not to Rheims, but the Maid was still of opinion that we should go to Rheims to consecrate the King, and she gave reason for her opinion saying that once the

TO RHEIMS AND BACK

The route to Rheims is marked by the continuous line: the return is marked by the dotted line.

King should be crowned and anointed (*sacré*) the strength of his adversaries would go on declining and that at last they would not be able to harm him or his kingdom. All rallied to her opinion." (R.135)

This decision was taken during a council held by the King and into which Joan burst in order to impose her will.

The Bastard of Orleans: "I well remember that when the King was at the castle of Loches, I went with the Maid, after the raising of the siege of Orleans, and while the King was in his chamber, in which were with him the lord Christophe de Harcourt, the bishop of Castres, confessor to the King (Gérard Machet) and the lord of Trèves who was otherwise [*sic*] chancellor of France (Robert le Maçon), the Maid, before entering into the chamber, knocked on the door, and, being in, fell on her knees and embraced the King's legs, saying these words or others like them: 'Noble Dauphin, hold not such, and such long, council but go to Rheims as soon as possible to receive a fitting crown (*digne couronne*, presumably "crown worthy of you").' Then the sire, Christophe de Harcourt, consulting with her, asked her if it was her counsel (i.e. her 'voice') which told her that and Joan answered 'yes' and that she was receiving pressing counsel on this subject. Then Christophe said to Joan, 'Will you not tell us here, in the King's presence, how (in what manner) your counsel speaks to you?' She answered, flushing, 'I see well enough what you would know and will tell you readily.' The King said to Joan: 'Joan, let it please you to say what he demands in the presence of those who are here.' And she answered the King, yes, and said these words or others like them: that when something was not going well because people would not easily repose their faith in her as to what was said to her from God, she went apart and prayed to God, complaining to Him that those to whom she spoke did not readily believe her; and, her prayer to God made, she heard a voice which said to her: 'Daughter-God (*Fille-Dé*), go, go, go, I shall be at your aid, go.' And when she heard this voice, she felt a great joy and desired to be always in that state. And what is more impressive, in thus repeating these words of her voices, she herself exulted in a marvellous fashion, raising her eyes to Heaven." (R. 134–135)

It is manifest here that it was Joan who forced them to a decision: while they were hesitating which way to go and opinions in Council were diverse, she it was, as all the documents prove, who carried her point and so got the royal army away to Rheims, with the object of crowning the King.

Meanwhile that army had been enlarged by an accretion of volunteers. And throughout the whole course of the Loire campaign, which was to take the army into Rheims, this "snowball" effect continued, as contemporary observers noted:

Gobert Thibault: "Joan had the fighting men assembled between the town of Troyes and that of Auxerre, and there were many there, for all followed her." (R.114)

That was the essence of Joan's mode of action. As it was magnificently expressed by the poet Alain Chartier:

"She raised (all) spirits towards the hope of better times" (*op. cit.*)

She restored their soul to a disunited and discouraged people who had lost all heart.

There is an echo of that ardour which was generated by her presence in the letter of a young gentleman, Guy de Laval, who came with his brother André to join the royal army at Saint-Aignan-en-Berry. These two brothers had an illustrious lineage since their grandmother, Anne de Laval, had been married to the Constable Bertrand Duguesclin. De Laval writes:

"Sunday, I arrived at Saint-Aignan, where the king is, and I sent to seek and to come to my lodgings the lord of Trèves who went away to the castle—to signify to the King that I was come and to learn when it would please him that I go to him; I had answer to go there as soon as I pleased and he made me right good cheer (made me very welcome) and spoke many good words to me. . . . And arrived the Monday at Selles my lord the Duke of Alençon who had a very great company; and today I won a game of fives with him. . . . And it is said here that my lord the Constable is coming also with six hundred men-at-arms and four hundred men of draft (*hommes de traits*—presumably 'pioneers' dragging the supplies) and that Jean de la Roche comes also, and that the King never had so great a company as are hoped for here (or expected here); nor ever did men go with a better will to a task than they go to this one."

He goes on to give his mother a long account of how he has seen *her*; who had obviously excited his admiration and whom he had impatiently been waiting to see:

"Monday I left the King's to go Selles-en-Berry at four leagues from Saint-Aignan and the King summoned before him the Maid who had been hitherto at Selles. And some say that this was done in my favour, that I might see her. And the Maid made my brother and me very good welcome, armed at all points save the head, and lance in hand. And after we were settled in Selles, I went to her lodging to see her; she sent for wine and told me that she would soon have me drinking wine in Paris. This seems a thing divine by her deeds, and also from seeing and hearing her. She set out Monday at vespers from Selle to go to Romorantin three leagues ahead. . . . And I saw her mount her horse, armed all in white excepting her head, a little axe in her hand (riding) a big, black charger which, at the door of her lodgings, cavorted very wildly and would not let her mount; then she said, 'Take him to the cross,' which was before the church, beside the road, and there she mounted without the horse moving, as if he were tied. And then she turned towards the door of the church which was quite near and said: 'You, the priests and churchmen, make procession and prayers to God.' And then she turned again into her road, saying, 'Forward, forward' (literally 'Draw forward, draw forward'), her standard unfurled, which was carried by a pretty page, and she having in her hand a little axe. And her brother, who came a week ago, departed likewise with her, all armoured in white. . . . The Maid told me at her lodgings, when I went there to see her, that she had sent to you, grandmother, a very small golden ring, that it was a very small thing and that she would rather have sent you a better, considering your renown." (Q. v, 105-111)

This letter, which was written on June 8, 1429, gives a clear idea of the general tone and atmosphere which distinguished the French court at the time. And the Burgundian chroniclers give us the reverse of the coin, the discouragement which had overtaken the English army.

"By the renown of Joan the Maid," wrote Jean de Wavrin, "the courage of the English was much impaired and fallen off. They saw, it seemed to them, their fortune turn its wheel sharply against them, for they had already lost several towns and fortresses which had returned to their obedience to the King of France, principally by the undertakings of the Maid, some by force, others by treaty; they saw their men stricken down and did not now find them of such or so firm and prudent words as they were wont to be. Thus they were all, it seemed to them, very desirous of withdrawing on to the Normandy marches, abandoning what they held in the country of France (en lieu de France) and thereabout." (Q. v, 418)

This piece of evidence is of particular value since the witness in question was well-informed. Jean de Wavrin, bastard son of the Robert de Wavrin who was killed at Agincourt, was chief of a company of mercenaries employed sometimes by the Duke of Burgundy and at others by the King of England: he fought in person at the battle of Patay, as we shall see.

To command the Loire campaign, the King chose the Duke of Alençon who directed all the operations as Dunois had directed those of Orleans. Meanwhile, the English had gathered their troops at Jargeau, or rather the remnant of the forces which had fought at Orleans, under Suffolk, while Bedford gave orders for the raising of another army which, under Falstaff's command, was to reinforce Suffolk.

The Duke of Alençon: "The King's men were gathered together to the number of six hundred lances, who wanted to go to the town of Jargeau which the English held in occupation; and that night they slept in a wood. On the morrow came other soldiers of the king led by the lord Bastard of Orleans and the lord Florent d'Illiers (captain of Chateaudun) and some other captains. Once all united they found that they numbered about twelve hundred lances, and there was then argument among the captains, because some were of opinion that they should assault the town, others of the contrary opinion, assuring that the English had great strength and were there in great number. Joan, seeing that there was difficulty between them, told them that they should fear no multitude, and should make no difficulty about attacking the English, for God guided their business. She said that if she were not sure that God was directing this business, she would rather keep the sheep than expose herself to such perils. Which being heard, they made their way to the town of Jargeau, thinking to take the suburbs and there spend the night; knowing this, the English came out to meet them and at the beginning drove back the King's men. Which seeing, Joan, taking her standard, went in to the attack exhorting the soldiers to have good courage. And they so wrought that that night the King's soldiers lodged in the Jargeau suburbs. I think that God guided this business, for that night there was hardly any guard set, so that if the English had come out of the town, the King's soldiers would have been in very great peril.

"The King's people prepared artillery and in the morning had the bombards and the machines dragged up against the town and, after several days, they held council among themselves as to what they should do against the English, who were in the town of Jargeau, to recover the town. At the time when they were holding council . . . it was decided that the town should be stormed and the heralds cried the assault. And Joan herself said to me: 'Forward, gentle Duke, to the attack!' and as it seemed to me that it was premature to begin the assault so swiftly, Joan said to me: 'Doubt not, the time is come when it pleases God,' and that one must act when God willed: 'Act, and God will act,' and saying to me later: 'Ah, gentle Duke, wast thou afeared? Knowest thou not that I promised thy wife to bring thee back safe and sound?' for in truth when I left my wife to go with Joan to the army, my wife said to Joanette (Jeanette) that she was greatly afraid for me and that I had formerly been a prisoner and that it had been necessary to give so much money for my ransom that she would readily have implored me to stay behind. Then Joan answered her: 'Lady, fear not, I will bring him back to you safe and sound and in such state or better than now he is.' "

The Duke continued,

"During the assault on the town of Jargeau, Joan said to me at a moment when I stood in a certain spot, that I should withdraw from that spot and that if I did not withdraw, 'that machine . . .' showing me a machine which was in the town, 'will kill thee'. I withdrew and shortly thereafter, at that spot whence I had withdrawn, someone was killed who was called my lord de Lude. That put me into a great fear and I marvelled at the sayings of Joan after all these events. Thereafter Joan went in to the assault and I with her. At the moment when the soldiers were invading the town, the Earl of Suffolk caused it to be cried that he wished to speak to me, but it was not heard and the assault was completed. Joan was on a (scaling) ladder, holding in hand her standard. This standard was pierced and Joan herself struck on the head by a stone which shattered on her light helmet. She herself was stricken to the ground and as she rose up she said to the soldiers, 'Friends, friends, up, our Lord has condemned the English, in this hour they are ours, be of good heart!' And at once the town of Jargeau was taken and the English withdrew towards the bridges and the French pursued them and in the pursuit were killed of them more than eleven hundred."

That happened on June 10, 1429, whereafter the French troops marched towards Meung and Beaugency.

The Duke of Alençon: "I spent that night with some soldiers in a church near Meung where I was in great peril. And on the morrow we went towards Beaugency, and in the fields we found other soldiers of the king and there an attack was made against the English who were in Beaugency. After this attack the English abandoned the town and entered into the castle, and guards were placed facing the castle in order that they might not get out. We were before the castle when the news reached us that the lord constable was coming with soldiers: myself, Joan and the others in the army, we were ill content, wishing to withdraw from the town, for we had orders not to receive the lord constable in our company. I told Joan that if the constable came, I should go away."

The constable in question was Arthur de Richemont who was then in disgrace. The King had forbidden him to reappear at court. The fact is that there were struggles between rival influences about the King's person throughout Charles's whole reign; and Richemont's rival was the famous La Tremoille who, at the time, was the royal favourite. Arthur de Richemont was a powerful personality, as the future was to show. His chronicler, Guillaume Gruel, a Breton like himself and his companion in many adventures, tells, in a quite entertaining style, how Richemont, having decided to go to the King's help despite the latter, nothing nor anybody could make him change his mind.

Guillaume Gruel: "My lord took his way to draw nigh to Orleans, and as soon as the King heard it he sent my lord de la Jaille to meet him and he found him at Loudun. He drew him aside and told him that the King ordered him to return to his house and that he be not so bold as to advance further, and that if he passed beyond (there) the King would fight him. Then, my said lord answered that what he did was for the good of the kingdom and the King and that he would see who tried to fight him. Then the lord de la Jaille said to him, 'My lord, it seems to me that you will do very well,' and took my lord his way and came near to the river of Vienne and passed it by fording and from there drew towards Amboise. And there learned that the siege was at Beaugency and took the straight road directly towards La Beauce to go and join them who laid the siege." (Q. iv, 316)

The Duke of Alençon: "On the morrow, before the arrival of the lord constable, came news that the English were approaching in great number, in company with whom was the lord de Talbot; and the soldiers cried alarm, then Joan said to me—for I wanted to withdraw because of the coming of the lord constable—that there was need to have help*. In the end the English yielded up the castle by a composition and withdrew with a safe conduct which I granted them, I who, at that time, was the King's lieutenant in the army. And while the English were retreating came one from La Hire's

* Or, "we must all help each other", i.e., instead of quarrelling.

company who said to me, as to the King's captains, that the English were coming, that we should soon be face to face with them and that they were about one thousand men-at-arms in number." (R.152)

This referred to the army raised by Bedford and commanded by Falstaff. It is obvious that, as Joan had said, "there was need to have help".

Meanwhile an agreement had been reached, not without difficulty, between the captains of the royal army and Arthur de Richemont. Guillaume Gruel has something to say about the meeting between de Richemont and the Maid: "He spoke to her and said: Joan, I have been told that you want to fight me. I do not know if you are from God or not. If you are from God I fear nothing from you, for God knows my good-will. If you are from the Devil, I fear you even less."

And the Duke of Alençon completes the account of this meeting thus: "Joan said to the lord constable: 'Ah! handsome* constable, you are not come for my sake, but because you are come you will be welcome.' "

It was felt by all that they were at a moment of decision and that the junction effected between Talbot's troops and Falstaff's, up river at Janville, put the royal forces in a position of some danger. Here we may let the Burgundians do the explaining:

Jean de Wavrin: "You might have seen on all hands amidst that Beauce, which is so ample and wide, the English riding in very handsome order. Then, when they came to about a league from Meung and quite near to Beaugency, the French warned of their coming, with about six thousand combatants, of which were chiefs Joan the Maid, the Duke of Alençon, the Bastard of Orleans, the Marshal de La Fayette, La Hire, Poton and other captains, ranked themselves and put themselves in battle on a little hillock the better to see the countenance (disposition) of the English. The latter, seeing clearly that the French were ranged in order of battle, believing that in fact they would come against them to fight, gave order particularly issued by King Henry of England that every man dismount and that all the archers have their pikes stuck into the ground before them, as they are accustomed to do when they expect to be attacked. Then they sent two heralds to the said French whom they saw not moving from their place, saying that there were three

---

* The word is, of course, *beau*. One wonders if there was a touch of hostility, of "Ah, my fine constable". But the epithet seems to have been a common courtesy.

knights who would fight them if they had the boldness to descend from the hill and come to them. Answer was made by the Maid's people: 'Go to your quarters for today, for it is rather late. But tomorrow, if it please God and Our Lady, we shall take a closer look at you.' " (Q. iv, 416–417)

The night of June 17th followed this challenge, both sides remaining in the field, the English camped towards Meung, the French in Beaugency. Statements subsequently made by Alençon and Dunois give us an idea of the uneasiness of the French captains. Indeed, that night spent by the two armies in their respective positions represents a case of what we should now call History in suspense.

The Bastard of Orleans: "These English combined into a single army in such fashion that the French saw that the English were taking up order of battle to fight. They therefore put their army into battle (order) and prepared to wait for the English attack. Then the lord Duke of Alençon, in the presence of the lord constable, of myself and several others, asked Joan what he ought to do. She answered him in a loud voice, saying, 'Have all good spurs,' which hearing those present asked Joan: 'What say you? Are we going to turn our backs on them?' Then Joan answered: 'No. But it will be the English who will not defend themselves and will be vanquished and you will need good spurs to run after them.' And it was so, for they took to flight and there were killed or captured of their number more than four thousand." (R.134)

The Duke of Alençon: "Many of the King's men were afraid, saying that it would be good to send for the horses. Joan said: 'In God's name, we must fight them; were they hung from the clouds, we should beat them, for God has sent them to us that we may punish them,' affirming that she was sure of the victory and saying in French: 'The gentle king will have this day greater victory than he ever had and my counsel has told me that they are all ours.' "

For an account of the actual battle of Patay, which was to make June 18th an important stage in the march on Rheims, we will pass the word to the Burgundian Jean de Wavrin, who was well-informed, since on that day he fought in the English ranks. He tells how the captains heard that the castle of Beaugency had surrendered: "Then, it was hastily ordered in all quarters by the English captains that . . . they were to make their way out into the fields and that as they reached the fields outside the town (of Meung where they were making a stand) every man should fall in to order of battle, which thing was done. . . . The van-guard set out first of all, which was led by an English knight who bore a white standard, then were placed between van-guard and battle (main body) the artillery, supplies and merchandise of all kinds. After came the battle of which was leader messire John Falstaff, the lord de Talbot, messire Thomas Rameston and others. Then rode the rear-guard who were all pure English.

"This company took the road, riding in good order towards Patay, which was reached in about a league, and there stopped, for came warning, in truth, by the runners from their rear-guard, that they had seen coming many men after them whom they thought to be French. Then, to know the truth of this, the English lords sent riding certain of their men who at once returned and related that the French were coming swiftly after them, riding in great strength, and so they were seen coming a little time thereafter. It was ordered by our captains that those of the van-guard, the sutlers, stores and artillery should go forward to take up a position all along by the woods (or hedges) which were near Patay. The thing was so done. Then marched the battle until it came between two strong coppices (or hedges), by which it was likely that the French pass, and there the lord de Talbot, seeing the place to be quite advantageous, said that he would dismount with five hundred picked archers, and remain there, guarding the passage against the French until the battle and rear-guard had joined together. And the said Talbot took his place at the woods of Patay with the van-guard which awaited them. And thus the lord de Talbot, guarding this narrow passage against the enemy, hoped to rejoin the battle by marching outside the woods . . . but it happened otherwise.

"Tensely came the French after their enemy, whom they could not yet see nor knew the place where they were, when it happened that their skirmishers saw a stag came out of the woods, which made for Patay and plunged into the midst of the English battle whence arose a great cry, for they knew not that their enemy was so close to them. Hearing this cry the French scouts were made certain that there were the English, and immediately afterwards saw them quite plainly. They sent certain of their number to tell their captains what they had seen and found, letting them know that they were riding forward in good order and that the hour had come to lay on. They (the captains) promptly prepared themselves in all respects and rode so hard that they came fully in sight of the English.

"When, then, the English saw the French draw so near, they hurried as much as they could in order to reach the woods before their coming, but they were able only to accomplish so much that, before they had joined up with their van-guard at the woods, the English (presumably 'the other English': the passage is involved and somewhat obscure) had come to the narrow passage where lay the lord de Talbot. And then, messire John Falstaff, riding towards the van-guard to join up with them, those of the van-guard thought that all was lost and that the men of the battle were in flight. Hence, the captain of the van-guard, taking it for true that it was so, with his white standard, he and his men, took flight and abandoned the woods. Hence, messire John Falstaff, seeing the danger of this flight, knowing that all was going very badly, had the notion of saving himself and it was said to him in my presence that he should take care of his person, for the battle was lost for them. And before he had gone, the French had thrown to the ground the lord de Talbot, had made him prisoner and all his men being dead, and were the French already so far advanced in the battle that they could at will take or kill whomsoever they wanted to. And finally the English were there undone at small loss to the French. . . . Which seeing, the lord Falstaff left with a very small company . . . and made his way towards Etampes, and me, I followed him as my captain whom the Duke of Bedford had ordered me to obey. We came, at about the hour of midnight, to Etampes where we spent the night, and on the morrow to Corbeil." (Q. iv, 421–424)

The Burgundians themselves estimated the loss on the English side at about two thousand. On the French side there had been three killed. Falstaff was in flight, Talbot a prisoner, the English army decimated.

"Thus," says Jean de Wavrin, "had the French the victory at the field of Patay where they passed that night, thanking Our Lord for their fine venture. . . . Because this place was so called, this battle will for ever bear as its name: the day of Patay. And they went away with their prey (booty) and prisoners to Orleans, where they were generally welcomed by all the people. After this fine victory, went away all the French captains who were there, and with them Joan the Maid, to King Charles who mightily rejoiced and greatly thanked them for their good services and diligence."

The *Journal d'un Bourgeois de Paris* has an echo of the panic which spread among the "Burgundians" of that city when the news of the victory of Patay reached them: "The Tuesday before Saint

John's Day (June 21, 1429) Paris learned in great uneasiness that
the Armagnacs were going to enter it that night, but nothing of the
kind happened. Since then, day and night the Parisians have
strengthened the watch and fortified the walls, placing on them a
quantity of cannon and other artillery." (p. 91-92)

More than ever, Joan was now insisting that they should make
for Rheims without further delay. "We went back to the King who
deliberated whether to go to the town of Rheims for his coronation
and sacring." At last the decision was taken and the troops assembled
at Gien, whence, following the custom obtaining in peace-time, the
King sent a letter of invitation to all the good towns of his kingdom
and to the great vassals both ecclesiastical and lay, calling upon them
to be present at his coronation. Joan, too, dictated a letter from Gien
to the inhabitants of the town of Tournai, the only place in the north
which, with Vaucouleurs, remained loyal to the King. Unfortunately
the original of this letter was destroyed with the greater part of the
town's archives when Tournai was burned during the war of 1940.
Another letter, also dictated by her, but the text of which has not
been preserved, was sent to the Duke of Burgundy, urging him to
come and join the other lords of the blood royal in paying homage
to the King of France. A well-informed witness, Perceval de
Cagny, friend and later chronicler of the Duke of Alençon, tells us
of Joan's impatience during those days of decision:

"The King was at the place of Gien until Wednesday twenty-
ninth day of June. And the Maid was mighty grieved at his long
lingering in that place because of certain men of his household who
advised him against undertaking the road to Rheims, saying that
there were many cities and towns closed (to him), castles and places
very well garrisoned with English and Burgundians between Gien
and Rheims. The Maid said that she knew this very well and that
she took no account of all that, and from disappointment she left
her lodgings and went out and camped in the fields two days before
the King's departure. And although the King had no money to
pay his army, all the knights, esquires, men of war and of the
commonality did not refuse to go with and serve him for that
journey in the Maid's company, saying that wheresoever she went
they would go, and she said: 'By my *martin*, I will lead the gentle
King Charles and his company safely and he will be crowned at
Rheims.'"

The first stage was Auxerre, where the army arrived on June
30th. The town belonged to the Duke of Burgundy, who had

appointed a municipality charged with its administration. For three days the troops camped beneath its walls while embassies between the King and the people of Auxerre went back and forth.

Monstrelet: "Finally, there was treaty between the two parties; and the people of the town of Auxerre promised that they would pay to the King the same obedience as should those of the towns of Troyes, Chalons and Rheims. And thus, providing the King's people with victuals and other goods for their money, they remained at peace and the King held them excused for that time." (Q. iv, 378)

The second important stage happened to be the town of Troyes itself, the very town in which, nine years before, had been signed that shameful treaty which disinherited the Dauphin Charles in favour of the King of England. What was the attitude of its citizens going to be? For, quite apart from their feelings in the matter, they might well fear reprisals. It was at least possible that the Burgundian garrison, five or six hundred strong, would offer active resistance.

From Saint Phal, where Joan camped on July 4th at twenty-two kilometres from Troyes, two letters were sent, one from her and one from the King himself. He promised to "put all in forgetfulness" while informing the inhabitants that "his intention was to go on the morrow to see the said town of Troyes". To this end he asked and commanded them to "render him that obedience which they owed him and to dispose themselves to receive him without making difficulties and without fear of things past".

As for Joan's letter, it bears the imprint of her particular style: "Loyal Frenchmen, come out to meet King Charles and let there be no failing and fear not for your persons nor your property if (you) do so; and if (you) do not so I promise you and certify on your lives that we shall enter with the help of God into all the towns which should be of the holy kingdom, and there make good and lasting peace (*y ferons bonne paix ferme*), let who will come against it. (I) commend you to God. God have you in his keeping if it please Him. Reply briefly (*Réponse brièvement*)."

The first move made by the people of Troyes was to send to Joan a certain Franciscan, Brother Richard by name, who was getting himself much talked of at the time. The *Journal d'un Bourgeois de Paris* mentions his presence in the town during the past April, where much attention had been paid to his predictions; but he had had to leave in haste, threatened with being thrown into

prison by the Burgundians. Joan herself has left us an account of
the encounters at Saint-Phal:

Question: Do you know Brother Richard?
JOAN: I had never seen him when I arrived before Troyes.
Question: How did Brother Richard receive you?
JOAN: They of the town of Troyes, as I think, sent him to me
saying that they feared lest I be not a thing of God. And when
he came towards me, as he approached he made signs of the
cross and sprinkled holy water, and I said to him: "Approach
boldly, I shall not fly away." (C. 98)

There were some days of waiting: neither in the town, nor in
the King's camp were all of the same opinion. The people of Troyes
sent two letters to their neighbours of Rheims, in which they
affirmed their willingness to remain loyal to the oath which they
had taken to King Henry and to the Duke of Burgundy; they also
let their fear of reprisals from the garrison appear between the lines:
"Whatsoever be our will, we the inhabitants, we must look to the
men of war who are in the town, stronger than us." As for Joan's
letter, it was cast into the fire and left unanswered.

The army's situation was critical. "There was in the army great
dearness of bread and other victuals, for there were there seven or
eight thousand men who had eaten no bread for eight days and were
living principally on beans and on wheat rubbed out of the ear."
Thus a contemporary chronicler, the Herald Berri (Q. iv, 73). The
time was, in fact, that of the harvest.

Moreover, the army's leaders were divided as to what they should
do.

The Bastard of Orleans: "The place where the King made a halt
with his army was before the city of Troyes. Once there, he held
council with the lords of his blood and the other captains of war to
consider whether they should set themselves before the city and
lay siege to it or take it, or if it would be better to march past it,
going directly to Rheims and leaving this city of Troyes. The
King's council was divided between diverse opinions and they
wondered what was best to be done. Then the Maid came and
entered into the council and spoke these words or nearly: 'Noble
Dauphin, order that your people go and besiege the town of Troyes
and stay no longer in council, for, in God's name, within three days
I will take you into the city of Troyes by love or by force or by

courage, and false Burgundy will stand amazed (*sera toute stupé-faite*).' Then the Maid crossed at once with the King's army and left the encampment beside the moats, and made admirable dispositions such as could not have done (better) two or three of the most famous and experienced soldiers. And she worked so well that night that on the morrow the bishop and the citizens of the city made their obedience to the King, shaking and trembling. And subsequently it was learned that from the moment when she advised the King not to go away from the city, the inhabitants lost heart and did nothing but seek refuge and flee into the churches. This city being reduced to royal obedience, the King went away to Rheims where he found total obedience and he was there consecrated and crowned." (R.136)

This deposition is confirmed by that of Simon Charles who was likewise present: "At the moment when the King was before the town of Troyes, and while the soldiers saw that they had no more victuals and were discouraged and ready to withdraw, Joan told the King that he should doubt not and that on the morrow he would have the town. Then she took her standard; many foot soldiers followed her to whom she gave order to make faggots to fill the moats. They made many of them, and on the morrow Joan cried the assault, signifying that they should put the faggots into the moats. Seeing this, the inhabitants of Troyes, fearing attack, sent to the King to negotiate a composition. And the King made composition with the inhabitants and made his entry into Troyes in great pomp, Joan carrying her standard beside the King." (R. 105)

This entry into the town took place on Sunday, July 10th, after negotiations carried on under the aegis of Jean Leguisé, bishop of Troyes, whom later, in gratitude, the King was to ennoble.

On July 12th the army resumed its march; on the 14th it was before Châlons. But as the royal advance towards Rheims became more and more decided, so hesitations in the towns diminished. Thus although the people of Châlons had hastened to send the news from Troyes to the people of Rheims, and to declare (it may simply have been a matter of form to cover them in case of an expected attack by the English): "That they had the intention of holding out and resisting with all their strength on meeting with the said enemies," that is the Dauphin's people, yet when the royal herald, Montjoie, appeared with letters from this same Dauphin, the bishop of Châlons, Jean de Montbéliard, went out in person to meet Charles VII and delivered over to him the city keys. On the same day Charles made his entry into the town, and all the chroniclers agree that the inhabitants were joyous at his coming.

At Châlons occurred a moving encounter: already the roads were busy with groups of people making their way from all the towns to which Charles had written announcing his coronation and sacring; among them, as may well be imagined, the people of Domremy were not the last to come running; for was it not to one of their number, still known to them as Jeanette, that the whole astonishing progress was due? Jean Moreau, her godfather, recalls this encounter in his deposition: "In the month of July, I went to Châlons, for it was said that the King was going to Rheims to have himself crowned. And there I found Joan and she gave me a red coat (veste) which she was wearing." (R.69)

Among her fellow townsmen was Domremy's "Burgundian", Gérardin d'Epinal: "I saw her afterwards at Châlons," he said, "with four from our town, and she said that she feared nothing excepting treason." (R.81)

And at last the final stage, Rheims itself, the town of the sacring of Kings.

Simon Charles: "The King went out of Troyes with his army and made for Châlons and thereafter for Rheims. As he was afraid that he might experience resistance at Rheims, Joan said to him, 'Doubt not; for the burgesses of Rheims will come out to meet you'; and before they drew near to the city of Rheims, the burgesses came over to him (se rendirent; surrendered). The King feared resistance from them of Rheims, for he had no artillery nor machines for a siege if they showed themselves rebellious. And Joan told the King to advance boldly and to fear nothing, for if he would advance courageously he would recover all his kingdom." (R.105)

It was in the castle of Sept-Saulx, an enormous dungeon built in the twelfth century by the ancestors of the archbishop of Rheims, Regnault de Chartres, that Charles VII received a deputation of the city's notables who came to offer him "full and entire obedience as to their sovereign". On the evening of the same day, July 16th, he made his entry into the town to cries of "Noel! Noel!" uttered by the population. The coronation and sacring were performed on the morrow.

For Joan this ceremony had a decisive importance. One of the King's councillors recalled this at the Trial of Rehabilitation.

François Garivel: "When Joan was asked why she called the King 'dauphin' and not 'king' she said that she would not call him 'king' until he had been crowned and consecrated at Rheims, in the town where she had made up her mind to take him." (R. 106)

On this point, however, she was only giving expression to what was commonly believed in her day: it was the sacring which made the King. And this argument took precedence of all strategic considerations, and alone explains the armed ride through Anglo-Burgundian country with the constant risk of coming up against the garrison forces which had remained in the towns, or roving bands of free-lances. Once crowned the King would be King indeed. Whereas, in his going out he had been obliged to halt and negotiate terms before each town, on his return he would meet with no obstacles. Wherever he appeared he was to find that his rights were recognized at once; and city gates opened to him as he approached. The English, likewise, felt, and felt cruelly, the effects of the new situation created by Charles's sacring. They attempted to counter it by bringing the boy-King Henry VI to France (April 23, 1430), and, six months after Joan's death, crowning him not, indeed, at Rheims, now loyal to Charles, but in Paris (December 16, 1431). It was a pointless gesture, however, since for the mass of the French people Charles VII was thenceforth the Lord's anointed, legitimate heir to the kingdom.

Everybody knows Joan's famous reply to the question touching the coronation at Rheims: "Why was your standard more carried in the church at Rheims at the consecration of the King than those of other captains?"

Joan: "It had borne the burden, it was quite right that it receive the honour (*il avait été à la peine, c'était bien raison qu'il fût à l'honneur*)."

After having described the sacring, one chronicler shows us Joan kneeling before the King "and embracing him round the legs, said to him whilst shedding copious tears: 'Gentle King, now is done God's pleasure, Who willed that I raise the siege of Orleans and that I bring you to this city of Rheims to receive your holy sacring, showing that you are true King and him to whom the kingdom of God should belong.' And causing great pity in those who beheld her." (J.S.O. 186)

Among the witnesses of this scene were two who must, surely, have been more moved by that than the rest: her father and mother.

The Rheims city account books mention their presence, and note that the municipality undertook to pay their expenses at the inn, the *Ane rayé*, where they put up.

COMMENTARY

This chapter raises no particular difficulties from the historical point of view. For the coronation ceremony reference may be made to the well-known work of J. de Pange, *Le Roi très chrétien*, Paris, 1949. We gave some details on this matter in our own work, written in collaboration with M. Rambaud, *Telle fut Jeanne d'Arc*, Paris, Fasquelle, 1957, pp. 160, et seq. Recourse may also be had to Henri Godart's *Jeanne d'Arc à Reims*, Rheims, 1887.

Curiously enough an attempt has been made to put forward the view that family affection played no part in Joan's life. The authentic texts prove the contrary. We may begin with those which show us two of Joan's brothers, Pierre and Jean, going to join her in Tours and taking their part in her feats of arms; one of them at least was to remain with her up to and including the time of her imprisonment. This was Pierre; Jean, on the other hand, cuts a rather sorry figure in history, for his principal aptitude seems to have been in exploiting his sister's renown for his own ends. These two persons are very carefully studied in Grosdidier des Mattons' *Le Mystère de Jeanne d'Arc*, Paris, 1935.

But there are very numerous small pointers to the affection in which Joan held her family: she was fond of kissing the ring which her parents had given her, "for her pleasure and for the honour of her father and mother". She was homesick for her family (see her remark, reported by Dunois, in the next chapter). Nor did she fail to write to ask forgiveness from her people after she had left them. Moreover her affection extended to the whole village, as witness the only favour she asked of the King after the coronation: exemption from taxes for the people of Greux-Domremy.

Reciprocally, her parents' affection for her is manifest in all sorts of ways: her father's remarks after having dreamed "that with soldiers would depart Joan his daughter"; that maternal solicitude which, sent to her, from Puy, Brother Jean Pasquerel who became her confessor; their coming to Rheims for the coronation. And then there is, of course (see Chapter 10), that pathetic supplication uttered by Isabelle Ramée when pleading with the judges who had been appointed to investigate the evidence for rehabilitation, "I had a daughter, born in legitimate wedlock. . . ." Guy de Laval's letter brings out a small point which is worth commenting on: Joan's sending of "a very small ring of gold" to Duguesclin's widow. Joan, at a time when she was aware that she herself was renewing the exploits of a hero whose popularity was such that he knew that "all the girls of France" would spin for his ransom, and who had crystallised the kingdom's resistance when, on a former occasion, it had nearly failed, thus paid homage to his memory. And contemporary folk legend was soon to assimilate her to the "*nine preux chevaliers*"* and make of her a tenth.

* The "neuf preux", nine valiant knights—champions of French history. Bertrand Duguesclin was twice captured and ransomed, on the second occasion by the Black Prince.

6

FROM RHEIMS TO COMPIÈGNE

"The French are come to Rheims where it is proper that all Kings of France be crowned, and there arrived the Dauphin, Saturday, 16th of this month; the town gates were opened to him without opposition and Sunday 17th he was crowned with great pomp. The ceremony lasted from the hour of tierce until Vespers."

It was thus that Morosini's journal, to which we have already referred, summed up the events. (*Ed. cit.*, pp. 10–11.) On the very day of the sacring itself, Joan sent to Philippe the Good, Duke of Burgundy, who had answered neither her invitation nor that of the King his cousin, the following letter:

"High and redoubted prince, Duke of Burgundy, the Maid requires you, on behalf of the King of Heaven, my right and sovereign Lord, that the King of France and you make good firm peace which last long. Forgive each other with good heart entirely as must faithful Christians do. . . . I beg and require you with clasped hands that you make no battle nor war against us, you, your men, and your subjects, and believe assuredly that what number soever of men you bring against us, they will not win, and will be great pity at the battle and at the blood which will there be spilt of those who shall come against us." (Q. iv, 127. *Original in the Archives départementales du Nord.*)

It happened that on the same day emissaries from the duke arrived in Rheims, led by one of his intimates, David de Brimeu. There was reason to hope that the King would take advantage of the exceptionally favourable turn in his affairs to conclude that "good firm peace" which Joan was counting on.

But no such thing; and in the course of the negotiations, from which Joan was carefully excluded and which were carried on in secret, Charles VII, henceforth King of France, concluded only a truce—of two weeks! This truce condemned the royal army to inaction; and in exchange the Duke made Charles the fantastic

I *This bronze statuette of Joan on horseback was cast in the fifteenth century. It is now in the Cluny Museum.*

1a

The bust of Charles VII from his tomb gives a rather less sulky impression of the man than the famous Fouquet portrait.

1b

Henry VI.

2   *Jean, Count of Dunois.*

e Judith la quelle Oloferne

3a

*The oldest miniature of
Joan is from a manuscript
executed in Arras in 1451
by Martin Le Franc, and
called* Le Champion des
Dames. *It depicts Joan,
with lance and shield, in
company with Judith
who is holding Holo-
fernes' head.*

3b

*A miniature from a later
manuscript of* Le Cham-
pion des Dames, *now in the
Grenoble Municipal Library.*

4 *This page of the official history of the siege of Orleans records the lifting of the siege on May 18, 1429. It was written by Clément de Fauquembergue, the scribe or greffier to the Parliament of Paris. In the margin he has scribbled a pen drawing of Joan from his imagination. It is the only pictorial representation of Joan done during her own life.*

5 *The inquiry into the circumstances of Joan's trial and condemnation which had been initiated by Charles VII was subsequently taken up by the Church. Its investigation was directed by Jean Bréhal who was appointed inquisitor of the Faith for France in 1452. This is a page from his "Summarium" of evidence.*

6　*A fifteenth-century Franco-Flemish miniature of Joan from a manuscript book of poems by Charles of Orleans.*

7 *The painting commissioned by the aldermen of Orleans and executed in 1581 was the prototype for much of the iconography during the next two centuries.*

TALIS INERMIS ERAT MULIEBRI VESTE PUELLA

IOHANNA DARC AVRELIANENSIS PUELLA VULGO NUNCUPATA

8a

Two frontispieces from Jean Hordal's dissertation on Joan, published at Pont-à-Mousson in 1612; 8a clearly is a derivative version of the "Aldermen's Painting"

8b

9   *The Bull of Canonization,* 1920.

10　Joan's last letter to the people of Rheims, March 28, 1430. The signature is in a different hand from the body of the letter. It may be an example of Joan's own hand.

11a   11b

Two folios from the letter John, Duke of Bedford, wrote to Henry VI, including the passage quoted on page 101: "And alle thing there prospered for you . . ."

12 *The sixteenth-century manuscript of
Diane de Poitiers contains a transcription
of the rehabilitation proceedings, and this
fine miniature, done from imagination,
of Joan's mother, Isabelle Romée.*

13 *Joan is brought to the Dauphin* (Vigils of Charles VII).

14   *Joan in the presence of the Dauphin at
Chinon.*

15   *Siege warfare.*

16 *Joan drives out the camp followers*
(Vigils of Charles VII).

Comme il se mestoit alabzy.
Pour regarder assus la Ville.

Si luy vint dire Vng de ses gens.
Monseigneur vous voulez a plain.

17   *The Siege of Orleans* (Vigils of Charles VII).

De son frere vint mener guerre.
Ou pais de france tresdure.

Si mist le siege deuant dreux.
Et leust par composition.
Auec autres places et lieux.

18   *The Siege of Dreux* (Vigils of
Charles VII).

19 *Charles receiving his crown from Archbishop Regnault* (Vigils of Charles VII).

20   *Joan directing her troops during the attack on Paris.*

21 *Joan is captured* (Vigils of Charles VII).

22   *Joan's trial. Bishop Cauchon is seated in
the high-backed chair.*

promise that he would hand over Paris to the King. In fact he, and Bedford with him, was simply seeking to gain time: Bedford had called for reinforcements from England immediately after the battle of Patay, and early in July three thousand five hundred knights and archers disembarked at Calais, raised, incidentally, with the funds collected for a crusade against the Bohemian heretics who were called Hussites. This army left Calais on July 15th for Paris where it arrived on the 25th.

The negotiations were a fraud practised on the King; they were, likewise, a betrayal by him of Joan and all who were animated by her spirit.

It must here be recalled how it was that the House of Burgundy had come to rely upon the English alliance, beginning in 1416 immediately after Agincourt. The duke—at that time John the Fearless—was dominated by his rivalry with the House of Orleans; it will be remembered that in 1407 he had had Louis, Duke of Orleans, assassinated. In 1418 John the Fearless had made himself master of Paris from which the Dauphin Charles had only escaped with great difficulty. An unbridgeable gulf had finally opened between Charles and the House of Burgundy when John the Fearless himself was assassinated on the bridge of Montereau (10 September 1419). He and the Dauphin—the future Charles VII—had met there to negotiate, it was hoped, a peace between Armagnacs and Burgundians; the negotiations having come to nothing, the two parties were withdrawing when, for some unknown reason, a dispute broke out, swords were drawn, and one of them struck the Duke of Burgundy on the brow. Since when his son, Philippe the Good, had resumed his policy of alliance with England. He it was who had dictated the signing of the Treaty of Troyes in the following year. His great aspiration was to play honest broker between England and France, and he missed no opportunity of making both sides feel his enormous strength: the possessions of this man, who was called "the grand-duke of the West", extended from the Alps to the North Sea; apart from Burgundy itself, his possessions included the country known as the County of Burgundy, i.e. Franche-Comté; Flanders, Artois and a part of the Ardennes; and nearly all present-day Belgium and Holland—Brabant, Limbourg, Hainaut, Zeeland, Frisia, etc.

Charles VII was still under the influence of his favourite La Trémoille, whose kinsman Jean de la Trémoille was in very good odour at the Burgundian court. This influence, combined with that of Regnault de Chartres, archbishop of Rheims, was used to make Charles think solely in terms of diplomatic action, negotiation at any cost. To make peace with Burgundy was the general wish; not least of Joan who "with clasped hands" implored Philippe to make peace as we have seen. But she was well aware that they ought not to be satisfied with misleading promises; the peace she asked for was "a good, firm one", and she knew that they would not get such a real peace excepting by virtue of courage and by proving their valour on the field of battle. Charles, on the other hand, preferred to make do with ridiculous promises which coddled his natural apathy; he hoped to conquer by diplomacy, and did not perceive until it was too late that he himself had been the Burgundian's dupe. From this it was that stemmed the ambiguity of his conduct from this point in his career.

His want of resolution was betrayed by the itinerary chosen for the return from the coronation; a glance at the map will show his goings and comings, his sudden changes of direction which were a torment to Joan and her followers, whose one idea was to make straight for Paris and take advantage of the general uncertainty and of the confusion in the Anglo-Burgundian ranks. But in signing the truce the King had signed away his chance, and without anything to show for it. Yet he should surely have been animated by the complete change in the spirit of the people which the sacring at Rheims had brought about:

"The burgesses of the city of Soissons brought him the keys and so did those of the city of Laon to whom he had sent heralds demanding that they open to him; he went away to Soissons where he was received with great joy by all those of the city who much loved him and desired his coming. And there came to him the very joyous news that Chateau-Thierry, Crécy-en-Brie, Provins, Coulommiers and many other towns had returned to their obedience. . . . And the King went towards Crépy-en-Valois, whence he sent his heralds to summon and require them of Compiègne that they place themselves under obedience to him, who sent answer that they would do so very willingly. At about this time . . . certain French lords went into the city of Beauvais of which was bishop and count master Pierre Cauchon, much inclined to the English side although he was a native of Rheims. But, however, the people of that city placed themselves in full obedience to the King as soon as his heralds came bearing his arms, and they cried all in great joy, 'Long live Charles, King of France!' and sang *Te Deum* and made great rejoicing. And that done they dismissed all those who would not stay under that obedience and let them go in peace carrying their chattels with them." (J.S.O. 187 and 190)

Dunois, giving evidence at the Trial of Rehabilitation, recalled the happy days of that armed excursion whose incidents roused strong feelings of tenderness in Joan: "And when the King came to La Ferté and to Crépy-en-Valois, the people came out to meet the King, exulting and crying 'Noel'. Then the Maid, riding between the archbishop of Rheims and myself, spoke these words: 'There is a good folk. I have never seen other people so greatly rejoice at the coming of so noble a King. May I be so fortunate, when my days shall be done, as to be buried in this ground.' The which hearing, the archbishop of Rheims said: 'O Joan, in what place do you hope to die?' To which she answered: 'Where it shall please God, for I am not sure either of the time or of the place, any more than you are. And please God, my Maker, that I may now withdraw myself, leave off arms, and go and serve my father and my mother by keeping the sheep with my sister and my brothers who will rejoice so greatly to see me again.'" (R.137)

The regent Bedford, meanwhile, was taking advantage of the unhoped-for respite. He was having Paris fortified and trying to diminish the prestige which the coronation had given Charles by discrediting (a foretaste of what was to be done at Rouen) Joan, who had accomplished that coronation. From Montereau he sent Charles a letter in the following terms:

"We, John of Lancaster, regent of France and Duke of Bedford, make known to you Charles of Valois who call yourself Dauphin of Viennois and now without cause call yourself King because you have abusively made enterprise against the crown and lordship of the very high and excellent prince, my sovereign lord, Henry by the grace of God true, natural and rightful King of France and England. . . . You who cause to be abused the ignorant people and take to yourself the aid of people superstitious and reproved, as that of a woman disordered and defamed, being in man's clothes and of dissolute conduct . . . who by force and power of arms have occupied in the country of Champagne and elsewhere cities, towns and castles belonging to my said lord and King . . . summon and require you that . . . taking pity on the poor Christian people . . . choose in the country of Brie where you and we are, or in the Ile de France, some place in the fields, convenient and reasonable, or one day soon and fitting . . . at which day and place, if you would appear there in person with the aforesaid defamed and apostate woman, we, at Our Lord's pleasure, will appear in person. . . ."

It was a formal challenge which Bedford was thus proclaiming, in the letter which is dated August 7, 1429. (Q. iv, 384.) A meeting between the two men was expected at an early date.

Back in Paris, Bedford had the cleverness to name the Duke of Burgundy as governor of the city; the Parisians could no longer complain of being under foreign tutelage; Philippe the Good was of the blood royal of France. Bedford took command of the army of reinforcement—seven hundred Picards—which the Duke of Burgundy had sent him in mid-July, and on August 14th the English army marched off towards Senlis. On the following day at dawn it halted at the village of Montepilloy where, on the evening of the same day, the French arrived. Was there to be a decisive battle? In his letter of challenge Bedford seemed to have been referring the outcome to a veritable "judgment of God".

"Sunday, fourteenth day of the month of August, the Maid, the Duke of Alençon, the Count of Vendome, the marshals and other captains, accompanied by six or seven thousand fighting men, were at the hour of vespers camped in a wood in the fields near Montepilloy, at about two leagues from the city of Senlis. The Duke of Bedford, the English captains, accompanied by eight or nine thousand English, were camped at half a league from Senlis, between our people and the said town on a little river, in a village called Nôtre-Dame de la Victoire. That evening our men went out skirmishing against the English, near their camp, and in that skirmish were men taken on both sides, and there died on the English side the captain d'Orbec and ten or twelve others and were men wounded on both sides. Night fell. All withdrew to their camp.

"Monday 15th day of this month of August 1429, the Maid, the Duke of Alençon and the company, thinking that day to join battle, all of the company, each for himself, put themselves in the best state which each in his conscience could do. And they heard mass as early in the morning as it could be done and thereafter to horse. And went to place their battle near to the battle of the English who had not moved from their camp where they had slept, and all night long had fortified themselves with stakes, ditches, and set their carts before them, and the river fortified them in the rear. There was still great skirmishing between one side and the other. The English never made any attempt at sallying out of their place excepting to skirmish. And when the Maid saw that they came not out, she went, standard in hand, and placed herself in the van and went striking at the very fortifications of the English . . . and she summoned them, with the Duke of Alençon and the captains, that if they would come out of their place and give battle, our people would withdraw and give them room to place themselves in (battle) order. Which they would not do and all day remained without coming forth excepting to skirmish. Night falling, our people returned to their camp. And the King was all that day at Montepilloy. The Duke of Bar (René of Anjou), who had come to the King at Provins, was in his company, the count of Clermont and other captains with them, and when the King saw that they could not make the English come out of their place and that night was falling, he returned to his billet in the place of Crépy." (Chronicle of Perceval de Cagny, Q. iv, 21–23)

"All day they were one before the other, without wood or thicket, near to each other a culverin shot (i.e., within culverin-shot) and fought not. . . ." Thus another eye-witness, the herald Berry, who concludes, "And that evening the King departed and went away with his army to Crépy and the Duke of Bedford went to Senlis." (Q. iv, 47)

The battle had not taken place.

At the same time negotiations had been started. On August 16th Philippe the Good received the archbishop of Rheims, Regnault de Chartres, who led the French delegation, which was closely watched by a Burgundian observer, Hugues de Lannoy, a member of the Royal Council of England. The French side declared themselves ready to make every concession, going so far as to offer to waive the homage and oath of loyalty due from the Duke of Burgundy, for the duration of Philippe's reign. There is a strange contrast between that offer, for which nothing was asked in exchange, and the enthusiasm for the King's cause which was manifest throughout the kingdom and is noted even by the Burgundian chroniclers themselves.

Monstrelet enumerates all the cities which have submitted their obedience to the King and he adds: "In truth, if, with all his power (forces), he had gone to Saint-Quentin, Corbie, Amiens, Abbeville and many other strong towns and castles, the greater part of their inhabitants were ready to receive him as lord, and desired in the world no other thing than to make their obedience to him and open fully to him. Nevertheless he was not advised to go so far forward on the Duke of Burgundy's frontiers, as much because some felt it strong in men-at-arms, as for the hope he had that a good treaty would be made between them." (Q. iv, 391)

The *Bourgeois de Paris* echoes the fears which were felt in that city on the Burgundian side: "Towards the end of the month Beauvais and Senlis went over to the Armagnacs who took Saint-Denis on August 25th. On the morrow they were up to the gates of Paris and nobody dared to go out to harvest the wine-grapes or the verjuice, nor to go and harvest anything at all in the marshes. In consequence everything soon became very dear." (P.93)

He goes on to mention the fortification hastily carried out by Bedford: "In the first week of September the *quarteniers* (heads of quarters or wards of the city), began, each in his quarter, to fortify the gates of the boulevards and the houses which were on the walls, to place canon on their carriages, to place tubs full of stones on the walls, to repair the outside moats and to construct barriers outside and in the town." (P.93)

In short everyone was expecting Paris to be attacked. Subsequently, at her Trial of Condemnation, Joan stated that though her voices had had nothing to say about the attack against the city, she herself had wanted to make that attack and that, probably, immediately after the coronation:

Question: When you went up before the town of Paris had you had a revelation from your voices to go there?

JOAN: No, but I went there at the request of noblemen at arms who wanted to make a skirmish or some valliance in arms against Paris and I had every intention to go further and to cross the moats of the town of Paris. (C.141)

And again:

Question: Did you do anything without the command of your voices?

JOAN: You are answered. Read well your book and you will find it. It was at the request of the men of war that was made a valiance in arms against Paris and also against La Charité at the request of my King. But it was neither against nor at the command of my voices. (C.160–161)

What is certain is that in the royal entourage the military men were all impatient to storm the city; the encounter at Montepilloy had made it quite clear that henceforth the Anglo-Burgundians were in no hurry to fight. We can see the events of September 7th and 8th from the Burgundian side by reference to the Bourgeois of Paris:

"In September, on the eve of the Nativity of Our Lady, the Armagnacs came and assailed the walls of Paris which they hoped to take, but won there only grief, shame and misfortune. Many among them were wounded for the remainder of their lives who, before the assault, were in good health. But a fool fears nothing so long as he is successful. I say this for them who sweated ill-luck and bad faith and who, on the word of a creature in the form of a woman who accompanied them—who was it? God knows—had conspired and agreed together to assail Paris on the day of the Nativity of Our Lady. They assembled to the number of more than twelve thousand and came with their Maid about the time of high mass between eleven and noon, accompanied by a rabble of carts, barrows and horses bearing great faggots with three ties, destined to fill the moats of Paris. Their assault, which was very cruel, began against the Saint-Honoré gate and the Saint-Denis gate and during the attack they shouted many insults at the Parisians. Their Maid was there, on the edge of the moat, and said: 'Yield to us quickly, for Jesus' sake, for if you yield not before night, we shall enter by force whether you will or no, and you will all be put to death without mercy.' 'Here's for you!' cried one. 'Cackling bawd!' and he shot straight at her with his cross-bow, transpierced her leg and she fled. Another transfixed her standard-bearer's foot, who, feeling himself wounded, raised his visor to try to draw the bolt from his foot, but another shot and wounded him mortally between the eyes. The Maid and the Duke of Alençon swore that they would rather have lost forty of their men at arms. The assault, which was very cruel on both sides, lasted until four in the evening without it being known who would get the better. A little after four o'clock the Parisians took heart and overwhelmed their adversaries with so many canon balls and arrows that the latter were forced to retreat, to abandon the assault, and go away." (B. de P., pp. 93–94)

At the same time Clément de Fauquembergue, Clerk to the Parliament, noted in his register: "Thursday, eighth day of September, Feast of the Nativity of the Mother (of) God, the people of Messire Charles of Valois, assembled in great number near the walls of Paris, near to the Saint-Honoré gate, hoping by commotion of people to stop the business of and damage to the town and people of Paris rather than by power or force of arms, at about two o'clock in the afternoon began to appear as if they would assail the town of Paris. And at that time there were inside Paris some (dis)affected or corrupted people who raised voice throughout the city on the hither and yon side of the bridges, crying that all was lost, that the enemy was inside Paris, and that every man should retreat and use deligence to save himself." (Q. iv, 457)

Which makes it clear that even in the town itself Charles VII had partisans who would not have failed to play their part had the business been managed with a little firmness. For the "Armagnac" version of what happened, we have the account written by the Duke of Alençon's chronicler, Perceval de Cagny:

"When the King was at the place of Compiègne," he writes, "the Maid was very vexed at his wanting to stay there, and it seemed from his manner that he was satisfied at that time with the mercies which God had granted him, without undertaking anything else. She called the Duke of Alençon and said to him: 'My handsome (fine) Duke, call your men and the other captains to arms. By my martin, I would go and see Paris closer than I have seen it.'

"And on the Tuesday twenty-third day of the Month of August, the Maid and the Duke of Alençon left this place of Compiègne and the King, with a fine company of men. . . . And the Friday following, twenty-sixth day of this month, were the Maid, the Duke of Alençon, and their company camped (billeted) in the town of Saint-Denis. And when the King learned that they were thus camped in the town of Saint-Denis, he went very reluctantly as far as the town of Senlis and it seemed that he was advised against the (course) wanted by the Maid, the Duke of Alençon, and those of their company.

"When the Duke of Bedford saw that the city of Senlis was French, he left Paris to the government of the burgesses, of the sire de l'Isle-Adam and of the Burgundians of his company, and were left there hardly any English. He went away to Rouen, very vexed, and in great fear that the Maid might restore the King to his lordship. Since she had arrived in the place of Saint-Denis, every day, two or three times, our men were out skirmishing up to the gates of Paris, now in one place, now in another, and sometimes at the windmill near the Saint-Denis gate and La Chapelle. And no day passed but the Maid had raids made by skirmishers. And eagerly studied the situation of the town of Paris and what place

would seem to her best for launching the assault. The Duke of
Alençon was most often with her, but because the King was not yet
come to Saint-Denis, what message soever the Maid and the Duke of
Alençon had sent him, the said Duke of Alençon went to him on the
first day of September following, and was told that on the second
day of the month the King would leave. D'Alençon returned to
his company, and, because the King did not come, the Duke of
Alençon went again to him on the Monday fifth day following. He
so wrought that the King set out and on the Wednesday dined at
Compiègne. At which the Maid and all the company were mighty
rejoiced and there was not a man, of whatever condition, but said,
'She will put the King in Paris if it be left to her.'

"Thursday, day of Our Lady, eighth day of the month of
September 1429, the Maid, the Duke of Alençon, the marshals de
Boussac and de Rais and other captains and great numbers of
men-at-arms and baggage men (*hommes de trait*) set out at about
eight in the forenoon from La Chapelle near Paris, in good order.
Some to go into battle, the others to guard and supply those who
would make the assault. The Maid, the marshal de Rais, the sire
de Gaucourt, called by order of the Maid, as seemed good to her,
were given the (task of the) assault on the Saint-Honoré gate.
The Maid took her standard in hand and among the first entered
the ditches (moat) near to the pigmarket. The attack was hard
and long and it was a marvel to hear the noise and din of the canon
and culverins which those within fired at those without, and all
manner of missiles in such great abundance as (to be) innumerable.
And although the Maid and great number of knights and esquires
and other men of war had gone down into the ditches at the edge or
thereabouts, very few were wounded, and there were many on foot
or mounted who were struck and thrown to the ground by blows
from canon stones. . . . The assault lasted from about the hour of
noon to about the hour of nightfall, and after sunset the Maid was
struck by a cross-bow bolt in the thigh. And since being struck
forced herself to cry louder than ever that every man should approach
the walls and that the place would be taken. But because it was night
and she was wounded and that the men at arms were weary from the
long assault which they had made, the sire de Gaucourt and others
went to fetch the Maid and against her will took her out of the moat
and so ended the attack. And she was very sorry indeed to leave in
that way, saying, 'By my martin, the place would have been taken.'
They put her on a horse and took her to her billet in the place of La

Chapelle near all the rest of the King's company: the Duke of Bar, the Count of Clermont, who that day were come from Saint-Denis."

For her and those of her company the game was not yet over:

"Friday, ninth day of this month, although the Maid had been wounded in the assault on Paris, she rose very early in the morning and sent for her fine Duke of Alençon, who was always her escort, and asked him to have the trumpets sound to horse to return before Paris and said that by her martin never would she leave until she had the town. The said d'Alençon and other captains were of the same wish to undertake to return, others not. And while they were still talking about it, the baron of Montmorency, who had always held to the party contrary to the King's, came from within the town, accompanied by fifty or sixty gentlemen, to join the Maid's company, whereby the heart and courage of those who were right willing to return to (the attack on) the town were more sustained. And when they were drawing near, came the Duke of Bar and the Count of Clermont from the King who was at Saint-Denis, and begged the Maid that, without advancing any further, she return to the King at Saint-Denis and also, on behalf of the King, begged Alençon and commanded all the other captains that they were to come and bring the Maid to him. The Maid and most of her company were very vexed at it and nevertheless obeyed the King's will, hoping to find their way to take Paris from the other side and cross the Seine by a bridge which the Duke of Alençon had had built across the river towards Saint-Denis; and so came to the King. . . . The Saturday following, some of those who had been before Paris, thought to go and cross the river of Seine early in the morning by this bridge, but they could not because the King, who had learned of the intention of the Maid, the Duke of Alençon and others of good will, during the night had the bridge demolished, and thus were they prevented from crossing. That day the King held council at which several opinions were voiced and he stayed in that place until Tuesday the thirteenth, still inclining to return to the (region) of the River Loire, to the Maid's great displeasure." (Q. iv, 25-29)

Before this retreat Joan hung up, as an *ex-voto*, a suit of armour taken from a prisoner she had captured before Paris.

Question: What arms did you offer in the church of Saint-Denis in France?

JOAN: A white harness entire for gentleman-at arms with a sword which I won before the town of Paris.

Question: Why did you offer these arms?

JOAN: It was in devoutness, as is the custom among men of war when they are wounded; and because I had been wounded before the town of Paris, I gave them to Saint-Denis because that is the (war)-cry of France. (C.170)

Today there is a plaque on the façade of the café de la Régence in the place du Palais-Royal, marking the spot where Joan was wounded near to the Saint-Honoré gate which opened unto the suburb of the same name, that of the bakers. As for the "white harness entire for gentleman-at-arms" it has been removed from the basilica of Saint-Denis and is preserved in the *Musée de l'armée* at the Invalides.

It is impossible to understand the sum of events and the incredible attitude of Charles VII, his changes of mind, that inexplicable halt at Senlis where the Duke of Alençon was twice obliged to return and urge him to rejoin his own army, without reference to the text of certain negotiations which, unknown to the Maid, had been conducted at Arras. A truce had been signed on August 21—initially of four months' duration but subsequently to be extended until April 16, 1430. The terms were altogether unfavourable to the King of France. The *status quo* was confirmed as regards all the towns important as communication links on the banks of the Seine; the truce applied to those regions on the right bank which lay between Nogent-sur-Seine and Honfleur, which prevented any French offensive against Normandy. But, on the other hand, the Duke of Burgundy, henceforth governor of Paris, was authorised to defend the city and moreover was to receive from the King the principal towns of the Oise-Compiègne, Pont Saint-Maxence, Créil and Senlis. Let us add that two memoirs of slightly later date than this treaty, drawn up in September or October by the King of England's counsellor, Hugues de Lannoy, show that an English offensive for the following spring had already been planned. The important things for the Regent of England were to strengthen the ties with his powerful ally of Burgundy; to ensure the Duke of Brittany's benevolent neutrality and, if possible, the Constable de Richemont's; and to detach the Scots from their French alliance since their military aid was redoubtable. Meanwhile, preparations for war were to be pushed along actively, while the King of France was to be kept amused with the promise of a peace conference to be held at Auxerre in the spring.

In point of fact, on October 13th Philippe the Good received from Bedford the title of Lieutenant-General of the King of England for the Kingdom of France; which meant that he held, after the Regent himself, the highest office in the kingdom.

A chronicle—actually it is hardly a chronicle but an account in verse more nearly related to a *Chanson de Geste* than to a historical narrative—gives an account of events as Charles VII's partisans would have liked them to happen. Written during the reign of Charles VIII, at the end of the fifteenth century, it is pure fantasy and of no historical value. In it Joan is depicted taking Bordeaux and Bayonne after Orleans! After the sacring at Rheims,* the Maid, seeing all accomplished, said to the King, " 'Now, let us go to Paris, there you shall be crowned.' Straight to Paris the road they took. When at Paris they appeared, all churchmen and noblemen to him presented themselves, received him in (*et se l'ont bouté*), the little children crying 'Long live the King!' The Maid always near him, by them of Paris much regarded was, saying 'Here is a maid greatly to be praised, God grants her the great mercy of making herself feared.' All the King's nobility to their lodging taken. Beside him the Maid did they house to serve God and make her welcome did they not delay. The morrow all the princes, Bourbon, Orleans, Nemours, Alençon, took the crown, on the King's head set it, saying, 'Long live the King.' They led him to Saint-Denis, eight days during were jousts, tourney and great bouts, dames and demoiselles set dancing, it was great pleasure.

"After that done, the Maid said to the King, 'Sire, since these English are all into Normandy retreated, all the army should be ready, should undertake driving them out, and that they return into England.' And said the King, 'My daughter, since you made a good beginning, must you make a good ending.' The King ordered all the army to be ready, and thanked them for the obedience and service which to the Maid they had given. 'I trust in you that with the Maid you will persevere, into Normandy she would lead you.' All the army promised him always to obey and to do so they prepared, the King to God commended them, and they set out." (Q. iv, 336)

It was thus that an optimistic imagination reordered events into a

---

* No attempt to reproduce the lame metre of the following doggerel has been made.—E.H.

might-have-been. The reality is very different, and Perceval de Cagny seems to give us the right note when he shows the King in a hurry to get back to the banks of the Loire, where his personal safety would be assured and where it would be possible, without for ever chasing about battle-fields, to construct elaborate diplomatic devices. "We are not of the court and council, we are of the field of battle," said one of the people who played an active part in Joan's saga, Poton de Xaintrailles. But it is easy to see that Charles VII was surrounded by both sorts: those who were "de l'exploit des champs" . . . of battle-field prowess—Alençon, La Hire, Dunois, Joan herself; and those who preferred to be "of the court and council"—the diplomats—men like Georges de la Trémoille and Regnault de Chartres whose influence is to be traced in events. And it was they who won the King over, thus wrecking the victory gained by the others. This situation was to last until the moment when Arthur de Richemont thrust de la Trémoille abruptly out of the picture, and by force rather than favour silenced the men of court and council and enabled the warriors to act; but by that time Joan had been sacrificed.

A part of that sacrifice was accomplished when, at Gien on September 21, 1429, the King gave orders to disband the fine army of the coronation adventure and condemned his war captains to inaction. "And thus," wrote de Cagny, "were the will of the Maid and King's army broken."

"I shall last a year, hardly longer," Joan had declared when she arrived at Chinon, adding that "it was necessary during that year to toil mightily." But from the moment that the man who was contemptuously known as "the little King of Bourges" became King of France, he seems to have had but a single care: to prevent Joan from "toiling". He began by separating her from the Duke of Alençon, whose warlike ardour accorded too well with hers. "The Duke of Alençon had been in the Maid's company and always escorted her on the road to the King's crowning at Rheims, and thence in coming to Paris; when the King was come to the place of Gien, Alençon went away to his wife and his viscounty of Beaumont, and the other captains each to his own frontiers. The Maid remained at the King's side, very vexed at their going and above all at the Duke of Alençon's whom she well loved and did for him what she would not have done for any other. A short time after, Alençon gathered together his men to return to the country of Normandy near the Breton and Maine marches, and to do so he requested and petitioned the King that it might please him to give him the Maid and that with her many (or several) would place themselves in his company who would not leave them if she set out with him. Messire Regnault de Chartres, the lord de la Trémoille, the sire de Gaucourt, who at that time governed the King's council and matters of war, would never consent, nor permit, nor suffer that the Maid and the Duke of Alençon be together, and since then he has not been able to recover her." (P. de Cagny, Q. iv, 30)

We rather lose track of Joan at this point. It is certain that she stayed for about three weeks at Bourges with Marguerite La Touroulde, and it is also known that she resided for some time at the castle of Sully-sur-Loire which belonged to La Trémoille. Another residence was Montfaucon-en-Berry; it was there that she met Catherine de La Rochelle, an "illuminata" who claimed, like Joan herself, to see visions and receive revelations.

Question: Did you know or meet Catherine de La Rochelle?
JOAN: Yes, at Jargeau or at Montfaucon-en-Berry.
Question: Did Catherine show you a certain lady dressed in white who she said sometimes appeared to her?
JOAN: No.
Question: What did Catherine say to you?
JOAN: Catherine told me that there came to her a certain lady clad in cloth of gold, telling her that she should go to the good towns and that the King would give her heralds and trumpets to make proclamation that all gold, all silver and all hidden treasure be at once brought to her, and that if those who had treasures hidden brought them not, she, Catherine, would know them well and that she would know where to find these treasures and that with them she would pay the men-at-arms in Joan's service. To this I answered this Catherine that she return to her husband and do her housework and feed her children. And to have certainty in the matter of this Catherine, I spoke with Saint Catherine and Saint Margaret and they told me that as for the matter of Catherine de la Rochelle, it was nothing but folly and nullity. And I wrote to my King telling him what he should do about it and when I went to him I told him that it was folly and nullity, this matter of Catherine. However, Brother Richard wanted Catherine to be set to work and they were very ill content with me, Brother Richard and this Catherine.

Question: Did you not talk with Catherine de la Rochelle in the matter of going to La Charité-sur-Loire?

JOAN: Catherine did not advise me to go there and said that it was too cold and that I should not go. I told her, when she wanted to go to the Duke of Burgundy to make peace, that it seemed to me we should find no peace but at the lance-point; and I asked Catherine whether this white lady who appeared to her came to her every night, telling her that I should like to sleep with her in her bed, to see her. And, in fact, I lay down and watched until about midnight and I saw nothing, and then I fell asleep. And when morning came I asked this Catherine whether the white lady had come to her. She answered me, yes, while I slept and that she had been unable to awaken me. And I asked her if this lady would come the following night, and this Catherine answered me, yes. Therefore that day I slept in the daytime to be able to watch all the following night, and I lay down that night with Catherine and I watched all night long, but I saw nothing, although often I questioned Catherine to know if the lady was going to come or not. And Catherine answered me, "Yes, presently." (C.104–106)

The siege of La Charité-sur-Loire, referred to in the above exchange, seems to have been suggested to Joan more or less by way of a distraction, inspired by La Trémoille.

Jean d'Aulon: "A certain time after the return from the King's sacring, he was advised by his council, being then at Mehun-sur-Yevre, that it was very necessary to recover the town of La Charité which was held by the enemy; but that it was first necessary to take the town of Saint-Pierre-les-Moutiers which was also held by the enemy.

"To do this and assemble the men, went the Maid to the town of Bourges in which she made her assembly, and from there, with a certain quantity of men-at-arms of which my lord d'Albret was chief, went to besiege the town of Saint-Pierre-les-Moutiers.

"After the Maid and her people had maintained the siege of the town for some time, it was ordered to storm the town. And so was it done and to take it did those who were there do their duty. But, because of the great number of men-at-arms being in the town, and of the great strength and also the great resistance which those within did make, the French were constrained and forced to retreat, and at the time I, who was wounded by an arrow in the heel, so that without crutches could I not stand or move, I saw that the Maid remained but very slightly accompanied by her men or others, and fearing lest some evil transpire, I mounted a horse and immediately made my way to her and asked her what she was doing thus alone, and why she did not retreat like the others. After she had removed her light helmet (*salade*), she answered me that she was not alone, and that still had she in her company fifty thousand of her men and that she would not leave there until she had taken the town.

"At that time, whatever she might say, she had not with her more than four or five men, and this I know certainly and many others who likewise saw her: for which cause I told her once more that she must come away and retreat as the others did. Then she told me to have them bring faggots and hurdles to make a bridge over the town moats so that we could better get at it. And as she spoke thus to me, she cried in a loud voice: 'Faggots and hurdles, everyone, to build a bridge!' which immediately was done. At this thing I marvelled greatly, for immediately the town was taken by storm without encountering too much resistance." (R.165–6)

As was usual, Joan had written to the good towns in the neighbourhood to get from them help in the siege of Saint Pierre-les-Moutiers and in the attempt made on La Charité. One of these letters has been preserved, the one she wrote to the inhabitants of Riom; it is still in the archives of that town. The scholar Quicherat, who had had the letter in his hands, saw its red wax seal in better condition than it is now. He wrote: "One can see the mark of a finger and the remains of a black hair which seems to have been originally put into the wax." It was a common custom at the time to put some personal mark into the seal, a finger-print or a hair. Was this one of Joan's own hairs? There would be nothing surprising in this, and from it we might deduce that she was a brunette.

But this letter is remarkable for another detail: it is the earliest in date which bears Joan's own signature. By this time, November 9, 1429, it is probable that she had learned, if not to read and write, at least to sign her name. Two other, later letters (March and April, 1430), bear her signature. In the case of the Riom letter the handwriting is, it must be confessed, very clumsy and the vertical strokes of the N badly executed; on the later letters the signature is written with far more assurance. Joan would have conformed to the custom of the time which was to dictate one's letters, but signed them herself, for the holograph signature was then beginning to replace the seal which, until that time, had been the usual personal mark. All contemporary letters from captains or other high personages, including the King and Queen, are likewise written by chancellery clerks but bear the author's holograph signature (see Q. v, 147).

The siege of La Charité-sur-Loire was a failure.

The herald Berry sums up the event as follows: "The sire de la Trémoille sent Joan with her brother, the sire d'Albret, in the depths of winter, and the marshal de Boussac with very few men, before the town of La Charité, and there they were for about a month and withdrew themselves shamefully without aid coming to them from inside and there lost bombards and artilleries." (Q. iv, 49)

"When Joan had been there a space of time, because the King made no diligence to send her victuals nor money to maintain her company, she was obliged to raise her siege and depart from it in great displeasure," adds Perceval de Cagny. Later Joan was to deny having been sent there by her voices:

Question: What did you do on the moats of the town of La Charité?
JOAN: I had an assault made there . . .
Question: Why did you not enter into the town of La Charité since you had God's commandment to do so?
JOAN: Who told you that I had God's commandment?
Question: Did you have council from your voices?
JOAN: Me, I wanted to go into France, but the men of war said that it was better to go first before the town of La Charité. (C.106)

It is of course possible that she was anxious to avoid any implication that her voices might have made a mistake. But it is perfectly clear that this operation was not one which she would have wanted to undertake; ever since Rheims she had lost her grip on the conduct of events for want of that acquiescence of the royal will in her own wishes which had been indispensable to the accomplishment of her earlier exploits.

Yet the King—who was nothing if not a good politician—was not grudging with his favours at the end of that year which had been so rich in events. In December 1429 he ennobled Joan and her family, making it clear that their nobility was to be transmitted to their posterity through either the male or female lines. (Q. v, 150–153) It is worth noting that the only favour which seems to have been asked for by Joan was that exemption from taxes which she had obtained for the people of Greux and Domremy, which had been granted on the morrow of the sacring, at the end of July 1429; it was enjoyed by the two towns until the Revolution.

Meanwhile, time was passing and even the blindest began to get a gleam of light on the true state of affairs. Philippe the Good, now all-powerful in "France" (the term meant, at that time, only the Ile de France, of course) and in all the region directly under his rule, was busy strengthening his territory. He was then at the zenith of his power. Having been widowed, on January 8th, 1430, he married the Princess Isabel of Portugal at Bruges, and his marriage feast was celebrated with unheard-of luxury. It was on this occasion that he founded the famous Order of the Golden Fleece, thus gathering round himself, like Arthur his "peers" in the romances of chivalry, the flower of the Burgundian Knighthood. Significantly Hugues de Lannoy, the negotiator who had rendered him such valuable service in his dealings with France, was one of their number. In February his States held a parliament at Dijon, and from them he obtained a war subsidy; and he persuaded the Duke of Bedford to grant him the counties of Champagne and Brie, their conquest to be carried out by himself. His attention, however, was first turned to the problem of those towns of the Oise which had been delivered up to him by the King of France and which, especially Compiègne, were refusing to recognize his authority. The much-talked-of peace conference which was to have been held in Auxerre was repeatedly postponed, and Burgundian troops established themselves firmly along the course of the Oise.

At last, in a letter dated May 6, 1430, and signed by his Chancellor Regnault de Chartres, Charles VII was forced publicly to recognize his mistake and admit that he had been duped by "the Burgundian adversary".

"After that he has, for some time, amused and deceived us by truces and otherwise, under the shadow of good faith, because he said and affirmed that he wished to arrive at the well-being of peace, the which, for the relief of our poor people who, to the displeasure of our heart, has suffered and every day suffer so much for the matter of the war, we greatly desired and do desire, he has set him-

self with certain forces to make war upon us and upon our countries
and loyal subjects."

Which was a fact; for, at this date, Philippe the Good was laying
siege to Compiègne.

Joan had not waited for the King to admit himself deceived
before resuming the struggle. It cannot have been without emotion
that she heard of the attitude of the people of Compiègne who,
rather than surrender themselves to the Duke of Burgundy in
accordance with the Arras agreement, had "resolved to lose their
lives, their own, their wives' and their children's". And she must
have been seething with impatience, for it was known that here
and there—in Melun, Saint-Denis, even in Paris itself—partisan
movements were coming into existence. Moreover, at the same
time, the English, resolved to play all their trumps under Bedford's
leadership, had landed an army of two thousand men in Calais, at
which port there also arrived, on April 23, the boy-King Henry
VI. On November 6 of the previous year he had been crowned
King of England at Westminster; and it was now hoped to crown
him King of France by way of riposte to the sacring of Charles
VII at Rheims.

"The King being in the town of Sully-sur-Loire, the Maid, who
had seen and heard all the matter and manner which the King and
his council held for the recovery of his kingdom, very ill content
with that, found means to separate herself from them and, unknown
to the King and without taking leave of him, she pretended to go
about some business and, without returning, went away to the
town of Lagny-sur-Marne because they of that place were making
good war on the English of Paris and elsewhere." (P. de Cagny,
Q. iv, 32)

The date of this departure is not exactly known; it was probably
towards the end of March or beginning of April. With her Joan
had her intendant Jean d'Aulon, her brother Pierre and a small
escort estimated at about two hundred men led by a Piedmontese
condottieri, captain of freelance mercenaries, Bartolomew Baretta.

It was at Lagny that the incident of the child baptised on Joan's
intervention took place:

Question: What age had the child which you held at the baptismal
font?

JOAN: The child was three days old and it was carried before the
image of Our Lady of Lagny; the maidens of the town were

before the image and me, I wanted to go and pray to God and Our Lady that life be given to the child. I went there with the other maidens and I prayed, and at last life appeared in this child who yawned three times and was immediately baptised; it died thereafter and was buried in holy ground. Three days had passed, so they said, during which no life had appeared in this child. It was as black as my coat, but when it yawned colour began returning to it. I was with the maidens, praying on my knees before Our Lady. (C.103)

There, too, occurred the incident of Franquet d'Arras which the judges tried to exploit against Joan in the course of her trial.

Question: Is it not mortal sin to receive a man to be ransomed and, once he is a prisoner, to bring about his death?
JOAN: I did not do that.
Question: Was there not the matter of one Franquet d'Arras whom you had killed as an enemy?
JOAN: I consented that he be put to death if he had deserved it, because he had admitted to being murderer, thief and traitor. His trial lasted fifteen days and the judge was the bailiff of Senlis and the justiciars of Lagny. I had asked to have this Franquet to have in exchange a man of Paris, master of the Hotel de l'Ours. And when I heard that this man was dead and when the bailiff told me that I was doing justice a great injury in liberating this Franquet, then I said to the bailiff: "Since that man is dead whom I wanted to have, do with this one what in justice you must do." (C.150–151)

Joan had gone first to Melun where her stay can be precisely dated thanks to a memory of her own; she was there in Easter week and Easter fell that year on April 22nd.

JOAN: In Easter week last, being upon the moat at Melun, it was told me by the voices of Saint Catherine and Saint Margaret that I should be taken before Saint John's Day, and that so it must be and that I be not dismayed, and take all in good part and that God would help me. (C.112)

And, in reply to other questions, she gave more details of her state of mind: "Since I received revelation at Melun that I should be taken, I submitted myself above all in the matter of war to the will of the captains, meanwhile however I did not tell them that I had had revelation that I should be taken." (C.141)

There are traces of Joan's passing through Senlis on April 24, then of her being at Compiègne on May 14. Meanwhile, Philippe the Good, having arrived on May 6 at Noyon, on the following day laid siege to Choisy-au-Bac and took the town on May 16. He then undertook the siege of Compiègne, disposing his forces along the course of the Oise. He set up his own G.H.Q. in the small fortress of Coudun-sur-l'Aronde, John of Luxembourg and Baudot de Noyelle being camped, respectively, at Clairoix and Margny, while Montgomery occupied Venette. On May 22, having learned of these dispositions, Joan and her small troop hastened to make their way, by night, into Compiègne.

Question: When you went for the last time to Compiègne, from what place did you set out?

JOAN: From Crépy-en-Valois.

Question: Did you remain some days in Compiègne before making any sortie or sally?

JOAN: I came in the morning at a secret hour and entered into the town without the enemy knowing much about it, as I believe, and the same day towards eventide I made that sally in which I was taken. . . .

Question: If the voices had ordered you to go out of Compiègne while signifying that you would be taken, would you have gone?

JOAN: If I had known the hour, and that I must be taken, I should not have gone willingly; nevertheless, I should have done their commandment in the end, whatever was to happen to me.

Question: When you went out of Compiègne, did you have voice or revelation to go and to make that sortie?

JOAN: That day I did not know that I should be taken and did not have precept to go out; but still it had been told me that I must be made prisoner.

Question: When you made that sortie, did you cross by the bridge of Compiègne?

JOAN: I crossed by the bridge and the boulevard and went with company of my men against the men of the lord John of Luxembourg and twice drove them back to the Burgundians' camp.

And then the English who were there cut the road behind me and my men. And me, in retreating I was caught in the fields, on the Picardy side, near the boulevard; and was the river between Compiègne and the place where I was taken. (C.112–113)

Perceval de Cagny gives some details of this capture: "The year 1430, the 23rd day of the month of May, the Maid being at the place of Crépy, heard that the Duke of Burgundy with great number of men at arms and others, and the Earl of Arundel, were come to besiege the town of Compiègne. At about midnight she left Crépy in company with about three or four hundred soldiers, and although her people told her that she had but few men to pass through the army of the Burgundians and the English, she said: 'By my martin, we are enough; I shall go and see my good friends of Compiègne.' She arrived at that place at about sunrise and without loss or damage to herself or her men entered into the town. . . . And about nine o'clock in the morning the Maid heard say that there was great and strong skirmishing on the meadows before the town. She put on her armour and ordered her men to arms and horse, and went out to join in the mêlée. As soon as she came the enemy fell back and was put to flight. The Maid charged hard against the Burgundian side. They of the ambush warned their people who fell back in great disorder.* Then they uncovered their ambush and spurring hard they went and placed themselves between the bridge into the town (and) the Maid and her company, and some of them turned straight upon the Maid in such great number that not well could they of her company hold them back and they said to the Maid: 'Take pains to (do your best to) get back to the town, or you and we are lost.' When the Maid heard them speak thus, very angry she said to them: 'Be silent. Their discomfiture depends on you. Think only of striking hard at them.' Whatever she might say, her men would not believe her and by force made her return directly to the bridge. And when the Burgundians and the English saw that she was coming back to get into the town, with a great effort they gained the end of the bridge. . . . The captain of the place, seeing the great multitude of Burgundians and English about to enter upon the bridge, for the fear he had lest he lose the town, had the bridge into the town raised and the gates closed, and thus

---

* It appears that the Burgundians had formed an ambush towards Clairoix. The falling back in great disorder was presumably to draw Joan and her company after them.

remained the Maid shut out and few of her men with her." (Q. iv, 32–34)

This shutting of the gates was long considered as having been an act of treachery; the governor of Compiègne, Guillaume de Flavy, was held responsible by historians who branded him as a traitor. But it now seems that he was no such thing: de Flavy had given and was still to give sufficient proof of his loyalty to the King of France to acquit him of any such imputation. The town gates were closed on his orders because the enemy was getting too close; Joan, as usual, was at the point where the danger was greatest; she had always been in the vanguard when it was a question of making an attack; and in the rearguard when a retreat had to be covered; her company had been thrown back upon Compiègne; and she happened to be one of the handful of combatants whom it was absolutely necessary to sacrifice if the town was to be saved.

The Burgundian Georges Chastellain has left us a very lively account of Joan's capture: "The French, with their Maid, were beginning to retreat very slowly, as finding no advantage over their enemies but rather perils and damage. Wherefore the Burgundians, seeing that and being flowing with blood, and not satisfied with having repulsed them in defence, since they could do them no more great harm than by pursuing them closely, struck among them valiantly both afoot and mounted, and did great damage among the French. Of which the Maid, passing the nature of women, took all the brunt, and took great pains to save her company, remaining behind as captain and bravest of her troop. And there Fortune allowed that her glory at last come to an end and that she bear arms no longer; an archer, a rough man and a sour, full of spite because a woman of whom so much had been heard should have overthrown (broken the bones of) so many valiant men, dragged her to one side by her cloth-of-gold cloak and pulled her from her horse, throwing her flat on the ground; never could she find recourse or succour in her men, try though they might to remount her, but a man of arms called the Bastard of Wandomme, who arrived at the moment of her fall, pressed her so hard that she gave him her faith (word, parole), for he declared himself to be a nobleman. He, more joyful than if he had had a King in his hands, took her hastily to Margny, and there held her in his keeping until that day's work was done. And there were taken with her also Poton the Burgundian, a gentleman-at-arms on the French side, the Maid's brother (Pierre), the master of her household (Jean d'Aulon) and others in small number, who were taken to Margny and placed under good guard." (Q. iv, 446–447)

Chastellain wrote his account only from hearsay, but another Burgundian chronicler, Enguerrand de Monstrelet, took part in the battle himself and gives us a clear impression of the effect of this unexpected news in both camps.

"The French entered into Compiègne, doleful and wroth at their losses, and above all had great displeasure at the taking of the Maid. And on the contrary, they of the Burgundian side and the English were very joyous at it, more than had they taken five hundred combatants, for they feared and redoubted no other captain or chief in war as much as they had always done, until that day, this Maid.

"Quite soon after came the Duke of Burgundy with his power (forces) to his camp of Coudun where he was camped in a meadow before Compiègne, and there gathered the English, the Duke and those of the other camps, in very great number, making together great outcry and jollity for the taking of the Maid. The Duke went to see her in the lodge (tent) where she was and spoke some words to her which I do not well remember, although I was present. After that the Duke retired, and all other people, each to his tent (*logis*) for the night. And the Maid remained in the keeping and governance of messire John of Luxembourg. He, some days thereafter, sent her under his safe-conduct to the castle of Beaulieu." (Q. iv, 402)

It is curious that Monstrelet, whose memory was so good, did not remember very well the details of so striking an encounter as that between the grand-duke of the West and Joan the Maid; but it is not the only time he can be faulted when dealing with Joan. Chronicler of the House of Luxembourg, he tends to slide over anything which might not be to the honour of that illustrious family, whence some surprising gaps: thus, he was not to mention the sale of Joan to the English, and he has not one word to say about her trial: he contented himself with inserting into his chronicle the letter which the King of England sent to diverse princes and prelates announcing the sentence of the court, and with mentioning the execution of that sentence.

Great, at all events, was the joy in the Burgundian ranks. Another chronicler, who was likewise an eye-witness, Jean Lefèvre de Saint-Remy, councillor to the Duke of Burgundy and king-at-arms of the Golden Fleece, echoes the feeling: "The Maid was taken with great joy to the Duke who was coming with all diligence to the aid and succour of his men. He was very joyous at her taking, for the great renown that she had, for it seemed to many of his side that her works could not but be miraculous." (Q, iv, 349)

Philippe the Good hastened to make his capture of Joan widely known; of the letters which were written to that end, we still have the one sent to the burgesses of Saint-Quentin. It is dated on the same day as the capture, May 23, 1430, and "at Coudun near Compiègne". The Duke writes thus:

"Very dear and well-beloved, knowing that you desire to have news of us, we signify to you that this day, twenty-third of May, at about six hours after noon the adversaries of my lord the King (of England) and ourselves, who had come together in very great force and had thrown themselves into the town of Compiègne before which we and the men of our army are camped, came out of the town against the camp of our vanguard nearest to them. In this sortie was she whom they call the Maid with several of their principal captains, in the encounter with whom our cousin, messire John of Luxembourg who was present and others of our people and some men of my lord the King whom he had sent to pass on and go to Paris, made very great and bitter resistance, and presently we arrived there in person and found that the adversaries had been repulsed already. And by the pleasure of our blessed Creator the thing thus came about and such mercy was vouchsafed us that she who is called the Maid was taken, and with her many captains, knights and esquires and others taken, drowned or dead, of whom at this time we know not yet the names." (Q. v, 166–167)

Official and private documents record the fact: Clément de Fauquembergue's register, for example, on May 25 when the news reached Paris; and the *Journal d'un Bourgeois de Paris* which notes: "The 23 May, *dame* Joan, the Maid of the Armagnacs, was taken before Compiègne by messire John of Luxembourg, his men, and a thousand English on their way to Paris. Four hundred at least of the Maid's men were killed or drowned." (P.99)

After some time spent in the fortress of Beaulieu-en-Vermandois Joan, who had tried to escape, was transferred to the castle of Beaurevoir, situated in the midst of woods between Cambrai and Saint-Quentin. In the course of her trial she was to be questioned about her two attempts to escape.

Question: How did you think to escape from the castle of Beaulieu between two pieces of wood?

JOAN: I have never been a prisoner in any place but I would try to escape from it. Being in that castle, I had shut up my keepers in the tower, excepting the porter who saw me and encountered me. It seems to me that it did not please God that I should escape that time and that I must see the King of the English, as my voices had told me. (C.155)

Question: Were you long in the tower of Beaurevoir?

JOAN: I was there for four months or thereabouts. When I heard that the English were coming to take me, I was very wroth at it, and however my voices forbade me often to leap from that tower. And at last, for fear of the English, I leapt and commended myself to God and the Virgin Mary and I was injured in that leap. And after I had leapt, the voice of Saint Catherine told me that I should be of good countenance and that they of Compiègne would receive succour. (C.107)

Question: What was the cause for which you leapt from the tower of Beaurevoir?

JOAN: I had heard say that all they of Compiègne down to the age of seven years were to be put to fire and to blood, and I preferred to die rather than live after such destruction of good people, and that was one of the causes of my leaping. And the other was that I knew that I was sold to the English and I would rather have died than to be in the hands of the English, my adversaries.

Question: Did you make that leap on the advice of your voices?

JOAN: Catherine told me almost every day that I must not leap and that God would help me and also them of Compiègne. And I said to Saint Catherine that since God would help them of Compiègne, I myself would (like to) be there. Then Saint Catherine said to me: "Without fail, you must accept your lot (be resigned, take what is happening in good part), and you will not be delivered until you have seen the king of the English." And I answered her: "Truly, I would rather not see him, and I would rather die than be put into the hands of the English."

Question: Did you say, to Saint Catherine and Saint Margaret, these words: "Will God let the good people of Compiègne die in so wicked a way (*si mauvaisement*)"?

JOAN: I did not say the word "*si mauvaisement*", but I said: "How can God let the good people of Compiègne die, who have been so faithful to their Lord?" After I had fallen from the tower I was, during two or three days, without will to eat. And I was so hurt in that leap that I could neither eat nor drink. And meanwhile I had comfort from Saint Catherine who told me that I should confess and ask forgiveness of God for having leapt, and that without fail the people of Compiègne would have succour before the feast of Saint Martin of the winter. Then I began to return to health and I began to eat and soon I was cured.

Question: When you leapt did you think to kill yourself?

JOAN: No, in leaping I commended myself to God, and I thought in making that leap to escape so that I should not be delivered over to the English. (C.143–145)

Of the time when she was a prisoner we have but little evidence. However, in the course of the Trial of Rehabilitation a Burgundian knight gave evidence. This was Haimond de Macy who was in John of Luxembourg's service:

"I saw Joan for the first time when she was shut up in the castle of Beaurevoir for the lord count of Ligny (John of Luxembourg). I saw her several (many) times in prison and on several occasions conversed with her. I tried several times, playfully, to touch her breasts, trying to put my hand on her chest, the which Joan would not suffer but repulsed me with all her strength. Joan was, indeed, of decent conduct (*honnête tenue*) both in speech and act.

"Joan was taken to the castle cf Crotoy where was held prisoner a man altogether notable, called master Nicholas de Queuville, chancellor of the church of Amiens, doctor of both civil and canon law, who often celebrated mass in the prison, and Joan, the most often, heard his mass. I later heard this master Nicholas say that he had heard Joan's confession and that she was a good Christian and very pious. He spoke much good of Joan." (R.186)

At Beaurevoir lived John of Luxembourg's wife, Jeanne de Béthune, and his aunt, the aged Demoiselle de Luxembourg, who was to die before Joan herself, on November 13, 1430. These two women seem to have shown Joan some kindness and she remembered them with affection.

Question: Were you required at Beaurevoir (to wear women's clothes)?

JOAN: Yes, truly, and I answered that I would not change clothes without the permission of Our Lord. The demoiselle of Luxembourg and the lady of Beaurevoir offered me a woman's dress or the stuff to make one, asking me to wear that habit, and I answered that I had not permission from God and that it was not yet time. . . . Had it been that I was to wear women's clothes, I should have done so more willingly at the request of those women than of any other woman in all France excepting my queen. . . . The lady of Luxembourg had requested my lord of Luxembourg that I be not delivered up to the English.

Joan was to remain in the fortress of Beaurevoir until the end of November 1430. In the meantime the English had not been inactive; they wanted the prisoner handed over to them. To handle the negotiations they applied to a man whose antecedents rendered him particularly apt for the work, the Bishop of Beauvais, Pierre Cauchon. In 1430 he was about sixty years of age, and he had had a brilliant career both as a diplomat and as a university man. He had been Rector of the University of Paris as early as 1403, and he had played a leading role throughout the troubles as a result of which the university had taken the Burgundian side against the Armagnacs. In 1419, at the time when the theory of the double monarchy was being worked out at the university, which placed the two kingdoms of France and England under the single crown of England, Cauchon was conservator of the university privileges. He was one of the negotiators appointed for the famous Treaty of Troyes, and immediately thereafter, on August 21, 1420, he was made Bishop of Beauvais. In 1424 he received the capitulation of the town of Vitry on behalf of the King of England; the town had succumbed despite the defence put up by La Hire, one of the captains who was to find himself fighting at Joan's side five years later. It is not difficult to imagine what Cauchon must have felt about the year 1429, in which he had been forced to flee first from Rheims, where he was living just before the coronation and where he had conducted the Fête-Dieu ceremonies, then from Beauvais when that town opened its gates to Charles VII. The negotiations entrusted to him would enable him both to avenge himself for that double humiliation and to vindicate the political theories dear to the heart of the Paris University men, and which he maintained throughout the whole course of his life. Checked in its progress by Joan's dazzling campaign and by the sacring of Charles VII at Rheims, the double-monarchy theory would recover all its prestige if it could be shown that the instrument of the French cause was nothing but a wretched heretic and a witch. There was another and still secret stimulus to his activity as a negotiator: the archbishopric of Rouen had recently fallen vacant and he, driven out of his own diocese, had good hopes of obtaining the preferment as a reward for his good offices.

The news of Joan's capture was, as we have seen, known in Paris on May 25 and recorded under that date in the Register of the Parliament. On the following day, May 26, the University of Paris sent a letter to the Duke of Burgundy, in the name of the Inquisitor of France, asking that Joan be handed over to him.

"Whereas all faithful Christian princes and all other true Catholics are required to extirpate all errors arising against the faith and the scandals which they entail among the simple Christian people, and that it be now of common renown that by a certain woman named Joan whom the adversaries of this kingdom call the Maid, have been in several cities, good towns and other places of this kingdom, broadcast* and published . . . diverse errors . . . we implore you of good affection, you, most puissant prince . . . that the soonest and most safely and conveniently it can be done, be sent and brought prisoner to us the said Joan, vehemently suspected of many crimes smacking of heresy, to appear before us and a procurator of the Holy Inquisitor, to answer and proceed as in reason bound with the good council, favour and aid of the good doctors and masters of the University of Paris and other notable councillors." (C.8-9)

On July the 14th following the university wrote, this time in its own name, to John of Luxembourg and to the Duke of Burgundy himself. And Pierre Cauchon appeared in person before John of Luxembourg, in the camp outside Compiègne, with letters of summons from the University requiring Joan to be delivered to him.

"It is by this (these presents) that it is required by the Bishop of Beauvais of my lord the Duke of Burgundy and of my lord John of Luxembourg and of the Bastard of Wandomme, in the name and on behalf of the King our sire and on his own behalf as Bishop of Beauvais: that the woman who is commonly called Joan the Maid, prisoner, be sent to the King to be delivered over to the Church to hold her trial because she is suspected and defamed to

---

* As of seeds in sowing: not an anachronism!—E.H.

have committed many crimes, sortileges, idolatry, invocations of enemies (devils) and other several cases touching our faith and against that faith." (C.90)

He offered, on behalf of the King of England, a sum of six thousand francs to those who had captured Joan, and to the Bastard of Wandomme a pension of between three and four hundred *livres*; for her actual ransom the sum of ten thousand francs was offered.

As we can see, neither time nor money were spared. And to this activity on the part of the English government the King of France opposed only a complete inertia. It is true that in Antonio Morosini's *Journal* we find references to a rumour passed on to him by a kinsman living in Bruges that Charles VII had instructed the Burgundians "that they should not for anything in the world lend themselves to such a transaction or, if they did, he would inflict similar treatment on those of their party whom he had in his hands". (Herval, p. 14) And in the university's letter to John of Luxembourg we read that it could happen "that this woman be delivered or lost, for it is said that some of the adversaries (i.e., of the King of England) are doing all in their power to accomplish and apply to that end all their understanding by extraordinary means and what is worse by money or ransom". (C.7) These are the only allusions, remote and indirect, to any effort the King of France might be making to save the girl to whom he owed his crown.

But need we be surprised? Contemporary accounts of Charles VII agree in showing him to have been of weak character and in telling us that he was "of a changeable condition". "There were frequent and diverse changes about his person, for it was his custom … when a man had raised himself high beside him, to the summit of the wheel, then he began to be troubled by it, and, on the first occasion which might give it countenance, readily reversed the wheel from high to low." Georges Chastellain, to whom we owe this portrait, adds that he "savoured of the fruit all he could suck from it". Moreover, it can be seen that the King was very careful to foster his own fame whenever he had a chance to do so: after the recovery of his kingdom he had innumerable medals struck on which he is entitled "Charles the Victorious". It may be, after all, that once, contrary to all expectation, he had received that crown and sacring which made him King of France, he was not sorry to see her to whom he owed them put out of the way.

Furthermore, there were not wanting envious persons in his

FROM RHEIMS TO COMPIÈGNE 159

entourage who might even go so far as to rejoice over Joan's capture. Most notable among these was the Archbishop of Rheims, Regnault de Chartres, who was hand-in-glove with La Trémoille and who was, as we have noted, at the head of the delegation which had presented itself to the Duke of Burgundy exactly one month after the sacring, at Arras, and, unknown to Joan, to sign the truces, which were a betrayal of the Maid. Events had shown his policy to have been wrong, and one may well wonder whether he did not bear Joan a grudge because he had been forced, willy nilly, to recognize that he had been duped in those negotiations and to come round to her view when it again became apparent that armed force alone would be effective. We have a reference to a letter which he had written to his diocesans in which he insinuates that "God had suffered that Joan the Maid be taken because she had puffed herself up with pride and because of the rich garments which she had adopted, and because she had not done what God had commanded her, but had done her own will". (Q. v, 169)

The negotiations touching Joan were to keep Cauchon busy for more than four months as we know from the receipt which he signed for Pierre Surreau, Receiver General of Normandy, declaring that he had received the sum of seven hundred and sixty-five pounds *tournois* "for seven score and thirteen days which we affirm to have spent in the service of the King our lord for his business, both in the town of Calais and in several journeys going to my lord the duke of Burgundy or to messire John of Luxembourg in Flanders, to the siege before Compiègne, to Beaurevoir, for the matter of Joan called the Maid, as for several other tasks and business of the King, our sire". Cauchon was, in fact, one of those men who know how to get their services well paid for: the diverse prebends and benefices which he accumulated represent about two thousand *livres* per annum.

One of the very few clerics of Rouen who had persisted in resistance to all political pressure, Nicholas de Houppville deposed, at the Trial of Rehabilitation, how he had seen Cauchon return from his various embassies and with what joy he had given an account of his transactions:

"I know very well," he said on that occasion, "that Joan was brought to this city of Rouen by the English and that she was put in prison in the castle of Rouen; the trial was held at the expense of the English, as I believe. As to fears and pressures, I believe no such thing as far as the judges are concerned; I think that on the contrary they did it voluntarily, and above all the Bishop of Beauvais whom I saw return after he had been to fetch her, and give an account of his embassy to the King and the lord of Warwick, saying with joy and exultation words which I did not understand. Then he spoke later in secret with the lord of Warwick; what he said to him I know nothing about." (R.261-262)

Joan's last long journey was to take her from the castle of Beaurevoir to Rouen, where she was to stand trial for heresy. The University of Paris would have liked this trial to be held in Paris, but Paris was much too exposed, too close to territory recently given back to the King of France. Whereas in Rouen the English felt quite sure of themselves, for Normandy had been a fief of the English crown for two centuries. The town had been in their possession for ten years, and it was there that the King of England resided with his tutor, Richard Beauchamp, Earl of Warwick.

The moment of Joan's delivery to the English coincided with the death of "the lady of Luxembourg" whom her nephew, John, Count of Luxembourg-Ligny, had probably hesitated to offend. It was at Arras that she was put into the charge of an English escort; she was then taken to the strong castle of Crotoy. A contemporary chronicle, Jean de la Chapelle's, says that she spent one night at the castle of Drugy near Saint-Riquier abbey. He was himself almoner of the abbey at the time, and he went with the provost of the same abbey, master Nicholas Bourdon, to visit Joan. (Q. v, 360). Studies of the tidal movements in the Somme bay have made it possible to determine when it was possible to cross the bay: Joan must have crossed it at about nine in the morning on December 20, 1430, to land at Saint Valery. The two gates of the town, the *porte du Bas* now called the *porte de Nevers*, and the *porte du Haut* now called the *porte Guillaume*, are still there. From there she must have been taken to the castle of Eu, going thence by way of Dieppe and Bosc-le-Haut to arrive at night-fall of December 23 in Rouen. There she was imprisoned in the castle of Bouvreuil under the guard of English gaolers.

On November 21st, when Joan was handed over to the English, the University of Paris had sent another letter to the King of England, signifying the joy felt by the worthy masters of that University on hearing that she was at last in the King's hands:

"To the most excellent prince, King of France and England. . . . We have newly heard that into your power is now delivered the woman called the Maid, at which are we mighty joyous, confident that by your good order this woman will be brought to justice for the repairing of the great malifices and scandals notoriously come about in this kingdom on her account, to the great prejudice of the divine honour, of our holy faith and of all your good people."

They ask that the mission of judging her be given to the Bishop of Beauvais and the Inquisitor of France, and it is at this point that they express the wish that she be judged in Paris. The King of England, as we have seen, was to decide otherwise, but was in agreement that the Bishop of Beauvais should be her judge. In principle a heretic was supposed to be judged by the bishop of his or her place of birth, or in the diocese where the heresy had been committed. The pretext, in this case, whereby it was possible to make Cauchon her judge, was that she had been taken at Compiègne which came into the diocese of Beauvais. But there was a difficulty: Cauchon, as Bishop of Beauvais, had no right to act as a judge in Rouen. But on the twenty-eighth of the previous December Bedford had made the chapter of Rouen grant him a "commission of territory" which enabled him to get round this rule.

A letter of January 3rd, written in the name of the king of England, stated: "It is our intention to recover and take back to ourselves that Joan if so be that she be not convicted or attainted of the case (of heresy) or other touching or regarding our faith." (C.15) This makes it quite clear that whatever the outcome of the trial the English intended to keep the prisoner. The duplicity of the trial is thus exposed: in theory Joan was judged by the Church in a matter of heresy; in point of fact she was simply a prisoner-of-war whose fate depended on the English government.

For that matter the political character of the Rouen trial was not doubted even at the time. When, during the later Trial of Rehabilitation, lips were unsealed—Rouen having at last been liberated after thirty years of occupation by the English—the evidence on that subject was unanimous. We will, to begin with, quote the evidence given by the notaries, or as we should say, clerks, appointed to make a written record of the Trial of Condemnation.

Guillaume Manchon: "Whether the judges proceeded from hate or otherwise, I leave to their conscience. I know however and firmly believe that had she been on the English side they would not have treated her so and would not have brought such proceedings against her. She was, indeed, brought to the town of Rouen and not to Paris because, as I believe, the King of England was in the town of Rouen as were the principal men of his council, and she was placed in the prisons of the castle of Rouen. I was forced, in that business, to act as notary, and I did it in spite of myself, for I would not have dared to go against the order of the lords of the King's council. And the English pursued this trial and it was at their expense that it was prepared. I believe, however, that the Bishop of Beauvais was not obliged to conduct this trial against Joan, nor was the promoter Jean d'Estivet. But it was voluntarily that they did it. As for the assessors and other councillors, I believe that they would not have dared contradict (refuse), and there was nobody who went not in fear." (R.193–197)

Boisguillaume, second notary: "I know well that the lord Bishop of Beauvais undertook the proceedings against her because he said that she had been made prisoner within the limits of the diocese of Beauvais; whether it was in hate or otherwise I leave to his conscience. I know, however, that all was done at the expense of the King of England and on the initiative of the English, and I know well that the bishop himself and the others who meddled with this trial obtained from the King of England letters of guarantee, for I saw them." (R.197)

One of the assessors, who was to play a great part in what remained of Joan's life, Brother Isambart de la Pierre, a Dominican of the convent of Saint Jacques at Rouen, sums up the situation as follows: "Some of them who took part in the proceedings were pushed to it, like the Bishop of Beauvais, by their partiality. Some others, like some of the English doctors, by appetite for vengeance. Others, the doctors of Paris, by the lure of gain. Others, again, were driven by fear, like the sub-inquisitor and some others whom I do not recall; and all this was done on the initiative of the King of England, of the cardinal of Winchester, of the Earl of Warwick and of other English who paid the expenses incurred on account of this trial." (R.199)

COMMENTARY

The exposition of military events takes, in the nature of things, more room in this chapter that in any other. For the sake of the reader who wishes to follow up points which we could not here treat in detail, here is a short bibliography.

On the military events in general:
Ed. Perroy, *La Guerre de Cent Ans.* Paris 1945.
Calmette et Deprez, La France et l'Angleterre en conflit. In *Histoire Générale* published under the direction of G. Glotz, Vol. VIII. Paris 1937.
On the military events of the year 1430 in particular:
A. Bossuat, *Perrinet Gressart et François de Surrienne, Agents de l'Angleterre.* Paris 1936.
On the Compiègne episode:
P. Champion, *Guillaume de Flavy.* Paris 1906.
J. M. Mestre, *Guillaume de Flavy, n'a pas trahi Jeanne d'Arc.*
On Joan's letters:
C. de Maleissye, *Les Lettres de Jehanne d'Arc.* Paris 1911.

In addition, of course, reference can be made to the diverse histories of Joan of Arc, the most reliable from the historical point of view still being Hanotaux's (1911); P. H. Dunand's, the most thorough, in three volumes (1899). There is also the excellent little *résumé* written by J. Calmette for the *Que sais-je?* series, *Jeanne d'Arc*, No. 211 of that collection.

A word must be said here touching the claim that the arms granted to Joan and her family contain "proof" of her "bastardy". (Though why, in that case, they were granted to the whole family is not clear. Is it claimed that her brothers were also Isabeau of Bavaria's bastards?) It is claimed that if Joan was permitted to display fleurs-de-lys on her arms, that was to affirm that she was of the blood royal. This misconception derives from the same ignorance as that which we pointed out in the matter of the "Orleans livery". The King, on this as on many other occasions, granted the right to bear the royal emblem to those he was particularly anxious to honour because their exploits had been outstandingly glorious. Examples are not far to seek: the arms granted, at the same period and for the same reasons to Gilles de Rais in September 1429, were *"fleurs-de-lys semées en orle"* (see the original deed preserved in the *Archives nationales* and to be seen in the *Musée de l'Histoire de France*, A.E. 11, 1715).

It is further claimed that the sword which appears on these arms constitutes a "brisure" (bar, bend sinister), the sign indicating bastardy. This is false: in heraldry the sword has *never* been a "brisure"; it is a "meuble" exactly like the crown, fleurs-de-lys, etc. But every bastard did invariably bear the customary "brisure" on his arms, that is to say the bar of bastardy which can be seen, for example, on the arms of Dunois, Bastard of Orleans. Reference can be made to the principal works on heraldry, among others Remy Mathieu's *Le système heraldique français*, Meurgey de Tupigny's work, and others.

7

THE TRIAL OF CONDEMNATION

The proceedings which ended in Joan's conviction were to last five months, from January 9 to May 30, 1431, and were in three phases. First came what was called the *procès d'office* which we should now call the instruction of the case*. This comprised investigations and interrogations lasting from January 9th to March 26th. Then came the ordinary trial, ending in the scene of Joan's "abjuration" (May 24th). Finally came the very short Relapse trial, on May 28th and 29th.

In trials touching the faith, the bishop and the Inquisitor sat together as judges. We have seen how Pierre Cauchon had been appointed by means of certain procedural artifices to judge the case: his whole past, a consistent story of attachment to the English cause, as well as his quality as a jurist, a doctor of both civil and canon law, guaranteed in advance the cleverness which, in the event, he deployed. With him sat Jean Lemaitre, vicar of the Inquisition at Rouen, designated for the task by Jean Graverent, Inquisitor of France. Lemaitre was to give a pitiful performance: he was present as rarely as possible; a month after the trial had opened he had not put in an appearance. On February 20th, expressly summoned by Cauchon, he did appear; but to declare "that he would not meddle in the matter as much for the scruple of his conscience as for the surety of the instruction of the trial, were it not for the fact that he had been given the authority and in so far as he had it." (C.29). He did not appear thereafter until March 13th, and although the minutes several times mention his presence, he did not once intervene.

These two were Joan's only judges. But in conformity with inquisitorial custom, to which we owe the idea of a jury in trials, a certain number of assessors had to take part, although their function was purely consultative. Cauchon, if only to add to the prestige of his court, did not fail to summon a large number of

* Investigation by an examining magistrate preceding the trial in open court. There is no equivalent in English or United States legal proceedings.

assessors, about sixty in fact, forty of whom sat fairly regularly: they were Norman and English prelates, canons of Rouen, masters of canon and civil law, advocates of the "*Officialité*", an ecclesiastical court of which there was one to each bishopric, etc. Among the most assiduous of these officers of the court were the Masters delegated to Rouen by the University of Paris, Jean Beaupère, Nicholas Midy, Jacques de Touraine, Gérard Feuillet, Pierre Maurice and Thomas de Courcelles. We may be quite sure that they brought to the trial the spirit which animated the university at the time. Also present at the trial was the cardinal of Winchester, Henry Beaufort, great-uncle of the King, usually referred to as the cardinal of England in contemporary texts; and the bishop of Thérouane, Louis of Luxembourg, brother of the man who had sold Joan. At the start of the trial on January 9th Cauchon named one of his own men, Jean d'Estivet, as promoter, ironically nick-named Master Benedicite because of his filthy language. As com-missioner he chose a clerk of the diocese of Bayeux, master Jean de la Fontaine. Finally, Cauchon chose his three notaries, clerks of the court, from the Rouen "*Officialité*", master Guillaume Manchon, master Guillaume Colles called Boisguillaume, and master Nicolas Taquel, while another priest of Rouen, Jean Massieu, filled the office of usher.

It is highly instructive, in measuring the worth of these men whom Joan had to face throughout her trial, to refer back to certain earlier documents, notably to the account rolls of the King of England. We note, for example, that Louis of Luxembourg, as Chancellor of France, draws a salary of 2,000 pounds *tournois*; the abbot of Fécamp, Gilles de Duremort, draws a thousand a year as does the abbot of Mont Saint-Michel, Robert Jolibet (he had long since fled from his valiant abbey whose resistance to English attacks during this last phase of the Hundred Years War is well known). Several other assessors, notably André Marguerie, Raoul Roussel and Denis Gastinel, picked out by Cauchon at the beginning of the trial, are also to be found in receipt of regular salaries noted in the account rolls, of diverse sums. (See Joseph Stevenson's *Letters and papers illustrative of the wars of the English*, London, 1864, Vol 11, pp. 561 *et seq*.) Nor were honours to be denied them: Gilles de Duremort was to be appointed Bishop of Coutances; another assessor, Robert Guillebert, became Bishop of London in 1436; Louis of Luxembourg became Archbishop of Rouen and Raoul Roussel succeeded him in 1444. Jean Fabri, or Lefevre, who survived at the time of the trial of Rehabilitation, became titular Bishop of Demetriade. And so forth, only Cauchon failing to obtain what he had hoped for. Hanotaux has this to say about Cauchon's failure, that there happened to him what does happen to over-complaisant servants, who in the long run earn nothing but contempt. Cauchon had expected the archbishopric of Rouen; he had to be satisfied with the bishopric of Lisieux.

In the course of the *proces d'office* diverse inquiries and examinations had to precede the interrogation. Thus, for example, and as the procedure laid down required, an inquiry was made in the neighbourhood of Joan's birth. But nothing about this is to be found in the records of the trial, nor, as we shall see, is that the only gap in those records. In fact this inquiry was not known about until very much later; it was not until the Trial of Rehabilitation that some of the commissioners who had carried out this inquiry were to come forward, among others Nicolas Bailly, *tabellion royal* in the provostry of Andelot:

"Joan came from Domremy and from the parish of that place and her father was Jacques d'Arc, a good and honest farmer (*laboureur*) as I saw and knew him; I know it also by hearsay and upon the report of many, for I was *tabellion* appointed by messire Jean de Torcenay, then bailiff of Chaumont, who held his authority from him who was then called King of France and England, at the same time as Gerard Petit, defunct, at that time provost of Andelot, to hold an enquiry in the matter of Joan the Maid who was, as it was said, detained in prison in the city of Rouen. It was I, *tabellion*, who made (compiled) in her time the information to which I was commissioned by messire Jean de Torcenay ... when myself and Gerard made (compiled) ... this information on Joan; by our diligence we so wrought that we procured twelve or fifteen witnesses to certify this information. We did this before Simon de Thermes, esquire, acting as lieutenant to the captain of Chaumont, on the subject of Joan the Maid; we were suspect because we had not done this information badly (evilly); these witnesses, before the lieutenant, attested the evidence which they had given and as it was written in their interrogatory; then the lieutenant wrote again to messire Jean, bailiff of Chaumont, that that which was written in this interrogatory made by us, *tabellion* and provost, was true. And when this bailiff saw the lieutenant's report, he said we the commissioners were false Armagnacs." (R. 89–90)

It seems quite clear from this that Nicolas Bailly and Gerard

Petit, having carried out their inquiry, were suspected of having done so in a cunningly sides-taking spirit, thus presenting a too favourable image of Joan. They were obliged to hail the witnesses before the bailiff of Chaumont's lieutenant in order to establish their good faith. Other depositions bore witness to this inquiry, and also to its outcome, wholly negative from the judges' point of view.

Jean Moreau, merchant: "I know that at the time when Joan was in Rouen and they were preparing a trial against her, someone important from the country of Lorraine came to Rouen. As I was of the same country I made his acquaintance. He told me that he had come from Lorraine to Rouen because he had been especially commissioned to gather information in Joan's country of origin to learn what reputation she had there. Which he had done. And he had reported his information to the lord Bishop of Beauvais, thinking to have compensation for his work and his expenses; but the bishop told him that he was a traitor and a bad man and that he had not done what he should have done and was ordered to do. This man complained of it to me for, from what he said, he could not get his salary paid him because his informations were not useful to the bishop. He added that in the course of (collecting) his informations he had found nothing concerning Joan which he would not have liked to find about his own sister, although he had been for information to five or six parishes near Domremy and in that town itself." (R.88–89)

The fact is further confirmed by yet other witnesses.

Michel Lebuin: "When Joan was taken, I saw one called Nicolas, bailiff of Andelot, who was come with many others to Domremy, and at the demand of messire Jean de Torcenay, then bailiff of Chaumont, in the name of the so-called King of France and England, made inquest into the repute and habits of Joan, as it was said. And, as it seems, he dared not force anyone to swear, for fear of the people of Vaucouleurs. I think that Jean Begot of that town was examined, for they were lodged in his house. I believe also that when they made this inquiry they found nothing evil touching Joan." (R. 87)

Joan was also forced to undergo an examination into her virginity which was carried out probably during the first days of January. The Duke and Duchess of Bedford were staying in Rouen from January 1st to the 13th and it was the Duchess of Bedford who took charge of this examination, which she had done by certain matrons of her choice. The evidence establishing this was given during the Trial of Rehabilitation.

Jean Fabri or Lefevre, one of the assessors at the Trial of Condemnation: "I know well that once, when Joan was asked why she was called the Maid and whether she was one, she answered: 'I can well say that I am so, and if you do not believe me have me examined by some women.' And she declared herself ready to suffer this examination provided it be done by decent women, as is the custom."

Boisguillaume, the notary: "I heard it said by one, whom I no longer remember, that Joan was examined by some matrons and that she was found to be a virgin and that this examination had been made by order of the Duchess of Bedford and that the Duke of Bedford stood in a secret place from which he could see Joan examined."

Jean Massieu: "I know well that she was examined to discover if she was a virgin or not by some matrons and midwives, and that on the orders of the Duchess of Bedford and notably by Anna Bavon and another matron whose name I do not remember. After this examination they declared that she was a virgin and intact and that I heard said by Anna herself for which cause the Duchess of Bedford had the warders and others forbidden to offer her any violence." (R.224–225)

No trace of this examination into Joan's virginity is to be found in the trial records either.

Throughout the whole course of the trial Joan was held in a civil prison, looked after by English gaolers and kept in irons. This was in flagrant disregard of the rule of Inquisitorial tribunals by which she had a right to be held in the archbishopric prison and guarded by women. Another irregularity: Joan had no advocate, and as we shall see anyone who tried to encourage or advise her, did so at his risk and peril.

The interrogatories began on February 21st. They began in open court in the Chapel of Rouen Castle; but after March 10th the proceedings continued in the prison itself, in camera, and with a much reduced court. Jean Massieu gives an account of how things were done: "On several occasions I took Joan from the prison to the place of jurisdiction and passing in front of the castle chapel; at Joan's request I allowed her, in passing, to make her orison. For this I was reproved by the said *Benedicite*, promoter of the cause, who said to me: 'Truant, who maketh thee so bold to allow that excommunicated whore to approach the church without permission? I will have thee put in a tower so that thou shalt see neither sun nor moon for a month if thou dost so again.' And when the said promoter perceived that I obeyed him not, he several times placed himself before the chapel door and Joan asked deliberately: 'Here is the body of Jesus-Christ?' ''

The interrogatories were conducted according to procedures which are still used by examining magistrates (*juges d'instruction*). Questions succeed each other without apparent order, some designed to distract the accused's attention, others, reverting suddenly to subjects already explored, intended to lead the accused to contradict himself. Joan, without any assistance, kept her end up superbly in the face of these attacks.

Jean Massieu: "When my lord of Beauvais, who was judge in the cause, accompanied by six clerks, to wit by Beaupère, Midy, Maurice, Touraine, Courcelles and Feuillet, or some other in his place, first interrogated her, before she had given her answer to one, another of the assistants interjected another question, whereby she was often precipitate and confused in her answers. . . . The assessors with the judges put questions to her, and sometimes at the moment when one was questioning her and she was answering his question, another interrupted her answer so much so that she several times said to those who were interrogating her: 'Fine lords, ask one at a time.' . . . And I was astonished to see how she could answer the subtle and captious questions which were put to her, which a lettered man would have had difficulty in answering. The examination lasted usually from eight o'clock to eleven." (R.208)

Guillaume Manchon, the notary, describes these interrogatories in the same way: "During the trial Joan was harassed by numerous and diverse interrogations and almost every day there took place interrogatories which lasted about three or four hours and sometimes, according to what Joan said, difficult and subtle questions were extracted on the subject of which they questioned her again after the midday meal for two or three hours, and often there was translation from one question to another while changing the manner of questioning. And notwithstanding this change, she answered prudently and with a very good memory, for very often she said: 'I have already answered on that point,' or, again, 'I refer to the clerk,' pointing at me." (R.209)

Manchon also throws some light on the circumstances under which he filled his office: "In the first of Joan's interrogatories there was great tumult on the first day in the chapel of Rouen Castle and almost every word of Joan's was interrupted when she spoke of her apparitions, for there were present certain secretaries of the King of England, two or three, who registered as they liked Joan's sayings and depositions, omitting her excuses and what might serve to acquit her. I therefore complained of that, saying that unless a better order were introduced I would no longer undertake the task of writing in that business. Because of that, on the morrow the place was changed and we gathered in the court of the castle near to the great court. And there were two Englishmen to guard the door. And as sometimes there were difficulties about Joan's answers and sayings and there were some who said that she had not answered as I had written it, wherever there was difficulty I put *nota* at the head, so that she could be questioned again and light thrown on the difficulty."

Joan's answers were, then, recorded as she gave them, then collated and examined by the judges and assessors who sought for weak points in her answers which might give them a basis for further questioning.

Certain inadmissible procedures were employed in the court itself. This is, again, revealed by Manchon: "At the beginning of the trial, during five or six days, while I set down in writing the Maid's answers and excuses, sometimes the judges tried to constrain me, by translating into Latin, to put into other terms, changing the meaning of the words or, in some other manner, my understanding (of what had been said). And were placed two men, at the command of my lord of Beauvais, in a window (embrasure) near to the place where the judges were. And there was a serge curtain drawn in front of the window so that they should not be seen. These men wrote and reported what was charged against Joan, and suppressed her excuses. I think it was Loiseleur (who was thus hidden). And after the session, while collating what they had written, the two others reported in another manner and did not put down Joan's excuses. On this subject my lord of Beauvais was greatly enraged against me." (R.49) . . . "Myself, I sat at the judges feet with Guillaume Colles and the clerk of master Jean Beaupère who wrote. But there were great differences between our writings, so much so that lively contestations arose between us." (R.49)

Apart from what was happening in open court, attempts were made to wring admissions from Joan by devious means:

Guillaume Manchon: "One named master Nicolas Loiseleur who was a familiar of my lord of Beauvais and held extremely to the English side—for formerly, the King being before Chartres (allusion to the siege of Chartres in 1421) he went to seek the King of England to get the siege raised—pretended to be of the Maid's own country and, by that means, contrived to have dealings, interviews and familiar talk with her, by giving her news from home which were pleasing to her, and he asked to be her confessor. And what she told him in secret he found means to bring to the ears of the notaries. And in fact, at the beginning of the trial, myself and Boisguillaume, with witnesses, were put secretly into a room near to where there was a hole through which one could listen, so that·we could report what she said or confessed to the said Loiseleur. And it seems to me that what the Maid said or reported familiarly to Loiseleur, he reported to us, and of that was made memoranda to find means of taking her captiously (catching her out)." (R.48)

The better to recreate the atmosphere of this trial, we give below the complete text of one day's interrogatories: that of Saturday, March 17th, 1431. The reader will get from this a clearer idea of the manner in which these proceedings were managed. On that day Joan was questioned on two occasions, morning and afternoon. Master Jean de La Fontaine was charged by the bishop to question her in his, Cauchon's, presence, and in the presence of the vice-Inquisitor Jean Lemaitre, two masters of the University of Paris, Nicolas Midy and Gerard Feuillet, Brother Isambart de la Pierre and the usher Jean Massieu. Joan was first required to take the oath, as was usual, and thereafter the questioning began:

LA FONTAINE: In what form, size, appearance and clothing does St. Michael come to you?

JOAN: He was in the form of a true and honest man,* and as for the clothes and other things, I shall not tell you any more. As for the angels, I saw them with my own eyes and you will get no more out of me about that. I believe as firmly the doings and sayings of St. Michael who appeared to me as I believe that our Lord Jesus Christ suffered death and passion for us. And what moves me to believe this is the good advice,

---

* Her word is *prud'homme*. I give the only approximate equivalent.—E.H.

the good comfort and the good doctrine that he did and gave
me.

LA FONTAINE: Will you leave to the determination of our Holy
Mother the Church, all your matters whether in good or in evil?

JOAN: As for the Church, I love her and would wish to sustain
her with all my power for our Christian faith. And it is not I
who should be prevented from going to church and hearing mass.
As for the good works which I have done and at my coming,* I
must put my faith in the King of Heaven, who sent me to Charles,
son of Charles, King of France, who is King of France. And you
will see that the French will soon win a great thing which God
will send to these French, such that it will rock the whole kingdom of France. I say it that when it happens you may remember
that I said it.

LA FONTAINE: After how long will this happen?

JOAN: In Our Lord's own time (*Je m'en attends à Notre Seigneur*).

LA FONTAINE: Will you abide by the Church's determination for
your sayings and deeds?

JOAN: I abide by God who sent me, by the Holy Virgin and all
the saints in paradise. And I am of opinion that it is all one
and the same thing, God and the Church, and that of that one
should make no difficulty. Why do you make difficulty over
that?

LA FONTAINE: There is a Church Triumphant where are God, the
Saints, the angels and souls already saved. And there is the
Church Militant in which are the Pope, God's vicar on earth,
the cardinals and prelates of the Church, the clergy, and all
good Christians and Catholics. This well-composed Church
cannot err and is ruled by the Holy Spirit. That is why I ask
you whether you are willing to abide by (put your trust in)
the Church Militant, that is to say, the one which is on earth,
as I have explained to you.

JOAN: I went to the King of France from God and the Virgin Mary
and all the saints in paradise and the Church Victorious above
and by their commandment. And to that Church I submit all
my good deeds and all that I have done and shall do. As for
submitting myself to the Church Militant, I shall answer you
nothing else for the time being.

LA FONTAINE: What say you of that woman's clothing which is
offered you that you may go and hear mass?

* I think she means "done because of my coming".—E.H.

JOAN: As for women's clothing, I shall not put it on until it please God; and if it should be that I must be brought even to judgment, I trust in the lords of the Church that they will grant me the mercy of having a woman's shift and a covering for my head. And I would rather die than revoke what God has made me do, for I believe firmly that God will not let it happen that I be brought so low without I have immediate succour, and by miracle.

LA FONTAINE: Since you say that you wear (a man's) habit by God's commandment, why do you ask for a woman's shift when it comes to dying?

JOAN: It will suffice if it be long.

LA FONTAINE: Your God-mother who has seen the fairy ladies, is she reputed a well-conducted woman?

JOAN: I hold and repute her a respectable woman* and not a diviner or witch.

LA FONTAINE: Since you have said that you would wear woman's clothes if you were allowed to go away, would that please God?

JOAN: If permission were given me to withdraw in woman's clothes, immediately (thereafter) I should dress myself in man's clothes and do what is commanded me by God; and I have answered elsewhere that not for anything whatsoever would I take oath not to put on armour and not to wear man's clothes to do the Lord's commandment.

LA FONTAINE: What ages (are), and what garments are worn by, Saints Catherine and Margaret.

JOAN: To that you shall have the answer you have already had from me and none other. I have answered as most certainly as I know.

LA FONTAINE: Did you believe before to-day that the fairy ladies were evil spirits?

JOAN: I know nothing about that.

LA FONTAINE: Do you know whether Saints Catherine and Margaret hate the English?

JOAN: They love that which God loves and hate that which God hates.

LA FONTAINE: Does God hate the English?

JOAN: Of the love or hate which God has for the English and of what He does to their souls, I know nothing; but well I know that they will be driven out of France, excepting those who will die

---

* *Prude femme:* it means, like *prud'homme*, a decent, sensible, well-mannered, 'respectable' person.—E.H.

there, and that God will send victory to the French over the English.

LA FONTAINE: Was God for the English when their cause was prospering in France?

JOAN: I know not if God hated the French, but I believe that it was His will to let them be stricken for their sins if there were sins among them.

LA FONTAINE: What guarantee and what succour do you expect from God for your wearing of man's clothes?

JOAN: For the clothes as for the other things I have done, I expect no other recompense than the salvation of my soul.

LA FONTAINE: What arms did you offer up in the church of Saint-Denis of Paris?

JOAN: I gave a white harness entire such as is fitting for a man of arms, with a sword which I won before the town of Paris.

LA FONTAINE: With what object did you give these arms?

JOAN: It was done in devoutness, as is the custom among men of arms when they are wounded; and because I had been wounded before the town of Paris I offered them up to Saint-Denis, because that is the (war-)cry of France.

LA FONTAINE: Did you do so that the arms might be worshipped?

JOAN: No.

LA FONTAINE: What was the purpose of the five crosses which were on the sword which you found at Sainte-Catherine of Fierbois?

JOAN: I do not know.

LA FONTAINE: Who was it led you to have painted on your standard angels with arms, feet, legs and clothes?

JOAN: You have been answered.

LA FONTAINE: Did you have the angels painted such as they come to you?

JOAN: I had them painted in the manner that they are painted in churches.

LA FONTAINE: Have you seen them like to the manner in which they were painted?

JOAN: I shall not tell you anything else about that.

LA FONTAINE: Why did you not have painted there that light which comes to you with the angel or with the voices?

JOAN: I was not commanded to do so.

The interrogatory was suspended at this point and resumed in the afternoon. In the second session there were more assessors present, since they now included Jean Beaupère, Jacques de Touraine, Pierre Maurice and Thomas de Courcelles in addition to those who had been present during the forenoon. Jean de La Fontaine continued the questioning:

LA FONTAINE: Did the two angels painted on your standard represent Saint Michael and Saint Gabriel?

JOAN: They were there only to honour God who was painted on the standard. I had that representation of two angels made only to do honour to God who was figured there holding the world.

LA FONTAINE: Those two angels figured on your standard, were they the two angels guarding the world? Why were there not more of them there, since it had been commanded you by God to take this standard?

JOAN: The whole standard was made at God's commandment by the voices of Saints Catherine and Margaret who said to me: "Take up the standard in the name of the King of Heaven." And because they said to me: "Take up the standard in the name of the King of Heaven," I had made that figure of God and of the angels, and in colours. And I did all by God's commandment.

LA FONTAINE: Did you then ask those two saints if, by virtue of that standard, you would win all the wars in which you would be, and whether you would be victorious?

JOAN: They told me to take it up boldly and that God would help me.

LA FONTAINE: Is it you who helped the standard or the standard which helped you, or the contrary?

JOAN: My victory or the standard's, it was all in our Lord.

LA FONTAINE: Was the hope of being victorious founded on the standard or on yourself?

JOAN: It was founded in our Lord and not elsewhere.

LA FONTAINE: If someone else had borne that standard, would it have brought as good fortune as when you had it?

JOAN: I do not know; I refer you to God (*Je m'en rapporte a Dieu:* God knows and I abide by Him).

LA FONTAINE: If someone on your side had given you his standard to bear, would you have carried it and would you have had in that one likewise as good hope as in your own standard which was given you in God's name, in particular the standard of your King, had you had it?

JOAN: I carried with a better will that which had been ordered me to carry by God, and yet in all I trust in God.

La Fontaine: What was the purpose of that sign which you put on your letters and those names: Jhesus-Maria?

Joan: The clerks who wrote my letters put it and they said that it was fitting to put those two names: Jhesus-Maria.

La Fontaine: Was it revealed to you that if you lost your virginity you would lose your (good) fortune and that your voices would come to you no more?

Joan: That was not revealed to me.

La Fontaine: Do you believe that if you were married, the voices would come to you?

Joan: I do not know and I (refer that to) trust in God.

La Fontaine: Do you think and firmly believe that your King did well to kill the lord Duke of Burgundy?

Joan: That was a great pity (brought great harm to) for the kingdom of France; and whatever may have happened between those two princes, God sent me to succour the King of France.

La Fontaine: Since you have told us, and also the bishop, that you would answer to us and our delegates as freely as you would do to our Most Holy Father the pope and that nevertheless there are many questions to which you will not reply, would you answer them more fully before the pope than you do before us?

Joan: I have answered all as truly as I could, and if I knew that in anything which I remember I have not spoken, I would willingly speak.

La Fontaine: Does it seem to you that you would be bound to answer, speaking the truth more fully, to our Lord Pope, vicar of God, of all that he might ask you touching the faith and the matter of your conscience, than you do to us?

Joan: I demand to be taken before our lord the pope and then I will answer before him all that I ought to answer.

La Fontaine: Of what material was one of your rings on which were written these names: Jhesus-Maria?

Joan: I am not sure, and if it was gold, it was not pure gold, and I know not whether it was of gold or base metal; and I think that there were on it three crosses and no other sign as far as I know, excepting Jhesus-Maria.

La Fontaine: Why did you like to look at that ring when you were going to do some war-like deed?

Joan: That was for my pleasure and in honour of my father and mother; and I, having that ring in my hand and on my finger, I touched Saint Catherine who appeared to me visibly.

LA FONTAINE: In what part of this Saint Catherine did you touch her?

JOAN: You will have nothing else on that.

LA FONTAINE: Did you kiss or embrace (*accolé*) Saints Catherine and Margaret?

JOAN: I embraced both of them.

LA FONTAINE: Had they a pleasant odour?

JOAN: It is good to know that they had a pleasant odour.

LA FONTAINE: When embracing them, did you feel any warmth or any other thing?

JOAN: I could not embrace them without feeling and touching them.

LA FONTAINE: In what part did you embrace them, the upper part or the lower?

JOAN: It is more fitting to embrace them by the lower part than the higher.

LA FONTAINE: Did you give these saints any garlands or chaplets?

JOAN: In honour of them I many times put such garlands on their images or representations in churches; and as to them who appeared to me, I never gave them any, that I remember.

LA FONTAINE: When you put garlands of that kind on the tree of which there was some talk before, did you put them in honour of them who appeared to you?

JOAN: No.

LA FONTAINE: When these saints came to you, did you make them a reverence by bending the knee and bowing?

JOAN: Yes, and as much as I could I made them my reverence, for I know well that they are of those who are of the kingdom of paradise.

LA FONTAINE: Know you ought of those who go wandering with the fairies?

JOAN: I have never been there and I know nothing else about it; but I have indeed heard it said that they went on Thursdays; but in that I do not believe and I believe that there is nothing in it unless it be witchcraft.

LA FONTAINE: Did someone make the other standards float around the King's head when he was consecrated at Rheims?

JOAN: Not as far as I know.

LA FONTAINE: Why was your standard more carried in the church of Rheims at the King's consecration than the standard of the other captains?

JOAN: That standard had borne the heat and burden; it was but right that it have the honours. (C.164–178)

To be glimpsed through these succeeding questions and answers are the principal accusations of which Joan was, if possible, to be convicted. There was the charge of witchcraft, to which we can refer those questions touching her standard and the story of it floating round the King's head; and those about her ring, with the suggestion that it had magical powers. Then there are the charges which, if proved, would convict Joan of impurity, of questionable intercourse with the beings whom, she claimed, appeared to her. And there are the questions relative to her deeds and prowess in war, with the possibility of convicting her of expressing hate or cruelty. Finally, there are the two charges which, cleverly confounded together, were, in the event, to enable the prosecution to convict her: wearing men's clothes; and the question of submission to the Church. It was on this point, and by making her male attire the symbol of her refusal to submit to the Church, that they contrived to give an appearance of justification to the final sentence; for Joan's answers gave the prosecutors absolutely no foundation upon which to build up a case against her in the matter of her morals, and still less in the matter of witchcraft. It is worth remembering that in the fifteenth century witchcraft trials were rare: there were to be some resounding ones, notably that of Gilles de Rais, which was as much a matter of morals as of magic, but they were not common, and did not become so until the end of the century, more so in the sixteenth and in the first half of the seventeenth centuries. On the other hand, trials for heresy had been common ever since the setting up, in the middle of the thirteenth century, of the Inquisition courts.

As the interrogatories proceeded, the charges which the prosecutors had in mind appear more and more clearly. We give here a complete calendar of the sessions, with Joan's principal answers, answers which, after five centuries, still fill us with admiration.

She first appeared before her judges on Wednesday, February 21st. It was at this first session that Cauchon adjured her to swear to tell the truth, and that Joan avoided the oath, saying that there were certain matters touching which she would not swear. She agreed to take the oath concerning anything to do with her father, mother, place of birth and incidents of her childhood, but not in the matter of her revelations. She made this reservation expressly, and she was never to go back on it.

CAUCHON: Swear to speak the truth with your hand on the Holy Evangels in all matters on which you will be questioned.

JOAN: I do not know on what you will question me. It may happen that you will ask me a thing which I shall not tell you.

CAUCHON: You will swear to speak the truth on what will be asked you concerning matters of faith and what you will know.*

JOAN: Of my father, of my mother, of all that I have done since I arrived in France, I will willingly swear; but the revelations made to me by God, I have not told nor revealed to anybody excepting only to Charles, my King, and I shall not reveal them though it cost me my head. I have had that by my visions and by my secret counsel, to reveal them to nobody. In the next eight days I shall know well whether I am to reveal them.

CAUCHON: Swear to tell the truth in everything touching our faith.

It was at this point, as we have said above, that Joan took the oath while maintaining that reservation in the matter of her revelations. She then complained about being kept in irons, to which Cauchon replied that it was to prevent an escape and to guard her more securely that orders had been given to keep her in irons.

JOAN: It is true that formerly I tried to escape from prison as it is licit for any prisoner to do. Even if I could escape I could not be reproached with having falsified or violated my word, for I have never given it to anybody.

At this the bishop made her three gaolers, John Grey, John Bernard and William Talbot, swear to guard her safely and in secret—that is to let nobody come near her. Which oath they took with their hands on a prayer-book. Another argument with the Bishop of Beauvais interrupted this session of questioning, in which Joan showed her mettle, proving that she was quite able to confound more than one kind of adversary.

CAUCHON: Recite *Pater Noster* and *Ave Maria*.

JOAN: I will say them willingly provided you hear my confession.

Cauchon, as may be imagined, dodged this request for, had he granted it, as a priest it would have put him in a very awkward

*i.e. what is within your knowledge.

situation. If he heard Joan's confession he would, thereafter, be prevented on his soul and conscience from declaring her guilty; on the other hand to refuse to hear her confession was to avoid doing his sacerdotal duty. The minutes of the trial mention that the bishop was obliged to admonish her "several times" and that in the end he attempted a compromise solution.

CAUCHON: Willingly will we order appointed for you one or two notable men who speak French to whom you can say *Pater Noster.*

JOAN: I shall not say it to them if they will not hear me in confession.

They were forced to drop the point and pass to the next subject.

Thursday, February 22nd

The second session was held on February 22nd and Master Jean Beaupère was appointed to undertake the questioning. His questions dealt chiefly with Joan's voices and with an account of the events which occurred at Vaucouleurs. This was after Cauchon had tried in vain to get the accused to take a more complete oath than she had taken the day before.

BEAUPÈRE: Are you going to speak the truth?

JOAN: You may well ask me some thing concerning which I will answer you the truth and to another I shall not answer. If you were well informed about me, you ought to wish that I were out of your hands. I have done nothing excepting by revelation.

Saturday, February 24th

On this day Cauchon again tried to get from her an oath free from reservations. Three times he required this of her: these were her answers:

JOAN: By my faith, you might ask me a thing that I would not tell you. . . .

JOAN: It may happen that on many things which you might ask me, I would not tell you the truth touching my revelations, for perhaps you would force me to say a thing which I have sworn not to tell and thus would I be foresworn, which you ought not to wish. And me, I tell you, consider well ere you call yourself my judge, for you are assuming a great charge, and you charge me too heavily. I have twice sworn in judgment and that is enough.

Questions and answers followed in the matter of this oath which Joan would not take.

JOAN: I will willingly tell anything I shall know and (but) not all. I am come by God's will and have nothing to do here, and demand that I be sent back to God from whom I am come.

On that day more than half the session was given up to this question of the oath, Joan remaining unshakable. After that Beaupère questioned her, notably about her voices.

BEAUPÈRE: Since what time have you neither eaten nor drunk?
JOAN: Since yesterday afternoon.
BEAUPÈRE: Since when have you heard your voice?
JOAN: I heard it yesterday and to-day.
BEAUPÈRE: At what time did you hear it?
JOAN: I heard it three times, one in the morning, one at the hour of vespers, and the third time when they were ringing the evening *Ave Maria*. And still have I heard it more often than I say.
BEAUPÈRE: What were you doing yesterday morning when the voice came to you?
JOAN: I slept and the voice awoke me.
BEAUPÈRE: Did the voice wake you by touching your arm?
JOAN: I was awoken by the voice without touch.
BEAUPÈRE: The voice, was it in your chamber?
JOAN: Not that I know, but it was in the castle.
BEAUPÈRE: Did you thank this voice and do you go down on your knees?
JOAN: I thanked it by rising and by sitting down on my bed and I clasped my hands and after that I asked it to come to my aid. The voice told me to answer boldly . . . (turning towards the bishop) you say that you are my judge. Consider well what you are about, for in truth I am sent from God, and you are putting yourself in great danger.
BEAUPÈRE: Has this voice sometimes changed its mind? (*Changé sa délibération.*)
JOAN: Never have I found it of two contrary minds. . . . (Lit: of two contrary sayings.)

BEAUPÈRE: This voice which you say appears to you, is it an angel
or does it come immediately (i.e., directly) from God, or is it
the voice of some saint?

JOAN: This voice comes from God and I think I (shall) tell you
not fully what I know; and I have a greater fear of being at
fault by saying something which displeases these voices than I
have of (not) answering you.

BEAUPÈRE: Do you believe that it displeases God that the truth
be told?

JOAN: The voices have told me that I should say a thing to the
King and not to you. This very night it has (sic) said to me many
things for the good of my King, that I would my King might
now know, though I had to drink no wine until Easter, for he
would be the more joyful for it at dinner. . . .

BEAUPÈRE: Could you not so manage things with this voice that
it would obey you and carry a message to your King?

JOAN: I know not if the voice would obey, unless it be the will of
God and that God consented to it. Were it not by God's grace,
I could do nothing. . . .

BEAUPÈRE: This voice, of which you ask counsel, has it face and
eyes?

JOAN: You shall not have that either. Little children say that
sometimes men are hanged for having spoken the truth.

BEAUPÈRE: Do you know if you are in God's grace?

JOAN: If I am not, may God bring me to it; if I am, may God
keep me in it.* I should be the most grieved woman in all the
world if I knew myself to be not in the grace of God, and were
I in (a state of) sin, I think that the voice would not come to
me, and I would that all could hear it as well as I.

After that answer the interrogation underwent a sudden change
of subject. This may be exactly what happened; or it may be one
of those deliberate omissions from the minutes of questions and
answers. Her enlightened answer on the state of grace had, indeed,
struck several of those present as it still strikes us to-day. During
the course of the Trial of Rehabilitation one of the notaries bore
witness:

Boisguillaume: "During the trial Joan very often complained
that she was being asked subtle questions without any bearing on

---

* G. B. Shaw's translation of this magnificent answer, in *Saint Joan*: but out of its proper
context.

the case. I well remember that once she was asked if she was in a state of grace. She answered that it was a great matter (*chose grande*) to answer on such a subject. And in the end she answered: 'If I am, may God keep me in it; if I am not, may God bring me to it, for I would rather die than not be in the love of God.' At this answer those who were questioning her were stupefied and at that time they stopped and questioned her no more that time." (R.211)

It is possible that Boisguillaume's memory was at fault and that the interrogatory was only suspended. At all events the following session was concerned with events in her childhood, the fairy tree at Domremy, and dealt with nothing of importance until the very end, when the matter of her male attire was raised, a matter which Joan did not yet consider of the slightest importance:

BEAUPÈRE: Will you wear woman's clothes?
JOAN: Give me a suit, I will take it and go away. Otherwise I will not take it. I am satisfied with what I have on since it pleases God that I wear it.

Tuesday, February 27th
The questioning was again left to Jean Beaupère and, after the usual argument about the oath, he again questioned her about the voices and on certain other details such as her sword.

BEAUPÈRE: Do you see Saint Michael and the angels corporeally and really?
JOAN: I see them with my corporeal eyes as well as I see you, and when they withdrew from me I wept and I should have liked them to take me with them. . . .
BEAUPÈRE: Is it Saint Catherine and Saint Margaret with whom you speak?
JOAN: I have told you often enough that they are Saint Catherine and Saint Margaret. And believe me if you will.
BEAUPÈRE: Is it forbidden you to say so?
JOAN: I have not yet fully understood whether it is forbidden or not.
BEAUPÈRE: How do you know how to make the distinction when you answer on certain points and others not?
JOAN: On certain points I asked permission and received it. I would rather be torn apart by four horses than to have gone to France without God's permission.
BEAUPÈRE: Did he command you to wear man's clothes?

JOAN: The clothes are a trifle, the very least of things. I did not put on man's clothes by the counsel of any man in the world and I did not put on the clothes and I did not do anything excepting by the commandment of God and the angels. . . .

BEAUPÈRE: Do you believe that you did right to put on man's clothes?

JOAN: All that I have done, I have done by God's commandment and I believe that I did right, and I expect from it good warrant and good succour.

BEAUPÈRE: In the particular case of taking on man's clothes, do you think that you did right?

JOAN: Of what I have done in the world I have done nothing but by God's commandment.

BEAUPÈRE: When you see this voice which comes to you, is there light?

JOAN: There is much light everywhere, and that is very fitting. Not all light comes only for you.

After this Beaupère made Joan explain in what manner she had found the sword of Sainte-Catherine de Fierbois.

BEAUPÈRE: Have you ever made a prayer that this sword be right fortunate?

JOAN: It is good to know that I should have liked that my harness be right fortunate!

BEAUPÈRE: Had you your sword when you were taken prisoner?

JOAN: No, but I had a sword that had been taken from a Burgundian.

BEAUPÈRE: Where has the sword been left, in which town?

JOAN: I gave a sword to Saint-Denis and a suit of armour, but it was not that sword. I had that sword at Lagny and from Lagny I carried the sword of the Burgundian to Compiègne. It was a good war sword and good for giving good buffets and good swipes. . . . (bonnes buffes et bonnes torchons).

BEAUPÈRE: Which did you like the better, your standard or your sword?

JOAN: I liked much better, even forty times, my standard than my sword.

BEAUPÈRE: Who made you have a painting done on the standard?

JOAN: I have told you often enough that I have done nothing without God's commandment.

Thursday, March 1st

On this day an attempt was made to confuse Joan by recalling a certain letter from the Count of Armagnac asking her which pope he ought to obey. We have here an echo of that great schism which divided Christendom for years, while first two and finally three popes wrangled over the pontifical office, until the election of Martin V put an end to the strife, although not everybody was willing to accept his supremacy without hesitation.

JOAN: To what he asked me: whom God would have him, the Count of Armagnac, obey, I answered him that I did not know, but I sent word to him of several things which were not put in writing, and as for my own part, I believe in the lord pope who is in Rome.

CAUCHON: Is it your custom to put on your letters the names Jhesus-Maria with a cross?

JOAN: On some I put them, and sometimes not. And sometimes I put a cross as a sign that he of my side to whom I was writing should not do what I wrote to him.

This cross then, which Joan drew on such letters which she dictated as contained false information or orders designed to deceive the enemy, was simply a war ruse. The detail has a certain importance, as we shall see when we come to the end of this chapter.

In this session, moreover, Joan was to fling down a veritable challenge before her judges, and that in the ironical style which she enjoyed using.

JOAN: Before seven years be passed, the English will lose a greater gage than they had at Orleans, and they will lose all in France. And the English will even suffer a greater loss than they ever had in France and this will be by a great victory which God will send to the French.

Question: How do you know that?

JOAN: I know it well by a revelation which has been made to me, and it will happen before seven years; and I should be very vexed should it be so long deferred. I know it as well as I know that you are there in front of me.

Question: When will this happen?

JOAN: I know not the day nor the hour.

Question: In what year will it happen?

JOAN: That too you shall not have, but I would that it might be before Saint John's Day.

Touching these words, which were noted down and registered in the month of March 1431, it is worth recalling that the liberation of Paris occurred on April 13, 1436. And it may be thought that she was alluding to the raising of the siege of Compiègne, a retreat to which the Duke of Burgundy was constrained on October 25, 1431, when she added:

JOAN: I have said that before the feast of Saint Martin of the winter we shall see many things, and it may well be that there will be Englishmen stricken to the ground.

It was Cauchon himself who conducted the interrogation on that day. One wonders whether it was this which stimulated Joan in her vein of insolence, for she rarely carried defiance and irony to such lengths. Thus, on the subject of her voices:

Question: What figures do you see?
JOAN: I see their faces.
Question: These saints which appear to you, have they hair?
JOAN: It's good to know!*
Question: How do they speak?
JOAN: This voice is beautiful, sweet and humble (low) and it speaks the French language.
Question: Does not Saint Margaret speak the English tongue?
JOAN: How should she speak English since she is not on the side of the English?
Question: Have you any rings?
JOAN: You have one of mine. Give it back to me. The Burgundians have another ring. You have that ring, show it to me.
Question: Who gave you the ring which the Burgundians have?
JOAN: My father and my mother, and I think that it had written on it the names Jhesus-Maria. I do not know who had them written; there was no stone, as I recall; it was given to me in the town of Domremy. It was my brother who gave me that ring. . . .
Question: What have you done with your mandragora?
JOAN: I have no mandragora and never had any. I have heard it said that near to my town there is one, but I have never seen any.

---

* *C'est bon a savoir!* Joan often used this phrase. I think it was a jeer—"Wouldn't you just like to know!"

I have heard it said that it is a thing evil and dangerous to keep.
But I know not what use it is . . . I have heard it said that it is a
thing to make money come. But I do not believe in that.

Question: Of what form was Saint Michael when he appeared to
you?

JOAN: I saw no crown on him; and of his clothes I know nothing.

Question: Was he naked?

JOAN: Do you think that God cannot afford to clothe him?

Question: Had he hair?

JOAN: Why should it have been cut off?

And finally, touching the King:

JOAN: I know well that my King will win the kingdom of France
and I know it as well as I know that you are before me as my
judge. I should be dead were it not for the revelation which
comforts me every day. . . .

Question: What sign did you give your King that you were come
from God?

JOAN: I have always told you that you will not drag that out of my
mouth. Go and ask him!

Saturday, March 3rd.

Jean Beaupère took over the interrogation, directing it towards
diverse questions such as the encounter between Joan and Catherine
de la Rochelle, her relations with Brother Richard; he tried to get
her to admit some deeds of witchcraft, such as having caused
standards to float round fortresses, etc. He also reverted to the
question of her revelations, on which Joan was as firm as ever, and
he tried to get from her some prediction touching her own fate.

BEAUPÈRE: Have you (fore) seen or known by revelation that you
will escape?

JOAN: That has nothing to do with your trial. Would you have me
say something against myself?

BEAUPÈRE: Your voices have told you nothing about it?

JOAN: It is not to do with your trial. I trust in Our Lord who will
do His own pleasure. I know neither the hour nor the day the
pleasure of God be done.

BEAUPÈRE: Have your voices said in general anything about that?

JOAN: Yes, truly. They have told me that I shall be delivered, but

I know neither the day nor the hour; and that I boldly put a cheerful face on it.

At this point the interrogations were suspended for one week.

Saturday, March 10th.
The interrogatory was resumed in the prison and in the presence of a small number of assessors. Jean de La Fontaine undertook the questioning and his questions bore chiefly on her last campaign, which had taken her to Melun, Crépy-en-Valois and Compiègne. He also alluded to the things which Joan was able to get from the King: horses, money; and to the ennobling of Joan's family.

LA FONTAINE: Have you an escutcheon and arms?
JOAN: I never had any, but the King has given arms to my brothers, to wit a shield of azure on which were two fleurs-de-lys in gold and in the middle a sword. I described these arms to a painter because he had asked me what arms I bore. They were given by my King to my brothers, without request from me and without revelation.

It was in the course of this interrogation that, asked once again about the "sign" given to the King, she began, possibly to throw her judges off the scent, to allude to that sign as to a concrete object, a crown brought by an angel. In the course of the following interrogations she amplified that image as if at random; it is easy to grasp the symbolic bearing.

LA FONTAINE: What is the sign which you gave to your King when it came to you?
JOAN: It is good and honourable and right credible and the richest there be in the world. . . . The sign is in my King's treasury.
LA FONTAINE: Is it of gold, of silver, of precious stones or a crown?
JOAN: I shall tell you nothing more. Nobody could describe a thing so rich as the sign.

Monday, March 12th.
Jean de La Fontaine again conducted the interrogation. He reverted to the beginnings of her mission, her vow of virginity, her setting out for Vaucouleurs, and he again put to her the question which had been put by Cauchon: would she recite *Pater Noster?*

LA FONTAINE: Did not your voices call you "daughter of God",
"daughter of the Church", "great-hearted daughter"?

JOAN: Before the raising of the siege of Orleans and since, every
day, when they speak to me, they have often called me "Joan
the Maid, daughter of God".

And, on the subject of angels, she added: "They come many
times among Christians but are not seen. And I have many times
seen them among Christians."

LA FONTAINE: Since you are daughter of God why will you not say
Pater Noster?

JOAN: I will say it willingly, and formerly when I refused to say
it, I did so with the intention that the Bishop of Beauvais should
hear me in confession.

Tuesday, March 13th.
Jean de La Fontaine continued his interrogation:

LA FONTAINE: How did the angel bring the crown. Did he place
it on the King's head?

JOAN: The crown was delivered to him by an archbishop, to wit
the Archbishop of Rheims, as I recall, in the presence of my King.
And the archbishop received it and gave it to my King. I was
present and the crown was placed in the treasury of my King. . . .

LA FONTAINE: The day when you yourself saw that sign, did your
King see it too?

JOAN: Yes, and it was my King himself who had it.

LA FONTAINE: Of what material was the crown?

JOAN: It is good to know that it was of fine gold and this crown was
so rich and opulent that I could not number or appreciate all
the riches which are in it, and this crown signified that the King
would hold the kingdom of France.

LA FONTAINE: Were there precious stones in it?

JOAN: I have told you all that I know.

There were more questions on the same theme. To one of the
following questions Joan made the answer which probably holds
the secret of her whole conduct:

Question: Why you rather than another?

JOAN: It pleased God thus to do, by a simple Maid to drive out the King's enemies.

Wednesday, March 14th.

Jean de La Fontaine was still the interrogator; dealing with events of mark in Joan's life, he questioned her especially on her leap from the tower at Beaurevoir; and again about her voices and what they could foretell for her.

JOAN: Saint Catherine has told me that I shall receive succour and I know not if it will be by being liberated from prison or rather whether, being brought to judgment, there would be some trouble (disturbance, confusion) by means of which I should be set free. I believe it will be by one or the other, and several times the voices have told me that I should be delivered by great victory. And thereafter my voices say to me: "Take all in good part, do not whine over thy martyrdom; by it thou shalt come at last to the kingdom of Paradise"; and this my voices say to me simply and absolutely, that is to say (meaning) without fail. I call it martyrdom because of the misery (*peine*) and adversity that I suffer in prison and I know not if I shall suffer greater misery, but I trust in God.

LA FONTAINE: Since your voices have told you that in the end you would go to Paradise, do you hold yourself assured of being saved and of not being damned in hell?

JOAN: I firmly believe what my voices have told me, to wit that I shall be saved, as firmly as if I were there already.

LA FONTAINE: After that revelation, do you believe that you cannot commit mortal sin?

JOAN: I know nothing about that, but in all things I trust in God.

LA FONTAINE: That answer is of great weight.

JOAN: Wherefore I hold it to be a great treasure.

On that day, as also on the preceding one, the interrogation was resumed in the afternoon. Jean de La Fontaine tried to catch her out in the matter of the assurance she seemed to have of her own salvation.

LA FONTAINE: Is there any need for you to confess yourself since you have revelation from your voices that you will be saved?

JOAN: I know not if I have sinned mortally, but if I were in mortal

sin I believe that Saints Catherine and Margaret would abandon
me at once. I believe that one cannot overdo cleansing one's
conscience.

The charge which was to assume substance later was here fore-
shadowed: the matter of her submission to the Church.

Thursday, March 15th.
The interrogation began with this question of her submission to
the Church:

Question: If it happens that you have done any thing which is
   against the faith, will you abide by the determination of our Holy
   Mother Church in whom you should trust?
JOAN: Let my answers be seen and examined by clerks (clergy) and
   let me be told thereafter if there be in them anything against the
   Christian faith. I shall be well able to say what there is in it,
   and thereafter I will say what I have found in it by my counsel.
   If there be anything bad against the Christian faith which God
   ordains, I would not maintain it and I should be right eager* to
   come to the contrary opinion.
Question: The distinction between the Church triumphant and militant and what pertains to the latter and to the former, has been
   explained to you. I now ask you to submit yourself to the
   determination of the Church upon what you have done and said
   of good, as of evil.
JOAN: I will make you no other answer for the present.

The remainder of this session was devoted chiefly to the
wearing of man's clothes and her apparitions, notably that of
St. Michael.

Saturday, March 17th
The interrogation for this day appears earlier in this chapter.
   Finally, March 24th and 25th, Joan was again visited in her
prison, still by only a restricted number of the assessors, but these
included all the delegates from the University of Paris. More
detailed answers were demanded of her in the matter of certain
questions, notably that of wearing man's clothes which she still
refused to change for female attire. It was on this occasion that

---

* Joan's words are *"bien irritée"*; we might say "on tenterhooks to come to, etc."

she gave the answer which, for her, summed up the whole business: "These clothes do not burden my soul and to wear them is not against the Church." (C.181–183)

That concluded the "instruction" of the case, that is the preliminary examinations.

Jean Beaupère was still alive, being seventy years of age, at the time of Joan's Rehabilitation. He was interrogated during the royal enquiry (preliminary to the Trial of Rehabilitation) in 1450. His memory was still coloured by resentment: "She was right subtle, with a subtlety pertaining to woman." (R.251)

As for the other assessors, it is obvious that they felt much what we feel ourselves when we read Joan's answers as they have been preserved for us. Martin Ladvenu, a Dominican of the convent of Rouen who was to be at Joan's side in her last moments, testified: "In my judgment she might be nineteen or twenty years of age; in her bearing she was very simple and in her answers full of discernment and prudence."

Others went a good deal further; Jean Riquier, who was not present in person at the trial but reported what he had heard, said, for example: "I heard it said that she answered with so much prudence that if certain of the doctors had been questioned as she was they would hardly have answered so well."

Jean Fabri or Lefevre: "They greatly fatigued her by long interrogations which lasted from two to three hours. . . . Sometimes those who questioned her cut into each other's questions to such an extent that she could hardly answer them. The wisest man in the world would have answered with difficulty. I remember that once, during the trial, while Joan was being examined on her apparitions and while a record of her answers was being read to her, it seemed to me that it had been wrongly recorded and that she had not answered thus. I told Joan to pay attention. She asked the notary who wrote the record to read it to her again and that done she told the notary that she had said the opposite and that he had not written it rightly. And that answer was corrected. Then master Guillaume Manchon told Joan that in future he would pay attention."

Pierre Daron: "I heard it said by several that during that trial Joan did wonders in her answers and that she had an admirable memory, for once when she was being questioned in a matter about which she had already been questioned a week before, she answered: 'I was already asked that on such a day' or 'A week ago I was

questioned about that and I answered in such-and-such way,'
although Boisguillaume, one of the notaries, told her that she had
not answered, some of those present said that Joan was speaking
the truth. The answer for that day was read and it was found
that Joan was right. She rejoiced greatly at it, saying to this Boisguillaume that if he made a mistake again, she would pull his ears
. . . ." (R.212–213)

The second phase of the trial, the ordinary hearing, began on
Monday, March 26th. On that day and the next, the act of accusation drawn up by the promoter (prosecutor), Jean d'Estivet, was
read to the assembled assessors. This act of accusation which is in
seventy clauses (C.192–286) goes interminably over the principal
points of the foregoing interrogations, without, moreover, taking
any account of Joan's replies. It was interrupted by her at the end
of almost every clause with a denial of its contents or with "I refer
you to what I said elsewhere." (Lit: *I abide in that by what I said
elsewhere*). It is worth our while to put some of Joan's answers
back into French, among others Joan's own prayer which, however, is not given in the minutes of the trial:

Questioned as to the manner in which she summons her voices,
she answers: "I call upon God and Our Lady that they send me
counsel and comfort and thereafter they send it to me." Asked by
what exact words she summons them, she replies in this fashion
in French: "Most gentle God, in honour of Your Holy Passion I
call upon You, if You love me, that You reveal to me how I should
answer these Churchmen. I know well, as to the clothes, the
commandment whereby I assumed them, but I know not in what
manner I should leave them off. For this, please You to teach
me." (C.252)

On Saturday, March 31st, Joan was again questioned in her
prison on the particular point of her submission to the Church.

Question: Will you confide yourself to the judgment of the Church
    which is on earth in all that you have said and done both good
    and evil, and especially in the cases, crimes and misdemeanours
    of which you are accused and in all touching your trial?
JOAN: On that which is asked of me, I will abide by the Church
    militant provided it does not command anything impossible to
    do, and what I call impossible is that I should revoke the deeds
    I have done and said and what I have declared concerning the
    visions and apparitions sent to me by God; I shall not revoke

them for anything whatsoever; that which Our Lord has made me do and commanded and will command, I shall not fail to do for any man alive, and in the case of the Church willing me to do otherwise and contrary to the commandment which has been given me by God, I should not do it for anything whatsoever.

Question: If the Church militant tells you that your revelations are illusions or things diabolical, will you abide by the Church?

JOAN: In that I will always abide by God whose commandment I have always done, and I know well that that which is contained in the proceedings (she is referring to the answers she has given) comes by the commandment of God, and that which I affirm in those proceedings to have done by God's commandment, it would have been impossible for me to do the contrary. And in the case of the Church militant commanding me to do the contrary, I should not abide by any man in the world but only by our Sire whose good commandment I have always done.

Question: Do you not believe that you owe submission to God's Church on earth, that is to our lord the pope, to the cardinals, archbishops, bishops and other prelates of the Church?

JOAN: Yes, our Sire being first served.

Question: Have you commandment from your voices not to submit yourself to the Church militant which is on earth, nor to its judgment?

JOAN: I shall not answer otherwise than I take into my head, but what I answer is by the commandment of my voices; they do not command me that I obey not the Church, God first served. (C.286–288)

Meanwhile another act of accusation, more precise than Jean d'Estivet's woolly and verbose prose, was drawn up to serve as a basis for the rest of the trial. During the course of the Trial of Rehabilitation, some interesting details were given about this proceeding, by the notaries.

Guillaume Manchon: "It was decided by the councillors and especially by those who had come from Paris, that, as was usual, out of all these articles and responses there should be made a few short articles and that the principal points should be summarized to present the matter briefly in order that the deliberations could be better done and more rapidly. It was for that (reason) that the twelve articles were drawn up, but it was not I who did them and I do not know who composed or extracted them."

"How was it done," asked the promoter of the Trial of Rehabilitation, "that such a multitude of articles and responses could be
reduced to twelve articles, especially in a form so remote from
Joan's confessions? It does not seem very likely that such important
men would have thus composed these articles."

MANCHON: I think that in the principal text of the proceedings done
in French, I inserted the truth of the interrogations and articles
drawn up by the promoter and the judges, and of Joan's answers.
As for the twelve articles, I refer them to those who composed
them, whom I did not dare to gainsay, any more than my companion.

Question: When the twelve articles were inserted, did you collate
those articles with Joan's answers to see if they corresponded
with those answers?

MANCHON: I do not remember.

Now at this point Manchon was shown a folio in his own handwriting, extracted from the dossier which he himself had produced
before the court of Rehabilitation and dated April 4, 1431. On
this folio Manchon had noted the discrepancies between certain of
the articles in question, and Joan's answers: the fact is that, as in
the earlier and longer act of accusation, certain of the articles
expressed the very opposite to what Joan had, in fact, answered.
For example, the reply given under the head of submission to the
Church becomes: "She will not submit herself to the determination
of the Church militant, but to God only."

Question: Do you believe that these articles were composed in a
spirit of truth, for there is a great difference between these
articles and Joan's answers?

MANCHON: What is in my text of the proceedings is true. As for
the articles, I refer them to those who did them, for it was not
I who did them.

Question: Were the decisions based on the whole proceedings (i.e.,
on the full record) or on these twelve articles?

MANCHON: I believe that the decisions were not based on the full
proceedings, for it had not yet been put in form and was not
drafted into the form it has now until after Joan's death, but the
decisions were made on the twelve articles.

Question: Were these twelve articles read by Joan?

MANCHON: No.

What Manchon said was confirmed by the other two notaries, Boisguillaume and Nicolas Taquel, who disclaimed all responsibility when confronted with the twelve articles and attested that they served as a basis for the subsequent judicial decisions. A witness who was particularly well informed, Thomas de Courcelles himself in fact, completed the detailed evidence taken on this point: "Certain articles, to the number of twelve, were edited and extracted from Joan's admissions and answers. This was done, as far as I can conjecture with some degree of likelihood, by the late master Nicolas Midy. It was on the twelve articles thus extracted that all the deliberations (i.e., decisions) and opinions were based and given, but I do not know if it was decided that they should be corrected or if they were corrected." (R.256)

Thus, then, the procedure followed could well seem correct and regular; the authorities did not fail to call the foreign doctors and jurists who were at the trial into consultation, as was the custom; nor to call the assessors to deliberate in complete freedom on the accusations brought against Joan; but the text which served as the basis of these deliberations was truncated, falsified and had never been read by the accused.

Consultations and deliberations went on from April 5th. On the 12th there was a deliberation in which the masters from the University of Paris played the preponderant part. A letter was subsequently drawn up by them accusing Joan of relying upon false revelations, of erring in her faith in claiming that the articles of faith were not better founded than her own revelations (a singular manipulation, as can be seen, of Joan's actual protestations), and finally of being guilty of idolatry, schism, heresy, blasphemy, vaingloriousness, etc. Cauchon was careful thereafter to place this letter with the twelve articles before the other assessors when they were called into consultation.

We shall not here go at length into the attitude of these other assessors. But at all events it should be noted that the majority of them had attended only the first of the interrogations during the "instruction" of the case and were judging the matter from articles of accusation which were a travesty of the truth. It is also the case that a fair number of them, chosen by Cauchon for their devotion to the English cause and the theory of the double monarchy, could without difficulty range themselves alongside the representatives of the university. Among these we may distinguish some more clearly decided in the hostility to Joan apparent in their answers: the Bishop of Lisieux, Zanon de Castiglione, for example, and Philibert de Montjeu, Bishop of Coutances; likewise Denis Gastinel, and the almoner of the abbey of La Trinité of Fécamp, Jean de Bouesgue. The same sort of response could safely be expected from the abbot of the same abbey, Gilles de Duremort, whose services, as we have seen, were generously rewarded by the King of England. The same may be said of several others, among whom we shall mention only the archdeacon of Eu, Nicolas de Venderès, whom we shall meet again.

Some, however, showed themselves less forthcoming. Between the lines of their answers we can read an uneasy feeling about the whole business. Thus the abbots of Jumièges and Cormeilles asked that the whole trial be transferred before the University of Paris. Then, in a second letter required of them by Cauchon who was not satisfied with this, they asked that Joan be better informed of the case and that the danger she was running be clearly expounded to her. They added: "As there are facts which we cannot know . . . more especially as we were not present at the examination of the said woman, we refer to and rely upon the masters of theology for an ulterior judgment."

Furthermore, eleven advocates of the Rouen Officiality expressed reservations, and three of the assessors, Bachelors of Theology, Pierre Minier, Jean Pigache and Richard de Grouchet, were in disagreement with Cauchon: "If these revelations proceed from God or from a good spirit, which however for us is not self-evident, they could not be taken as evil."

Richard de Grouchet, giving evidence at the Trial of Rehabilitation: "Myself and the two called Pigache and Minier, gave our opinion in writing according to our conscience. It was not agreeable to the bishop and his assessors, who said to us: 'Is this what you have done?' " (R.198)

And finally there was Raoul le Sauvage, Bachelor of Theology, who, albeit far from favourable to Joan, considered that the case should be taken before the Holy See.

It is only from certain indications and from the evidence given at the Trial of Rehabilitation, when Rouen had been liberated and lips could be unsealed, that we know of the resistance which Cauchon encountered. It should be noted, to start with, that the canons of Rouen were in no hurry to give their opinion. Having called an assembly of the chapter for the first time on April 13th, they found that there were too few of them present to enable them to deliberate. There was another chapter meeting on the next day at which they agreed to ask that the twelve articles be read to Joan in French and that she be better instructed in the matter of submitting to the Church. Their letter, as if accidentally omitted, is not to be found in the definitive text of the proceedings. Cauchon had summoned them to hold a third chapter which they did on May 4th, and at this one (and we can imagine the pressure which was brought to bear on it) the canons pronounced Joan guilty.

Also missing from the final text of the proceedings is a letter written by the Bishop of Avranches, Jean de Saint-Avit, and we only know of its existence from the evidence given by Isambart de la Pierre during the Rehabilitation proceedings:

"Myself, in person, I was called before the Bishop of Avranches, a very old and good cleric, who like the others had been summoned and requested to give his opinion on this case. For that, the bishop questioned me, asking what my lord Saint Thomas said and determined touching the submission which was owed to the Church. I gave the bishop, in writing, the determination of Saint Thomas, who says: 'In things doubtful regarding the faith, recourse should be had to the pope or the general council (synod).' The good bishop was of that opinion and seemed to be very ill-pleased with the deliberation (decision) which had been taken already. This deliberation (the bishop's) was not put into the writing, it was left out by malice." (R.269)

His conduct in this matter earned the Bishop of Avranches the rancour of the English and of Cauchon. In the following year, 1432, accused of having taken part in a plot designed to liberate Rouen, he was to be imprisoned despite his great age. And this is the place to mention two other people who, despite the danger they ran, had the courage to oppose Cauchon. "Threats were uttered against master Jean Lohier and master Nicolas de Houppeville, under pain of being drowned because they would not attend the trial," declared Guillaume de La Chambre, one of the Rehabilitation witnesses. And Guillaume Manchon himself was to give details of Jean Lohier's conduct on this occasion:

"When the trial was started," he says, "master Jean Lohier, a learned Norman clerk, came to the town of Rouen and there was communicated to him by the Bishop of Beauvais, what was in writing. Lohier asked for a delay of two or three days to see (consider) it. He was told that he must give his opinion at once and to that he was constrained. And Master Jean Lohier, when he had seen (read) the proceedings, said that it was worthless for several reasons: for as much as it had not the form of an ordinary trial. It was carried on in a place closed and locked where those present were not at liberty to say their full and pure will; they were dealing in this matter with the honour of the King of France whose cause Joan supported, without calling himself or anyone from him; neither libels nor articles had been delivered (to the prisoner) and this woman, who was a simple girl, had no counsel to answer so many doctors and masters and on great matters, especially those touching her revelations, as she said. And for all that, it seemed to him that the proceedings were not valid.

"My lord de Beauvais," he went on, "was very indignant against Lohier, and although he had told him to remain and see the said trial carried on, Lohier replied that he would not stay, and at once my lord de Beauvais . . . sought out the Masters (of the university) to whom he said: 'Here is Lohier who wants to wreck our trial with his interlocutory judgments.* He would calumniate the whole thing and says it is worthless. If he is to be believed, everything is to be done over again, and what we have done is good for nought.' And, reporting the reasons why Lohier wanted it annulled, he said, 'It is easy to see which side he is lame. By St. John we shall do nothing of the sort and will continue our trial as it began.' It was then the Saturday afternoon in Lent. On the following morning I spoke to Lohier in the church of Our Lady of Rouen, and asked him what he thought of Joan's trial. He answered: 'You see the manner of their proceeding. They will catch her if they can by her own words, that is to say in the assertions where she says, "I know for a certainty" touching her apparitions, whereas if she said, "it seems to me", instead of "I know for a certainty", there is not a man living who could condemn her. It seems that they are proceeding more from hatred than otherwise, and for that cause I shall stay here no longer, for I want nothing to do with it.' And, in fact, he always thereafter remained in the Court of Rome and he died dean of the Rota."† (R.259–61)

At the time of the Trial of Rehabilitation there still survived one of those righteous souls for whom the word justice really meant something, Nicolas de Houppeville. He himself was thus able to

---

* *bailler belles interlocutoires en notre proces.*
† Rota: a court judging appeals to the Holy See.

give an account of the sanctions which were applied to him: "I was sent for one day at the beginning of the trial and I did not go because I was prevented by another case. When I went, on the second day, I was not received; I was, indeed, ordered out (of court) by the lord Bishop of Beauvais, and that was because I had said earlier, when I was discussing it with Master Colles, that there was a danger in bringing this case for several (many) reasons. This remark was reported to the bishop. That was why the bishop had me put into the royal prisons at Rouen from which I was delivered at the prayer of the then lord abbot of Fécamp. I heard it said that, on the advice of certain people whom the bishop had called together for that (purpose), it was decided to send me into exile in England or elsewhere, out of the city of Rouen, which would have been done but for the intervention of the abbot and some of my friends." (R.262)

It is well known, of course, that after Joan's burning, a Dominican, Pierre Bosquier, was cast into prison for having given his opinion of her condemnation.

Meanwhile Joan, in her prison, had fallen ill. The Duchess of Bedford's* physician, Jean Tiphaine, was sent to treat her. He gave an account of this occasion during the Trial of Rehabilitation:

"When Joan was ill the judges sent me to visit her and I was taken to her by the man d'Estivet. In the presence of d'Estivet, of Master Guillaume de la Chambre, Master of Medicine, and of several others, I felt her pulse to learn the cause of her sickness and I asked her what was the matter and where she felt pain. She answered me that a carp had been sent to her by the Bishop of Beauvais, that she had eaten of it, and that that was the cause of her sickness. Then d'Estivet scolded her saying that that was false and he called her wanton, saying, 'It is thou, wanton, who hast eaten shad and other things which have done thee harm.' She answered that she had not and many injurious (insulting) words were exchanged between Joan and d'Estivet. Later, wishing to know more of Joan's sickness, I heard it said by people who were there that she had vomited many times." (R.204-205)

The other physician, Guillaume de la Chambre, was also alive at the time of the Rehabilitation, and was called to give evidence: "In what concerns her sickness, the cardinal of England† and the Earl of Warwick sent for me. I presented myself before them with

* Anne of Burgundy, sister of Philippe the Good.
† Cardinal Beaufort, Bishop of Winchester.—E.H.

Master Guillaume Desjardins, Master of Medicine, and other physicians. Then the Earl of Warwick told us that Joan has been (taken) ill, as had been reported to him, and that he had sent for us that we might take care of her, for not for anything in the world would the King have her die a natural death. The King, indeed, held her dear for he had bought her dear, and would not have her die excepting at the hands of justice, and that she be burnt. And we so wrought, visiting her with care, that she was cured. I went to see her, as did Master Desjardins and the others. We palpated her on the right side and found her feverish. We therefore decided to bleed her. When we made our report to the Earl of Warwick he said: 'Be careful when bleeding her, for she is cunning and might kill herself.' Nevertheless, she was bled, which gave her immediate relief. As soon as she was thus better, came one Master Jean d'Estivet who exchanged insulting words with Joan and called her 'whore, wanton'. She was by this so irritated (excited) that she became feverish again and fell ill again. That came to the earl's knowledge who forbade d'Estivet to insult Joan thenceforth." (R.205-206)

From the point of view of proper procedure, the next stage was that of the so-called "charitable admonitions". This was the regular thing in the Inquisition courts: when the preliminary examination (instruction) of the case had revealed that the accused was guilty, he must be brought either to a full admission of guilt, or to repentance. That was the aim of the admonitions. In cases where there was a beginning of proof of guilt in the accused, the use of torture was permissible.

On Wednesday, April 18th, Joan being still sick and confined to her bed, the first charitable admonition was administered to her. Into her cell went Cauchon, the Vice-Inquisitor Jean Lemaitre, three Masters from the University of Paris, Jacques de Touraine, Nicolas Midy and Gérard Feuillet, an English clerk William Haiton, and three other men whose names appear only rarely in the minutes of the proceedings, Guillaume Boucher, Maurice Du Chène, Guillaume Adelie. It was Cauchon himself who undertook the admonitions. He first proposed to Joan that she should choose among the assessors composing the court who would be her counsel. He pointed out that if she would not take counsel or follow the Church's advice, she was in great danger.

JOAN: It seems to me, in view of the sickness that I have, that I am in great danger of death; and if it be so that God would do

His will upon me, I ask to have confession and the sacrament
of the Eucharist and to be buried in holy ground.

CAUCHON: If you have the sacraments of the Church you must
declare yourself a good Catholic and submit to the Church.

JOAN: I am not able to say anything else to you at present.

CAUCHON: The more you fear for your life because of the sickness
which you have, the more should you amend your ways. . . .

JOAN: If my body dies in prison, I expect you to put it in holy
ground, and if you do not have it put there, I expect it of God. . . .
(Or, "I put my trust in God").

CAUCHON: Since you ask that the Church give you the sacrament of
the Eucharist, will you submit yourself to the Church Militant
and a promise to give you that sacrament would be given you?

JOAN: I shall not do otherwise about that submission.* God I
love, I serve Him and am a good Christian and I would help and
sustain the Church with all my power.

CAUCHON: Would you have us order a beautiful and notable procession to restore you to a proper state if you are not in such a state?

JOAN: I should indeed like the Church and Catholics to pray for
me. (C.329–333)

A second admonition took place on May 2nd. With her health
restored Joan had recovered her attitude of defiance. It is probable
that an episode which the official account leaves out, as it leaves out
the opinions given by Jean de Saint-Avit and Jean Lohier, should be
placed here, just before this solemn admonition. This episode was
not known until later, when it came out at the Trial of Rehabilitation.

Guillaume Manchon: "Master Jean de La Fontaine, from the
beginning of the trial until the week after Easter 1431, was substitute
for my lord of Beauvais in questioning her when the bishop was
absent. Nevertheless he was always present with the bishop during
the argument of the trial, and the Maid was hard pressed to submit
herself to the Church by this La Fontaine and brother Isambart de
la Pierre and Martin Ladvenu, by whom she was warned that she
must believe and hold by our Holy Father the pope and those
who presided over the Church Militant and that she must not
doubt that she ought to submit to our Holy Father the pope
and the Holy Synod, for there were both, at her side and elsewhere,

---

* There is no equivalent to the form of words Joan used here but the implication was not
quite so downright. A modern equivalent might be "I cannot handle myself differently."—
E.H.

many notable clerks; and that, if she did not so, she would put
herself in great peril; and on the day after she had been thus warned,
she said that she would readily submit herself to our Holy Father
the pope and to the Holy Synod. When my lord of Beauvais heard
of this remark, he demanded to know who had been to see her the
day before. He sent for the Maid's English guard and asked who
had spoken to her. The guard answered him that it had been the
said La Fontaine and the two religious. And for that, in the absence
of La Fontaine and the religious, the bishop became furiously angry
with Jean Lemaitre, vicar of the Inquisitor, loudly threatening to
cause them distress (or, "do them mischief", "bring them to grief").
And when La Fontaine had word of this and that he was menaced for
that cause, he left that city of Rouen and since came not back. And
as for the two religious, had it not been that Lemaitre made their
excuses and supplicated on their behalf, saying that if any grievous
thing was done to them never would he appear at the trial, they would
have been in danger of death. And thenceforth it was forbidden by
my lord of Warwick that any go into the Maid, excepting my lord
of Beauvais or on his behalf, and whenever it should please the
bishop to go to her. But the vicar was not to go to her without
him." (R.218–219)

Guillaume Duval, who belonged, like the two other Dominicans
and the vice-Inquisitor, to the convent of Saint-Jacques of Rouen,
confirmed this evidence. And in the event neither La Fontaine nor
Ladvenu were among the sixty-three assessors present at the
charitable admonitions of May 2nd, which is what makes it likely
that the scene described above may have occurred on May 1st.

The questioning was undertaken by Jean de Chatillon.

Question: Will you correct and amend yourself according to the
decision of the doctors?
JOAN: Read your book and then I will answer you. I trust in God
my creator, in all. I love Him with all my heart.
Question: Will you answer more fully to this general admonition?
JOAN: I trust in my Judge, that is King of Heaven and earth. . . .
Question: Will you submit to the Church Militant?
JOAN: I believe indeed in the Church here below, but for my deeds
and sayings, as I said formerly, I trust in and abide by Our Lord.
I do believe that the Church Militant cannot be at fault nor fail,
but as for my sayings and deeds, I place them and refer them in
all to God who has made me do all that I have done.

Question: Do you mean that you have no judge upon earth? Our Holy Father the pope, is not he your judge?

JOAN: I shall say nothing else to you about this; I have a good master, God to wit, in whom I trust in all things and not in another.

Question: If you will not believe in the Church and believe in the article *Unam sanctam Ecclesiam catholicam,* you are a heretic in maintaining that, and other judges may punish you with the pain of fire.

JOAN: I shall say nothing else to you about this. And if I saw the fire, I should say all that I am saying, and do not otherwise.

Question: If the Holy Council General (Synod) and our Holy Father the pope, the cardinals and others of the Church were here, would you refer (the matter) and submit to that holy council?

JOAN: You will get nothing else out of me.

Question: Will you submit to our Holy Father the pope?

JOAN: Take me to him and I will answer him. (C.342–343)

Did this interrogation in fact occur exactly as it appears in the record? It may be doubted that it did if we can rely upon some of the witnesses at the Trial of Rehabilitation. For several of them affirmed that Joan said more than once that she would abide by the pope's decision. Here, as an example, is Richard de Grouchet's deposition: "I saw and heard, at the time of the judgment, that when Joan was asked if she would submit herself to the Bishop of Beauvais and to certain among those who were there and were named, Joan answered that she would not, and that she submitted herself to the pope and to the Catholic Church, demanding that she be taken to the pope. When she was told that the proceedings would be sent to the pope that he might judge them, she answered that she would not have them do so, for she knew not what they would put in the proceedings, but that she wanted to be taken there that she might be questioned by the pope. I do not know if it was put or written in the proceedings that she did not submit herself to the Church and I did not see that putting it in was prevented, but I know that in my presence Joan always submitted herself to the judgment of the pope and the Church."

And we may also quote the deposition of Isambart de la Pierre: "Joan, asked if she would submit herself to our Holy Father the pope, answered yes provided she was led and taken to him, but that she would not submit herself to those who were present, that is to say the Bishop of Beauvais, for they were her mortal enemies. And when I persuaded her that she should submit herself to the Council General then assembled, at which were many prelates and doctors of the King of France's party, that heard, Joan said that she submitted herself to the Council. Then the Bishop of Beauvais called upon me violently, saying, 'Be silent, by the devil!' That heard, Master Guillaume Manchon, notary of the trial, asked the bishop if he should write down her submission. The bishop answered no, that it was not necessary. And Joan said to him: 'Ah, you take care to write down what is against me, and will not write down what is for me'; and I believe that it was not written down, whence arose a great murmuring in the assembly." (R.222–223)

The record shows that Isambart was indeed present at that session of May 2nd. After Joan's answer, "Take me to him and I will answer him," the text of the proceedings notes simply: ". . . and otherwise would not answer." (Lit: ". . . and more about it would not answer.") After that the subject of questioning was changed completely: woman's clothes, the sign given to the King, etc.; the change occurring from the direct style to the indirect, and from one question to another, leads us to think that it is here that the incident reported by Isambart should be placed.

Wednesday, May 9th, Joan was taken to the Great Tower of Rouen Castle—it still survives and is the only vestige of the ancient fortress of Bouvreuil. The judges were accompanied by only a reduced number of assessors; and in their presence Joan was threatened with torture. She was called upon thereafter to speak the truth on various points in the trial "which she has denied or in which she has answered in a lying fashion".

JOAN: Truly, though you were to have my limbs torn off and send the soul out of my body, I should not say otherwise; and if I did tell you otherwise, I should always thereafter say that you had made me speak so by force.

And she added:

At the last feast of the Holy Cross (May 3rd) I had comfort from Saint Gabriel, and I believe that it was Saint Gabriel, and I learned it from my voice, that it was Saint Gabriel. I asked counsel of my voices if I should submit myself to the Church, since Churchmen were pressing me hard to submit myself to the

Church: and these voices told me that if I wanted God to help me I must trust in him for all I did. I know well that God has always been the master of all that I have done, and that the devil has never had power over my deeds. I have asked my voices whether I shall be burnt and my voices have answered me that I should trust in Our Lord and that he would help me.

Question: About the sign of the crown of which you say that it (the crown) was delivered to you by the Archbishop of Rheims, will you abide by what that archbishop says?

JOAN: Bring him here and then I will answer you. I would not dare to say the opposite of what I have told you.

Thereupon, the masters present decided to put off the torture and to deliberate first as to whether or not it should be applied to her. The record mentions the presence of some "officers" who were there in readiness to put John to the torture. The principal man among them was the executioner, Maugier Leparmentier: he was still living at the time of the Rehabilitation and he remembered the episode perfectly. "I met Joan at the time when she was brought to the town of Rouen and I saw her at Rouen Castle when me and my companion were sent for to put Joan to the torture. She was then questioned for some time and she answered with much prudence, so much so that those who were there marvelled. Finally we withdrew, I and my companion, without having laid hands on her person." (R.215)

Saturday, May 12th, Cauchon assembled twelve of the assessors to discuss the question of whether Joan was to be put to the torture. Only three among them gave an affirmative opinion: Thomas de Courcelles of Paris University; Nicolas Loiseleur, the man who had passed himself off as a fellow-countryman of Joan's in an attempt to extract damaging confessions; and one Aubert Morel, Doctor of Canon Law, whose appearance at sittings of the court were few and far between. The details of this discussion do not appear in the definitive text of the proceedings drafted by Thomas de Courcelles; it is only to be found in the text of the "French Minute" given in the Urfé MS. and in that of Orleans. (See Commentary, p. 227.)

The English, however, were becoming impatient. A document recently brought to light, the Beauchamp Household Book now preserved in the Earl of Warwick's archives and not yet published,* yields fresh confirmation of the texts we already possessed.

* See Pernoud, R., *Jeanne d'Arc prisonnière, Revue de Paris*, June, 1960.

In this register of accounts for the year 1431–32 are entered, day by day, the names of all the guests entertained by the then Earl of Warwick, who lived in Rouen as Governor representing the King of England. On Sunday, May 13th, the earl gave a grand dinner; first among the guests were the Bishop of Beauvais, Pierre Cauchon, and the Bishop of Noyon, Jean de Mailly. Also present wei ∴ certain persons who had played important parts in Joan's life, John of Luxembourg, his brother Louis, Chancellor of France, Humphrey, Earl of Stafford, one of the principal English captains, and the wife of John Talbot who had been captured by the French at Patay and was still held by them; she was Richard Beauchamp, Earl of Warwick's daughter.

After the list of names the Beauchamp's major domo entered in his register the expenses necessitated by their keep. We thus know the details of an entertainment which seems to have been very grand, if we are to judge by the substantial purchases made on that day. (Folios 68 V. and 69 of the MS.)

It is very probable that we may ascribe to this Sunday, May 13th, the scene recounted by one of the witnesses at the Trial of Rehabilitation, Haimond de Macy, who, it will be recalled, had had some conversation with Joan in her prison at Beaurevoir; among the guests of that day the Account Book mentions "*duo milites Burgonie*," two Knights of Burgundy, one of whom must be Haimond himself. Here is what he had to say about the matter:

"(After her stay at the castle of Beaurevoir and the castle of Crotoy) Joan was brought to the castle of Rouen, to a prison on the country side (of the castle). In that town, at the time when Joan was held there, the Count of Ligny (John of Luxembourg) went to see her, and me with him. One day this Count of Ligny wanted to see Joan. He went to her, accompanied by the lord Earls of Warwick and of Stafford, and the present Chancellor of England, at that time Bishop of Thérouanne and brother of the Count of Ligny, and myself. This Count of Ligny addressed himself to Joan, saying: 'Joan, I am come to ransom you provided you will promise that you will never take up arms against us.' She answered: 'In God's name, you are making game of me, for well I know that you have neither the will nor the power.' And she repeated that several times because the count persisted in saying the same. And she said next: 'I know that these English will put me to death, because they think, after my death, to win the Kingdom of

France. But were they a hundred thousand godons* more than they are now, they will not have the Kingdom.' At these words the Earl of Stafford was angry and he half-drew his dagger to strike her, but the Earl of Warwick prevented him." (R.187)

This Earl of Stafford, one of Warwick's intimates (his name constantly recurs in the pages of the register) seems to have been one of the most implacable against Joan. An episode recounted by Guillaume Manchon shows him as a man of quick and violent temper: "One day someone whose name I do not remember said something about Joan which displeased the lord of Stafford; this sire of Stafford pursued him who had spoken to a place of sanctuary, with drawn sword; to the point that, if the sire of Stafford had not been told that the place where this man was, was a holy place and enjoying the right of asylum, he would have struck the man."

What decisions were taken at that dinner on May 13th? What is certain is that thereafter events came much faster.

On the following day, May 14th, the University of Paris met in plenary session to deliberate on the twelve articles of accusation which had been sent to it with a letter from Cauchon and another from the King of England, which letters can have left no doubt as to what the tendency of the deliberations ought to be. Not that there was any need to bring pressure to bear on that assembly as to the conclusion it was desired to come to, considering the unequivocal proofs of devotion which the University had long given to the English cause. The deliberations concluded by finding Joan guilty of being a schismatic, an apostate, a liar, a soothsayer, suspect of heresy; of erring in the faith, and being a blasphemer of God and the saints. A letter to the King of England, in support of these conclusions, was drawn up by the masters, who wrote:

"Your Most Noble Magnificence . . . has commenced a right good work touching our holy faith: to wit the judicial proceedings against the woman known as the Maid and her scandals, faults and offenses so manifest throughout this Kingdom. . . .

"We humbly implore your Excellent Highness, that very diligently this matter be brought swiftly to an end, for verily length and dilation is most perilous and it is very necessary to make in this (matter) notable and great reparation for that the people who, by this woman, have been mightily scandalised†, be led back into good and holy doctrine and belief." (C.355–356)

---

* i.e., *goddams* the nickname for English soldiers.
† Led into scandalous conduct.—E.H.

As soon as he received these conclusions, so favourable to his cause, Cauchon hastened to assemble the assessors for a session of the court on Saturday, May 19th. After the letters and conclusions from the university had been read, the assessors were called upon, each for his opinion. Most of them, as we might expect, gave an opinion in the same sense as that of the authority *par excellence* of that time, the University of Paris. A few only had reservations, notably Brother Isambart de la Pierre, who referred the court to the first deliberations he had put before it and who insisted that Joan be warned again.

On Wednesday, May 23rd, Joan appeared before the court in a room in the castle near to her prison cell, to be solemnly exhorted by one of the university Masters, Pierre Maurice, to "renounce her errors and scandals". A long and verbose exhortation was answered by Joan as follows:

"The way that I have always spoken and held to in this trial, that will I still maintain. And if I was brought to judgment and saw the fire lit and the faggots ready, and the executioner ready to stoke the fire and that I be within the fire, yet should I not say otherwise and should maintain what I have said in the trial even unto death." (C.384)

It was at this point that it was decided to set a scene designed to shake her. On Thursday, May 24th, in the cemetery of Saint-Ouen, a scaffold and tribune were erected. Here Joan was to be brought and threatened with burning unless she made public abjuration.

The great prelates were all present; the scene was presided over by the Bishop of Winchester, Henry Beaufort, known as the "Cardinal of England". He was Bedford's uncle and Henry VI's great-uncle. With him sat the Bishop of Beauvais and Noyon; Louis of Luxembourg, Bishop of Thérouanne; and William Alnwick, Keeper of the Privy Seal and Member of the Grand Council of the Crown. The principal assessors were also present, and a crowd had collected all round the platforms. Joan was brought out to a tribune facing the prelates; at her side was the usher, Jean Massieu, who was, as always, delegated to accompany her.

A sermon was preached to her, for which office Master Guillaume Erard had been chosen, a university man, a friend of Cauchon, and politically devoted to the English cause; he was to die in England, in 1439.

Isambart de la Pierre: "I was present at the first preaching to Joan which was done by Master Guillaume Erard who took as his text: the branch can produce no fruits if it stay not on the vine—

saying that in France there never had been such a monster as Joan was, who was a magician, heretic, schismatic, and that the King who was favourable to her was like unto her in that he had tried to recover his kingdom with the help of such a heretical woman. He added, 'Because of that, I believe that they were moved, among other things, by the desire to defame the royal majesty'." (R.226) This impression was confirmed by other witnesses, such as Martin Ladvenu and Jean Massieu himself.

Jean Massieu: "When she was brought to Saint-Ouen, to be preached to by Master Guillaume Erard, during the preaching, at about half way, when Joan had been greatly blamed by the preacher's words, he began to shout in a loud voice, saying: 'Ah! France, thou art much abused, thou hast always been the most Christian country; and Charles, who calls himself King and of thee ruler, has adhered like a heretic and schismatic to the words and deeds of a woman vain and defamed and of all dishonour full; and not him only but all the clergy in his obedience and lordship, by whom she was examined and not corrected, as she has said'. . . . Then, addressing himself to Joan, he said, raising his finger: 'It is to thee, Joan, that I speak, and I tell thee that thy King is a heretic and schismatic.' To which she answered: 'By my faith, sir, with respect, I dare to tell you and swear to you on pain of my life that he is the noblest Christian of all the Christians, and who better loves the faith and the Church, and is not such as you say.' Then the preacher said to me, 'Make her be silent.' " (R.227)

We read as follows in the record of this session: "After his sermon the preacher said to Joan: 'Here be my lords the judges who many times have summoned and required of you that you submit all your deeds and sayings to our Holy Mother the Church, and that in those deeds and sayings there be many things which, as it seems to the clerks, were not good to say and maintain.' "

JOAN: I will answer you. As for the matter of submission to the Church, I have answered on that point; of all the works I have accomplished, let them be sent to Rome to our Holy Father the Sovereign Pontiff, in whom, and in God first, I trust. As for my sayings and deeds, I have done them as from God. And with them I charge no man, neither my King nor any other; and if fault there be, it is in me and no other.

Question: Will you revoke all your sayings and deeds which are reproved by the clerks?

JOAN: I abide by God and our Holy Father the pope.

The text of the record continues here: "And it was said to her that this did not suffice, and that to go for the pope to such a great distance could not be done, that the Ordinaries (diocesan bishops) were judges, each in his own diocese, and that it was necessary that she throw herself upon the Holy Church and that she abide by what the clerks and other learned men said and had determined on her sayings and deeds."

It should be noted here that in Joan's own epoch there were several precedents for what she asked: heretics who, having appealed to the Pope, were in fact taken before his court in Rome; in fact that was the rule in cases of judgment by the Inquisition.

Guillaume Erard repeated his exhortation three times. Here follows what Massieu, charged with reading to Joan the form of abjuration which she was called upon to sign, had to say: "When Joan was required to sign this document (*cédule*) there was a great murmuring among those who were present, to the point that I heard the bishop say to someone: 'You will make reparation for that' ('You shall pay for that') asserting that he had been insulted and that he would proceed no further unless he received an apology. Meanwhile, I warned Joan of the danger which threatened her in the matter of signing this abjuration document. I saw well that Joan understood neither the document nor the danger which threatened her. Then Joan, pressed to sign, answered: 'Let this paper be seen by the clerks and by the Church into whose hands I must be put. If they advise me that I should sign it, and to do as I am told, I will do it willingly.' Then Master Guillaume Erard said to her: 'Do it now, if not this day shalt thou end thy days by fire.' Then Joan answered that she would rather sign than be burnt, and at that moment there was a great tumult in the crowd which was there and stones were thrown. By whom? I know not." (R.227–228)

Other details were given by one who was on the prelates' tribune, Jean Monnet who was then clerk, that is secretary to Master Jean Beaupère: "I was at the sermon preached at Saint-Ouen and was myself on the tribune, seated at the feet of master Jean Beaupère. When the sermon was finished, as they began to read the sentence, Joan said that if she was advised by the clerks according to their conscience as it would seem to her (as best she could judge), she would willingly do what she was advised. That heard, the Bishop of Beauvais asked the cardinal of England, who was there, what, given Joan's submission, he should do. The cardinal then answered the bishop that he should admit Joan to penitence. Thereupon the sentence which they had started to read was withdrawn and Joan was admitted to penitence (received as a penitent). I saw at the time a *cédule* of abjuration which was read, and it seems to me that it was a little *cédule* of five or six lines: and I remember that she threw herself upon the conscience of her judges as to whether she ought to recant or not." (R.228–229)

The intervention of the English in this scene was constant, as it was behind the scenes throughout the trial. This was attested by Haimond de Macy: "Some time thereafter (i.e., after the above scene of May 13th) I was still in Rouen. Joan was taken to a place before Saint-Ouen where was preached to her a sermon by Master Nicolas Midy. (Here he is confusing the occasions; Midy was to preach the sermon at the Vieux-Marché.) Among other things he said to her, as I heard, 'Joan, we have such pity for you: you must retract what you have said or we shall hand you over to secular justice.' But she answered that she had done nothing bad and that she believed in the twelve articles of the faith and in the ten precepts of the Decalogue, saying thereafter that she referred her case to the court of Rome and would believe all that the Holy Church believed. Despite that, she was hard pressed to retract; but she said to them: 'You take great pains to lead me astray that, and, to avoid the danger she would do all that they wanted. Then the secretary of the King of England who was there, called Laurent Calot, drew from his sleeve a little written *cédule* which he held out to Joan that she might sign it; and she answered that she could neither read nor write. Despite which this Laurent Calot, secretary, handed Joan the paper and a pen that she might sign, and by way of derision Joan drew a circle. Then Laurent Calot seized Joan's hand with the pen in it and made Joan make a mark which I no longer remember."

Laurent Calot was a man well-known in other aspects: secretary to the King of England, he several times signed the official acts for the provisioning of the English armies in France and he was an intimate of the Earl of Warwick, often a guest at his house, as witness the Beauchamp Household Book.

What exactly had Joan abjured?

The record is very brief on the circumstances in which Joan made her submission: "As the sentence was begun to be read, she said that she would hold all that the judges and the Church said or pronounced, saying that in all she would obey our order. She said several times that since the men of the Church said that the apparitions and revelations she said she had had were not such as should be maintained or believed in, she would not maintain them and in all referred herself to Holy Mother Church and to us, judges. Then, in the presence of the above-named and in view of a great multitude of clerks and people she made and produced her revocation and abjuration according to the form of a *cédule* which was read to her, written in French, which she repeated: and signed this *cédule* with her own hand under the form which follows." (C.388–389)

Now the *cédule* of abjuration which follows in the record is a very long document (forty-seven lines of type in the French version) in which Joan accuses herself in great detail of having 'feigned lyingly to have had revelations and apparitions from God", of having blasphemed God and his saints, of having worn "Clothes dissolute, mis-shapen and indecent, against natural decency", of having "desired cruel effusion of human blood . . . despised God and his sacraments . . . been a schismatic and many ways erred from the faith. . . ." She declares that she "abjures, detests, denies, and entirely renounces and separates herself from" her "crimes and errors". (C.388–389)

But during the Trial of Rehabilitation the notaries and other witnesses revealed the existence of another *cédule* of abjuration, differing from the one contained in the official record of the trial.

Nicolas Taquel: "I was present in Rouen when the first preaching was delivered, but I was not on the tribune with the other notaries. I was, however, near enough and in a place where I could hear what was done and said. I remember well that I saw Joan when the *cédule* of abjuration was read to her. There were in all six lines of coarse handwriting. This letter (*sic*) of abjuration was in French, beginning with 'I, Joan, etc.' "

Another witness, Guillaume de la Chambre, confirmed this evidence: "I was present at the sermon made by Master Guillaume Erard. I do not remember the abjuration which Joan made, although she had much deferred making it. Master Guillaume Erard, however, decided her to make it and telling her that she should do what she was advised, that afterwards she would be delivered from prison; and it was on this condition and not otherwise that she did it, reading thereafter another little *cédule* containing six or seven lines on a sheet of paper folded in two. I was so near that I could easily see the lines and how they were disposed." (R.60–61)

Better than anybody the usher Jean Massieu, charged with reading aloud the form of abjuration, could recall the scene: "In what concerns the abjuration, when she was preached to by Master Guillaume Erard at Saint-Ouen, Erard held in his hand a *cédule* of abjuration and said to Joan: 'Thou shalt abjure and sign this *cédule.*' Then this *cédule* was handed to me that I might read it and I read it to Joan; and I well remember that in this *cédule* it was noted that in the future she would no longer carry arms nor wear man's clothes, nor shorn hair, and many other things which I no longer remember. And I know well that this *cédule* contained about eight lines and not more. And I know absolutely that it was not that of which mention is made in the proceedings, for that which I read to her is different from that which was inserted into the proceedings, and it was the former which Joan signed." (R.62)

As a result of this the judges of the Trial of Rehabilitation called Thomas de Courcelles, who had drawn up in form the record of the Trial of Condemnation, to give explanations of the real nature of the abjuration:

Question: Who composed the *cédule* which is contained in the proceedings and which begins with "I, Joan, etc."?

COURCELLES: I do not know. Nor do I know that it was read to Joan or that it was explained to her. A sermon was preached to her at Saint-Ouen by Master Guillaume Erard: I was on the tribune behind the prelates. I do not, however, remember the preacher's words excepting that he said "the pride of this woman". Afterwards the bishop began to read the sentence. I do not remember what was said to Joan nor what she answered. However, I remember well that Master Nicolas de Venderès made a *cédule* which began with, "When the eye of the heart", but if that be the one which is contained in the proceedings, I know not. I do not know if I saw this *cédule* in the hands of Master Nicolas before the Maid's abjuration, or after, but I believe it was before. And I did hear it said that some of those present spoke to the Bishop of Beauvais because he did not apply his sentence and admitted Joan to repentance. But as for the words spoken and who spoke them, I do not remember." (R.61–63)

However wanting in precision were these explanations given by Courcelles whose memory, at the Trial of Rehabilitation, proved grievously faulty whenever his own actions were in question, what he did say was enough to establish that there had been a substitution of texts. The *cédule* inserted into the official proceedings was not the one which had actually been read to Joan at Saint-Ouen. The promoter of the Rehabilitation, Simon Chapitault, in his summing-up, declared that the document in the record was an abjuration "artificially fabricated".

In our own time Father Doncoeur believed that he had found the text of the *cédule*, which was actually read to Joan and signed by her with a cross, in the text of the abjuration contained in the Orleans MS.; a document of six or seven lines, which corresponds with what Jean Massieu said. This would be quite likely if, as may be presumed, that MS. is a copy of the notes taken during the hearing by Guillaume Manchon. (See Commentary, p. 227.) The question, at all events, remains undecided: not all historians are of that opinion.

The circumstances in which the "abjuration" occurred were recounted by various witnesses whose words evoke Joan's curious attitude and the misunderstandings which arose between Cauchon and the English who were present.

Guillaume Manchon: "Two sentences had been prepared: one of abjuration and another of condemnation which the bishop had with him, and while the bishop was reading the sentence of condemnation, Master Nicolas Loiseleur was telling Joan that she should do what she had been told and accept woman's clothes. And as there was then a small interval of time, one of the English who was there told the bishop that he was betraying (them). The bishop answered him that he lied. And meanwhile Joan answered that she was ready to obey the Church. They then made her speak an abjuration which was read to her, and I do not know if she spoke it after whoever was reading it, or whether, once it had been read to her, she said that she accepted it. She was laughing.* The executioner was there with a cart in the vicinity, waiting for her to be delivered to him, to be burnt. I did not see the letter of abjuration," he added, "but it was written after the conclusion of the deliberations and before she came to that place. I do not remember that this letter of abjuration was ever explained to Joan nor that she had been given to understand or read it, excepting at the very moment when she made that abjuration." (R.60)

Another witness, Guillaume du Desert, an assessor at the trial, declared: "I was present at the sermon preached at Saint Ouen.

* It could mean only "smiling". —E.H.

There I saw and heard the abjuration made by Joan submitting herself to the determination, judgment and mandate of the Church. There was there an English doctor who was present at the sermon, and who was displeased at Joan's abjuration being accepted. And as she was laughing while uttering certain words of that abjuration, he said to the Bishop of Beauvais, the judge, that he did ill to admit this abjuration and that it was a derision. The bishop, furious, answered that he lied; and that, being judge in a case of (the) faith, he must rather seek her salvation than her death.

That laugh of Joan's, so unexpected at such a moment, needs an explanation. It may be that we can find it in a detail given above (and provided that the witnesses may not have recalled correctly the precise moment of her laughter), to wit that Joan—we have seen that she could sign her name—was obliged by the King of England's secretary to sign with a cross. It will be recalled that this cross was the sign agreed upon with those of her own side to warn them not to believe the contents of a letter. It was surely curious that the English should now be making her use it to sign a document whose contents she considered false. This may be the explanation of her laughter which, moreover, must have exasperated the English present who, baffled by Cauchon's attitude, saw their prey escaping them. There was a complete muddle of misunderstandings.

Jean Fave, an eye-witness of the scene: "After the first preaching . . . according to what I heard said, the leading Englishmen were very angry with the Bishop of Beauvais, the doctors and other assessors at the trial, because she had not been convicted, and condemned and delivered over to execution. I even heard it said that some of the English, in their indignation, raised their swords to strike the bishop and the doctors on their way back from the castle—but they did not strike them—saying that the King had ill spent his money on them. I heard people tell, moreover, that when the Earl of Warwick was complaining to the bishop and the doctors saying that all was going badly for the King because Joan was escaping them, one of them answered him: 'My lord, have no care, we shall catch her yet.' "

Following this event and contrary to her expectation, Joan was to be condemned to imprisonment for life. In the course of the Rehabilitation the judges showed surprise at this, and asked Guillaume Manchon this question:

Question: Who urged the judges to condemn her to perpetual imprisonment, whereas they had promised her that she would not be punished?

MANCHON: I think that happened because of the diversity of powers (the two powers who then shared France between them) and because they were afraid that she might escape.

And in answer to later questioning Manchon added: "On leaving the preaching at Saint-Ouen, after the Maid's abjuration, for as much as Loiseleur said to her: 'Joan, it has been well for you this day, if it please God, and you have saved your soul,' she asked: "Come now, among you men of the Church, take me to your prisons and let me be no longer in the hands of these English.' Whereupon my lord of Beauvais answered: 'Take her to where you found her'; wherefore she was taken back to the castle whence she had set out." (R.231)

Cauchon's "Take her to where you found her" was Joan's real sentence of condemnation. For there is a fact which dominates the whole trial, the fact that Joan was detained in a lay prison and guarded by English warders, while being tried for heresy: now she should have been held in an ecclesiastical prison—in the prison cells of the archbishopric where she would have been guarded by women. This is the fundamental contradiction which makes it impossible to see this trial as a normal trial for heresy—although Cauchon insisted that it was so—and which underlines, quite clearly, its political character. Joan was a political prisoner whose enemies contrived to get her dealt with as a heretic in order to destroy the prestige which her personal saintliness and her extraordinary exploits had made for her.

Now Cauchon, as an advocate experienced in dealing with the law, knew that, according to the rules of the Inquisition courts, none but those who, having recanted their heresy, had relapsed, could be condemned to suffer death by burning. And having succeeded in making the wearing of man's clothes (it is certain, from the evidence given by Jean Massieu, that the wearing of such clothes was expressly mentioned in the *cédule*) the symbol of Joan's failure to submit to the Church, he might be fairly sure that she would, without much delay, show herself to have relapsed by retaining her male attire. Events were soon to prove him right.

The importance given to the matter of her male attire for the conclusion of Joan's trial and condemnation was felt and understood by an observer as impartial as he was well-informed, Aeneas Sylvius

Piccolomini, the future Pope Pius II. He summed up the business in his Memoirs, as follows: "It is known that, taken in the war, the Maid was sold to the English for ten thousand gold crowns and conveyed to Rouen. In that place she was diligently examined to discover whether she used sortileges (spells) or diabolical aid or whether she erred in any way in her religion. Nothing worthy to be censured was found in her, excepting the male attire which she wore. And that was not judged deserving of the extreme penalty. Taken back to her prison she was threatened with death if she resumed the wearing of man's clothes." (Q.517) And he added that her gaolers brought none but male attire.

Two different versions have been given concerning the male attire which Joan was to resume on the following Monday, May 27th. One by Jean Massieu according to which Joan, on that day, when she woke up, found only a suit of man's clothes, her gaolers having hidden her woman's clothes: "That day, after dinner, in the presence of the council of the Church, she put off male attire and assumed female attire, as she was ordered to do. It was then the Thursday or Friday after Pentecost, and the male attire was put into a bag in the same room. And when came the Sunday morning following, which was the day of the Trinity, and she had to rise, as she told it to me, she asked the Englishmen, her guards, 'Take off my irons and I will get up.' And then one of the Englishmen took away her woman's clothes which she had upon her, and they emptied out the bag in which were the man's clothes, and flung this attire upon her, saying, 'Get thou up.' And hid the woman's clothes in the bag. And, by what she said, she put on the male attire which they had given her, saying, 'Gentlemen, you know that it is forbidden me, without fail I will not wear it.' And nevertheless, would they not give her other, so that in this argument they remained until the hour of noon; and finally, for the necessity of the body, was she constrained to go out, and to wear that attire, and after she had returned within would they not give her other, notwithstanding the supplications or requests which she made them."

The other version is given by several witnesses. Among others is one called Pierre Cusquel, a burgher of Rouen who, apparently, was a master mason in the service of the "master of masonry works of the castle"; for, he says, it was by that officer's permission that he twice entered Joan's cell and was able to talk to her. He declared: "People were saying that her condemnation had no other cause excepting that she had resumed man's clothes; and that she had not worn and was not wearing this male attire excepting in order not to give herself to the soldiers with whom she was. Once, in the prison, I asked her why she was wearing this male attire and that was what she answered me." (R.232)

Martin Ladvenu's evidence is in the same sense: "As for knowing whether anyone approached her secretly at night, I heard it from Joan's own lips that a great English lord entered her prison and tried to take her by force. That was the cause, she said, of her resuming man's clothes."

Again, there is Isambart de la Pierre: "After she had renounced and abjured and resumed man's clothes, I and several others were present when Joan excused herself for having again put on man's clothes, saying and affirming publicly that the English had had much wrong and violence done to her in prison when she was dressed in woman's clothes. And in fact I saw her tearful, her face covered with tears, disfigured and outraged in such sort that I had pity and compassion on her." (R.268)

THE TRIAL FOR RELAPSE

Sunday, May 27th, Cauchon learned that Joan had resumed male attire. On the following day he went to the prison, accompanied by the vice-Inquisitor and several assessors. The following is from the official record:

"The Monday following, 28 of the month of May, on the day following Holy Trinity, we, judges aforesaid, went to the place of Joan's prison to see her state and disposition. Were present the lords and Masters Nicolas de Venderès, Thomas de Courcelles, Brother Isambart de la Pierre, Guillaume Haiton, Jacques Camus, Nicolas Bertin, Julien Floquet and John Gray.

"Joan was dressed in a man's clothes, to wit tunic, hood and gippon (a short robe worn by men) and other man's clothes, attire which on our order she had formerly left off and had taken women's clothes: therefore did we question her to know when and for what cause she had again put on man's attire."

JOAN: I not long since resumed man's attire and left off woman's attire.

Question: Why have you assumed this male attire and who made you take it?

JOAN: I have taken it of my own will. I have taken it because it is more licit and fitting to have man's clothes since I am with men than to have woman's clothes. I have resumed it because what had been promised me has not been observed, to wit that I should go to mass and should receive the Body of Christ and should be taken out of irons.

PIERRE CAUCHON: Have you not made abjuration and promised especially not to resume man's clothes?

JOAN: I would rather die than remain in irons; but if it be permitted me to go to mass and I be taken out of irons and that I be put in a pleasant (*gracieuse*) prison, and that I have women, I will be good and will do what the Church wishes. (The item "have women" is down in the French Minute but not in the official text of the proceedings.)

CAUCHON: Since that Thursday, have you heard the voices of Saints Catherine and Margaret?

JOAN: Yes.

CAUCHON: What did they tell you?

JOAN: God has sent to me by Saints Catherine and Margaret great pity for the mighty betrayal to which I consented in making abjuration and revocation to save my life, and that I was damning myself to save my life.

(Here the clerk has noted in the margin, *responsio mortifera*, mortal (fatal) answer.)

JOAN: Before Thursday my voices had told me what I was going to do that day, and what I then did. My voices told me, when I was on the scaffold and the tribune before the people, that I should reply boldly to that preacher who was then preaching. He was a false preacher and he said I had done many things which I have not done. If I said that God had not sent me, I should damn myself; it is true that God sent me. My voices have since told me that I did a great injury in confessing that I had not done well in what I had done. All that I said and revoked that Thursday, I did only because of fear of the fire.

CAUCHON: Do you believe that the voices which come to you are those of Saints Catherine and Margaret?

JOAN: Yes, and that they are from God.

CAUCHON: And the crown which you mentioned?

JOAN: In all, I told you the truth at the trial, as best I could.

CAUCHON: You said, upon the scaffold and the tribune, before us,
  judges, and before others and before the people, when you made
  abjuration, that it was falsely (lyingly) that you had boasted that
  those voices were the voices of Saints Catherine and Margaret.
JOAN: I did not mean to do and say so. I did not say or mean to
  revoke my apparitions, to wit that they were Saints Catherine
  and Margaret. And all I have done I did for fear of the fire and I
  revoked nothing but it (the revocation) was against the truth. I
  would rather make my penitence once and for all, that is to say
  die, than to suffer any longer the pain of being in prison. I have
  never done anything against God and against the faith, whatever
  I may have been made to revoke; and for what was contained
  in the *cédule* of abjuration, I did not understand it. I did not mean
  to revoke anything unless provided it pleased God. If the judges
  wish it I will resume woman's clothes; for the rest, I will do
  nothing about it.

"That heard," continues the record, "we went away from her
to proceed thereafter according to law* and reason." (C.395-399)

Isambart de la Pierre, who was present at this exchange, adds
an epilogue which, needless to say, does not appear in the official
record: "Before all present," he says, "when she was reputed heretic,
obstinate and relapsed, she answered publicly: 'If you, my lords
of the Church, had kept and guarded me in your prisons, peradventure would it not be so with me.' After the issue and end
of this session and instance the lord Bishop of Beauvais said to
the English who awaited without: 'Farewell, it is done.'"
(R.268)

In one of his depositions at the Trial of Rehabilitation Martin
Ladvenu also recalled the bishop's attitude at the time; and in that
attitude saw, in his opinion, proof of the bishop's partisanship:
"The first (sign): When the bishop offered himself as judge, he
commanded that Joan be kept in a secular prison and in the hands of
her mortal enemies, although he could very well have had her
detained and guarded in an ecclesiastical prison. As it was, he
permitted, from the beginning of the trial until the consummation,
that she be tormented and treated cruelly in a secular prison. Moreover, at the first session and instance, the said bishop required and
asked the advice of the whole court to know which was the most

* Or "according to right and reason".—E.H.

fitting, to keep her in a secular prison or in the prisons of the Church. Whereupon it was decided that it was more decent to keep her in the ecclesiastical prisons than the others. Then answered this bishop that he would not do that for fear of displeasing the English.

"The second sign is that, the day when the bishop with some others declared her a heretic, recidivist and backslider into her misdeeds, because she had within the prison resumed male attire, coming out of the prison, he perceived the Earl of Warwick and a multitude of English about him, to whom, laughing, he said aloud, intelligibly: 'Farewell, farewell, it is done, farewell' or words to that effect."* (R.266)

Cauchon wasted no time in bringing Joan to trial for her "relapse". After the interrogation set out above, on May 28th, he summoned the principal assessors to meet on the 29th, and gave them a brief *exposé* of the state of her case: after the solemn preaching and admonitions addressed to her, Joan had renounced the error of her ways and signed an abjuration with her own hand. . . . However, at the suggestion of the devil she had started saying again that her voices and spirits had come to her, and having rejected woman's clothes, had resumed the wearing of male attire. Which was why he was now asking the assessors to give their opinion on what should now be done.

The first asked to speak happened to be Master Nicolas de Venderès, the man who had drawn up the false abjuration document, the one which was not read to Joan. As may well be imagined, his opinion was clear: Joan must be held to be a heretic and without further delay handed over to the secular arm, "with a recommendation to be gentle with her". This was a conventional formula (employed by Inquisition courts) and everyone knew what it implied.

But Giles de Duremort, abbot of Fécamp, asked next to give his opinion, introduced a request which must have made Cauchon uneasy. "It seems to me," he said, "that she is a relapsed heretic and that the word of God should be preached to her; that the *cédule* which was read to her shall be read to her again and explained; that done, the judges will have to declare her a heretic and abandon her to secular justice."

Of the forty assessors listed as giving their opinion in the text of the proceedings, after the first two had spoken, only two were for passing sentence at once: Denis Gastinel—a canon of Rouen

---

* Farewell, farewell are in English in the text. The words I have translated literally by farewell are *faites bonne chère*.—E.H.

who was, as we have seen, in receipt of regular payments from the English crown; and Jean Pinchon, archdeacon of Jouy-en-Josas, with canonical stalls in Paris and Rouen. All the rest, including those who had shown themselves most implacable to Joan, rallied to the abbot of Fécamp's opinion, some going further—Isambart de la Pierre, for example—and insisting that it should be made perfectly clear to Joan that the matter was one of life or death for her. Thus, of forty-two, thirty-nine demanded that more light be thrown, in the first place, on the abjuration question.

Whereupon—we are still quoting the official proceedings— "Having heard the opinion of each one, we, the judges, thanked them and thereafter concluded that the said Joan be proceeded against as a relapsed heretic according to law and reason." (C.408)

The assessors having only a consultative voice, it is perfectly obvious that Cauchon was not going to hamper himself with a formality which would be doubly awkward for him, since the *cédule* which had been put into the file of the proceedings was not the one which had been read to Joan.

During the afternoon of the same day a missive was sent, by the notaries, to all the assessors, informing them that Joan, having fallen again into the errors which she had abjured, would be taken the next day to the Old Market Place in Rouen, at eight o'clock in the forenoon, to be declared "relapsed, heretic and excommunicate".

COMMENTARY

The reader will already have formed some idea of the manner in which the proceedings of this trial were drawn up, from the texts quoted in this chapter. While Joan was being questioned, the notaries wrote down her answers; and they were also responsible for the record or minute of each session with such details as the list of persons present, the place in which the court was sitting, and so forth. The notaries also added to the dossier all other papers involved in the proceedings, assignations and convocations addressed to the assessors, letters from people who were implicated in some way or other, these ranging from the King of England when, for example, he entrusted judging Joan, a prisoner-of-war, to Pierre Cauchon, down to the usher Jean Massieu, charged with the task of producing the prisoner to the court whenever it sat in public, and of returning her to her cell thereafter.

The whole formed a stout file which was not to be arranged in formal order, as we can tell from the texts, until after Joan's death. By "arranged in formal order" we mean what follows: all the questions and answers were translated into Latin and the diverse papers, after classification according to the actual order of the proceedings, were copied into a register which the notaries were then called upon to "authenticate". This authentication consisted in signing the bottom of every page to attest the conformity of the text with their own notes, and to prevent the addition of any document or writing whatsoever, contrary to juridical custom. At the end of the file they placed their "sign manual", that is a signature accompanied by a flourish which was personal to each clerk, a copy of which was deposed at the Officiality, the seat of the archbishopric's ecclesiastical court, exactly as, nowadays, we depose a copy of our signature at the bank when opening an account.

This formality, it should be noted, assumed its full import in the case of the proceedings of the trial of condemnation, when it came to the matter of those *Posthumous Informations* (Chapter 8) which Cauchon wanted to integrate into the file itself. For the simple fact of their not being included in the authenticated pages and of their being filed after the signs manual of the notaries, is a proof of their misleading character: the notaries were able to plead the illegality of what was proposed to them in refusing, out of professional honesty, to carry out Cauchon's orders. The bishop was obliged to resign himself to having the *Posthumous Informations* put into the file only outside the limits of the authenticated proceedings. He was able to substitute a bogus *cédule* for the real one, by doing it without the knowledge of the notaries at a time when the file was composed of loose leaves not yet copied into the register; but he was not able to do likewise with those "informations" which had nothing whatever to do with the declarations properly heard or received by the court in session.

We know from the depositions of Guillaume Manchon that there were five authenticated copies of the proceedings of the Trial of Condemnation. Three were for the Inquisitor, one for the King of England, and one for Cauchon. Of these five, three have come down to us. One, the most carefully produced, written on parchment, is now in the library of the National Assembly; a facsimile reproduction of this was made, thanks to J. Marchand, the chief librarian, and published in 1956. The two others are in the Bibliothèque Nationale (Fonds Latin 5965 and 5966). Several copies of the original five were made, but they have not the value as juridical instruments given to the remaining three originals by the notaries' signatures.

It was this official and authentic text of the Trial of Condemnation in Latin which was published by the scholar Jules Quicherat, forming the first volume of that important work which anyone wishing to know about Joan will always have to refer to (*Procès de condamnation et de réhabilitation de Jeanne d'Arc, dite la Pucelle*, Paris 1841–1849). The publication of this work marks the beginning of any real knowledge of Joan of Arc, in her person and in the events of her life. For it is self-evident that, so long as the documents in the two cases remained in MS. only, then only those few scholars who had access to them, and who knew both mediaeval Latin and palaeography, could be exactly informed as to Joan's answers, and what the people who knew her really said about her when they gave evidence. Until Quicherat published his great book, the story of Joan could only be followed in the works of chroniclers, whose information, gathered at second-hand, could not have the same value as a direct reading of the questions and answers at the trials. In point of fact only one scholar, in the seventeenth century, had both the idea and the occasion to read the MSS. of the trial proceedings. This was Edmond Richer, whose work was not published in his lifetime and was not, in fact, to be published until the twentieth century (1911–12) by Canon P. H. Dunand. In its MS. form, however, Richer's work served as the basis for Lenglet-Dufresnoy's *Histoire de Jeanne d'Arc, vierge, heroine et martyre d'Etat, suscitée par la Providence pour rétablir le monarchie françoise*, which appeared in 1753; but the abbé Lenglet-Dufresnoy made but indifferent use of it.

All this explains, of course, the errors, nonsense, and in general the want of exact knowledge of Joan, which were the rule until the nineteenth century. We have dealt elsewhere with this aspect of the matter (see our *Jeanne d'Arc*, Ed. du Seuil, 1959), and a more thorough treatment of the same subject will be found in a scholarly work by Pierre Marot (*Memorial de la Réhabilitation*), published in 1956 (see Commentary to Chapter 10).

Before Quicherat only one scholar, Clement L'Averdy, had had the idea of publishing *Extraits des manuscrits des procès*; but his publication, which appeared in 1790, was incomplete and remained little known.

In our own time we have at our disposal a publication of the highest order in which to study the Trial of Condemnation; this we

owe to Pierre Tisset and Yvonne Lanhers; it appears under
the aegis of the *Société de l'Histoire de France*, and replaces
Quicherat, now unobtainable excepting in the major libraries. This
re-edition gives not only the Latin text of the proceedings, but
also that of the "French Minute".

For in fact, while Joan was being questioned, the notary Guillaume Manchon was taking down her answers in French; he had
kept for himself, among his personal papers, the MS. of the questions
and answers in French (he refers to this MS. as the *notula in gallico*),
and he handed this over to the judge at the Trial of Rehabilitation,
on December 12, 1455, when this last trial was opening. Now
of this French Minute, which has unfortunately disappeared, copies
were made, and these are to be found notably in two of the MSS.;
the so-called Urfé MS., preserved in the Bibliothèque Nationale
(Fonds Latin 8838), and another which is now kept at the Bibliothèque d'Orléans and bears the number 518. It is probably in this
French text that the least attenuated echo of Joan's own language
is to be found, a language full of freshness and which is well worth
reading in the original text despite the difficulties which that may
entail for us.

Excellent translations of the Trial of Condemnation have been
made, among others those of Pierre Champion (Paris, 1920–21, 2
vols.), which had both Latin text and translation; and of Robert
Brasillach, which happily combines a translation of the Latin with
the text of the French Minute (Paris, Gallimard, 1939, and often
reprinted).

8

DEATH

On Wednesday, May 30th, in the morning there came to Joan in her cell Brother Martin Ladvenu, chosen by Cauchon to inform her of the fate in store for her. A young Brother of Ladvenu's convent, Brother Jean Toutmouillé, went with him and he has left us an account of the scene:

"The day that Joan was abandoned to secular justice and delivered up to be burned, I went in the morning to the prison with Brother Martin Ladvenu, whom the Bishop of Beauvais had sent to her to announce her imminent death and to induce in her true contrition and penitence, and also to hear her confession. The which the said Ladvenu did very thoroughly and charitably. And when he announced to the poor woman the death which she must die that day, that so had her judges ordained, and understood and heard the hard and cruel death which was almost upon her, she began to cry out grievously and pitiably pulled and tore out her hair. 'Alas! Do they treat me thus horribly and cruelly, so that my body, clean and whole, which was never corrupted, must be this day consumed and reduced to ashes! Ah! I had rather seven times be decapitated than to be thus burned. Alas! Had I been in the ecclesiastical prison to which I submitted myself, and been guarded by men of the Church and not by my enemies and adversaries, it had not so wretchedly happened to me as now it has! Ah! I appeal before God, the Great Judge, from the great wrongs and grievances (*ingravances*) being done to me.' And she complained marvellously in that place of the oppressions and violences which had been done to her in the prison by the gaolers and by others who had been let in against her.

"After these complaints came the aforesaid bishop to whom she immediately said: 'Bishop, I die by you.' He began to remonstrate with her, saying: 'Ah! Joan, have patience herein, you die because you held not to what you had promised and are returned to your first evil-doing.' And the poor Maid answered him, 'Alas! if you had put me in the prisons of the court of the Church, and into the hands of competent and fitting ecclesiastical keepers, this would not have happened. That is why I appeal against you before God.' That done, I went out and heard no more." (R.234–235)

This deposition is completed by that of the usher Jean Massieu:

"The Wednesday morning, the day that Joan died, Brother Martin Ladvenu heard her confession, and Joan's confession heard, he sent me to the Bishop of Beauvais to notify him that he had heard her in confession and asked that the sacrament of the Eucharist be given her. The bishop called together several persons on that matter. After their deliberation, he told me to tell Brother Martin that he was to give her the sacrament of the Eucharist and all that she asked for. . . . The Body of Jesus Christ was carried to her irreverently without stole or light, at which Brother Martin, who had confessed her, was ill-pleased. Wherefore I was sent back to fetch a stole and the light, and so Brother Martin administered it. And that done, she was taken to the Old Market, and at her side were Brother Martin and me, accompanied by more than eight hundred men of war with axes and swords, and she, being at the Old Market and after the preaching during which she showed great constancy and very peaceably listened to it, showing great sign and evidence and clear appearance of her contrition, penitence and fervour of faith, as much by her pious and devout lamentations and invocations of the blessed Trinity and of the blessed glorious Virgin Mary and of all the blessed saints of Paradise, naming expressly several of these saints in the which devotions, lamentations and true confessions of faith, as in requesting also of all manner of people of what condition and estate soever, whether of her own party or the other, pardon most humbly, requesting that they would pray for her, forgiving them the evil that they had done her, she persevered and continued a very long space of time, as about half an hour, and so to the end, at which the judges there present and even several Englishmen were provoked to tears and to weeping and indeed most bitterly wept at it." (R.236–237)

The text of the Condemnation proceedings gives the official account of the scene, which took place in the Old Market Place of Rouen, near to the church of Saint-Sauveur. In this are particularly mentioned, as being with Cauchon and the vice-Inquisitor Jean Lemaitre, Louis of Luxembourg, Bishop of Thérouanne, Jean de Mailly, Bishop of Noyon, Jean de Chatillon, André Marguerie, Nicolas de Venderès, Raoul Roussel, Denis Gastinel, Guillaume

Haiton—all of them men in whom there is no difficulty in discovering the most ardent partisans of the English cause. And there were some others, like Guillaume le Boucher, Jean Alepée, Pierre de Houdenc and, of course, the University Masters. Among these were Pierre Maurice; and above all Nicolas Midy whose task it was to preach a final sermon to Joan.

After his sermon, the definitive sentence was spoken by Pierre Cauchon himself:

"We declare that thou, Joan, commonly called the Maid, art fallen into diverse errors and diverse crimes of schism, idolatry, invocation of devils and numerous others. . . . And thereafter, after abjuration of thine errors, it is evident that thou hast returned to those same errors and to those crimes, your heart having been beguiled by the author of schism and heresy. . . . Wherefore we declare thee relapsed and heretic." (C.411–412)

Joan should, at this point, have been conducted to the secular judges, who alone were qualified to decide the actual sentence and apply it. But Cauchon, in haste to have done with it, neglected that formality.

Martin Ladvenu: "It was evident, to the judges, that she had submitted herself to the determination of the Church and that she was a believer and Catholic and repentant, and it was by permission and on the order of the judges that I gave Joan the Body of Christ. She was handed over as relapsed to the secular judges, and I believe that had she gone over to the side of the English, she would not have been so treated. I am certain that after she had been abandoned by the Church, she was taken by the English soldiers who were there in great number, and without any sentence by the secular judges, although the sheriff of Rouen and the council of the lay court were there. I know it, for I was with Joan all the time from the castle until the moment when she yielded up the ghost and it was I who, on the order of the judges, administered to her the sacraments of penitence and of the Eucharist."

His evidence was confirmed by the sheriff's lieutenant, Laurent Guesdon: "I was at the last sermon delivered at the Old Market of Rouen; I was there with the sheriff for at the time I was lieutenant of the sheriff. The sentence was pronounced whereby Joan was abandoned to secular justice. As soon as possible after this sentence, immediately and without delay, she was delivered into the hands of the sheriff, and without the sheriff or myself, to whom it appertained to pronounce sentence, having pronounced one, the executioner, without further ado, seized Joan and took her to the place where the wood was ready and she was burned." (R.233–234)

Jean Massieu also bears witness to this haste: "While she was making her devotions and pious lamentations, I was hard-pressed by the English, and even by one of their captains, to leave her in their hands the sooner to put her to death, saying to me, who according to my understanding comforted her at the scaffold: 'What, priest, will you make us dine here?' And incontinent, without other form or sign of judgment, sent her to the fire, saying to the Master of the Work (executioner), 'Do thine office.' And so was she taken and bound, still continuing praises and lamentations to God and the saints, and whose last word, in departing this life, cried in a loud voice: 'Jesus'." (R.237)

The apparitor of the archiepiscopal court, Maugier Leparmentier, who had, it will be recalled, been sent for two weeks before this event to put Joan to the torture, was present: "The day when Joan was burned, the wood was got ready to burn her before the sermon was finished or the sentence had been pronounced. And no sooner the sentence uttered by the bishop, without any delay, she was taken to the fire, and I did not see that there was any sentence pronounced by the lay judge. But was at once taken to the fire. And in the fire she cried more than six times 'Jesus', and above all with her last breath she cried in a loud voice 'Jesus!' so that all present could hear her. Almost all wept with pity, and I have heard say that the ashes, after her burning, were gathered up and cast into the Seine."

The most detailed accounts of Joan's last moments are provided, as we might expect, by those who accompanied and supported her to the scaffold itself. There was, in the first place, the usher, Jean Massieu: "When she was abandoned by the Church I was still with her and with great devoutness she asked to have the cross. Hearing that, an Englishman who was present made a little cross of wood from the end of a stick, which he gave her and devoutly she received and kissed it, making pious lamentations to God our Redeemer who had suffered on the Cross, for our redemption, of which Cross she had sign and representation. And she put this cross into her bosom, between her flesh and her clothes, and furthermore asked humbly that I enable her to have the cross from the church so that she could have it continually before her eyes until death. And I so contrived that the parish clerk of Saint-Sauveur brought it to her. Which being brought, she embraced it long and closely and retained it until she was bound to the stake. Brother Isambart had gone with the parish clerk to fetch the cross. The pious woman asked, requested and begged me, as I was near her at her end, that I would go to the near-by church and fetch the cross to hold it raised right before her eyes until the threshold of death, that the cross which God hung upon be continually before her eyes in her lifetime. Being in the flames she ceased not until the end to proclaim and confess aloud the holy name of Jesus, imploring and invoking without cease the help of the saints in paradise. And what is more, in giving up the ghost and bowing her head, uttered the name of Jesus as a sign that she was fervent in the faith of God." (R.270)

Martin Ladvenu: "As to her great and admirable contrition, repentance and continual confession, she called still upon the name of Jesus and devoutly invoked the help of the saints in paradise, as Brother Isambart, who had supported her to her passing and addressed her on the way of salvation, has already deposed." (R.207)

Among other depositions touching her end, and they were numerous since that end was public, there is that of Jean Riquier, parish priest of Heudicourt at the time of the Rehabilitation. At the time of the Condemnation he was a boy of about fifteen who, as a chorister in the church of Rouen, moved much in that town's ecclesiastical circles: "Master Peter Maurice visited her in the morning, before she was brought to the sermon in the Old Market. And Joan said to him: 'Master Peter, where shall I be this evening?' And Master Peter answered her: 'Have you not good hope in God?' She said that she had and that with God's help she would be in paradise. That I had from Master Peter himself. When Joan saw the fire kindled she began to cry out in a loud voice 'Jesus, Jesus', and still until her death she cried 'Jesus'. And when she was dead, as the English feared lest it be said that she had escaped, they told the executioner to push back the fire a little so that those present could see her dead, that it be not said she had escaped. . . . I heard Master Jean Alepée, then canon of Rouen, present at Joan's execution, weeping copiously, say in my presence and the presence of those about me: 'I would that my soul were where I believe this woman's soul to be.' "

And here is what was being said among the people, passed down to us by the voice of the stone-mason Pierre Cusquel: "I was not present at the last preaching, and the condemnation and execution of

Joan," he said, "because my heart would not have been able to bear and suffer it, out of pity for Joan, but I did hear say that she received the Body of the Lord before her condemnation. . . . I heard say that Master Jean Tressard, secretary to the King of England, returning from Joan's execution afflicted and groaning, wept lamentably over what he had seen in that place and said indeed: 'We are all lost, for we have burnt a good and holy person,' and that he believed that her soul was in God's hands and that, when she was in the midst of the flames, she had still declaimed the name of the Lord Jesus. That was common repute and more or less all the people murmured that a great wrong and injustice had been done to Joan. . . . After Joan's death the English had the ashes gathered up and thrown into the Seine because they feared lest she escape or lest some say she had escaped." (R.240–241)

And there is the contrition of an Englishman, notably of the executioner Geoffroy Therage, as recounted by Brother Isambart de la Pierre: "One of the English, a soldier who detested her extraordinarily, and who had sworn that with his own hand he would bear a faggot to Joan's pyre, in the moment when he was doing so and heard Joan calling upon the name of Jesus in her last moment, stood stupefied and as if in ecstasy, and was taken thence to a tavern near the Old Market so that, drink helping, he might regain his senses. And after having eaten a meal with a Brother of the Order of Preaching Friars, this Englishman confessed, by the mouth of this Brother who was himself English, that he had sinned gravely and that he repented of what he had done against Joan whom he held to be a saintly woman for, as it seemed to him, this Englishman had himself seen, at the moment when Joan gave up the ghost, a white dove coming out on the side towards France. And the executioner, on the same day after the mid-day meal, came to the convent of the preaching friars and said to me, as to Brother Martin Ladvenu, that he greatly feared to be damned for he had burned a holy woman."

Jean Massieu: "I heard it said by Jean Fleury, clerk and writer to the sheriff, that the executioner had reported to him that once the body was burned by the fire and reduced to ashes, her heart remained intact and full of blood, and he told him to gather up the ashes and all that remained of her and to throw them into the Seine, which he did."

Isambart: "Immediately after the execution, the executioner came to me and my companion Martin Ladvenu, struck and moved to a marvellous repentance and terrible contrition, all in despair, fearing never to obtain pardon and indulgence from God for what he had done to that saintly woman; and said and affirmed this executioner that despite the oil, the sulphur and the charcoal which he had applied against Joan's entrails and heart, nevertheless he had not by any means been able to consume nor reduce to ashes the entrails nor the heart, at which was he as greatly astonished as by a manifest miracle." (R.270)

As for the feelings of the man who had managed the whole business, Pierre Cauchon, we know nothing unless we judge by the steps he took during the days following the execution and which seem to reveal in him at least a certain nervous irritability. There was first the imprisonment of the preaching friar Pierre Bosquier, condemned to prison on bread and water until the following Easter for having said, on the afternoon of the day of the execution, that they who had judged Joan had done ill. Then on June 7th Cauchon assembled some of the assessors and made them say what he would have liked Joan herself to say: that she had been misled and deceived by her voices. We need not doubt that Nicolas de Venderès, Thomas de Courcelles, Nicolas Loiseleur, Pierre Maurice, readily and abundantly said what was required of them: Joan said that her voice had told her that she would be liberated from prison and she had seen clearly and knew that she had been misled by them. . . . She had been deceived and would not have faith in her voices. . . . She referred the matter to the ecclesiastics to know whether they were good or bad spirits. . . . She said: "Truly, I see well that they have deceived me. . . ." It is unpleasant to find, among those who thus answered the judge's questions, Brother Martin Ladvenu and that same Brother Jean Toutmouillé who, obviously, had been overcome by Joan's lamentations when he went to announce to her that she was about to die by burning. At all events, Cauchon tried to get these Posthumous Informations inserted into the official record, but came up against an unexpected resistance, that of the notary Guillaume Manchon, who subsequently declared: "I was at the continuation of the trial until the end, saving at some examinations of people who spoke to him aside, like private persons. Nevertheless, my lord of Beauvais tried to constrain me to sign them, which thing I would not do." (R.243)

And in effect the MS. book of the proceedings, as it has come down to us in the three surviving copies already referred to, are significant in their arrangement: after the record of the definitive sentence, the

three notaries Guillaume Colles, called Boisguillaume, Guillaume
Manchon and Nicolas Taquel, in that order, appended, as was
customary, each a note of the registration, followed by signature
and sign manual. On the master MS., written on parchment, are
thereafter appended the red wax seals of the notary, the bishop and
the vice-Inquisitor. Then, on the following pages, are transcribed,
but this time without the notaries' signatures at the bottom of the
pages and without any note of registration, the Posthumous Informations. Thus we have proof of the illegality of a proceeding which the
notary, recovering some of his courage, refused to sanction: it was
really altogether too easy to put words into Joan's mouth after she
was dead.

Then again, on June 12th following, Cauchon obtained for
himself and the principal assessors "letters of warranty" from the
King of England. By these letters the King promises that: "On
the word of a King, if it come about that any one of the persons who
worked in the trial be brought to trial (summoned, sued) for that
trial or its dependences. . . . we will aid and defend, have aided and
defended in court of law and without, such persons at our own cost
and expense. . . ." One of the prelates who had taken an active
part in the trial, the Bishop of Noyon, Jean de Mailly, was greatly
embarrassed when, at the Trial of Rehabilitation, he was reminded
of these letters of warranty: of the three prelates mentioned at the
time of the promulgation of the definitive sentence, he was the sole
survivor, since Cauchon and Louis of Luxembourg were both dead.

The text of the Rehabilitation proceedings runs: "The witness
was questioned on the letters of warranty which the King of England
gave to the Bishop of Beauvais and to the others who were involved
in that trial. From those letters it emerges that the bishop of Noyon
was included in the safeguard given.

"I do believe, he answered, that there were some. I do not
remember it very well. I know, however, that it was not at his own
expense that the Bishop of Beauvais held that trial, but at the
expense of the King of England, and that the expenses which were
incurred in it were on the account of the English." (R.253)

For the English, Joan's death was followed by an immediate
resumption of military operations. On June 2nd that same Laurent
Calot who had guided Joan's hand in making her sign the abjuration
with a cross, signed an indent on the English crown treasurer,
Thomas Blount, for money to finance the construction of war
machines for the siege of Louviers. (The original document is in

the National Archives, AF II, 448.) This was a vindication of the rumours which were circulating among the people of Rouen.

Jean Riquier: "It was commonly said that the English did not dare lay siege to Louviers until Joan was dead. . . . Among others I heard Master Pierre Maurice, and Nicolas Loiseleur and others whom I no longer remember, say that the English so feared her that they did not dare, while she still lived, lay siege to Louviers, and that it was necessary to humour them, that a trial would be quickly made against her and that therein they would find occasion for her death." (R.194)

This remark was also reported by Brother Jean Toutmouillé: "Before her death the English were proposing to lay siege to Louviers, but soon ate their words, saying that they would not besiege the town until the Maid had been examined. Of which what follows is manifest proof, for immediately after her burning, they went and set siege to Louviers, estimating that never in her lifetime would they get glory or prosperity in deeds of war." (R.194)

This was also the opinion of another witness, prior of the convent of Saint-Michel near Rouen, who had not personally taken any part in the trial but who, inhabiting Rouen, had followed the whole business from outside.

Thomas Marie: "As Joan had done wonders in the war and as the English are generally superstitious, they thought that there was in her something of magic. That was why, as I believe, in all their councils and otherwise, they desired her death."

Question: How do you know that the English are superstitious? THOMAS MARIE: Everyone knows it, it is even a current proverb.* (R.191)

Meanwhile, the University of Paris and Bedford himself, acting for the King of England, hastened to make known to all that Joan had died at the stake as a heretic. An official letter from the King was sent "to the emperor, to the King, to the dukes and other princes and all Christendom, 8th June 1431 (text in C.423–426); it is written in Latin, the European language and the language of all official documents. Another letter, dated June 28th, was written in French and sent to "the prelates of the Church, to the dukes, counts and other nobles and cities of the Kingdom of France";

* It is a fact that both Henry V and his brother, the Regent Bedford, had a particular fear of witchcraft.—E.H.

it was only a translation of the other one but it was important that to the French people of France it be written in their own language. The letter sums up the events following which "This woman, who had herself called Joan the Maid, had, for two years and more, against divine law and her condition as of the feminine sex, worn male attire, a thing abominable to God, and in that state conveyed to our capital enemy, to whom and to those of his party, Churchmen, nobles and common people, she gave it often to be understood that she was sent by God."

The trial and the Saint-Ouen "abjuration" were next described, after which ". . . for the which things, according to what the judgments and institutions of holy Church ordain, in order that henceforth she contaminate not the other members of Jesus Christ, she was forthwith preached to publicly and as a backslider into the crimes and faults to her habitual, abandoned to secular justice which without delay condemned her to be burned."

The University of Paris, meanwhile, was sending its own letter to the pope and the College of Cardinals to inform them of what had been done with its full approbation. It has often been asked what the court of Rome had known about the trial. In fact, Pope Martin V, who without any doubt had heard of Joan and her victories, had died on February 20, 1431, on the eve of the first phase of Joan's trial. His successor, Gabriel Condulmaro, Bishop of Siena, elected on March 3rd and taking the name Eugenius IV, was obliged, from the very beginning of his pontificate, to deal with that series of disturbances which were to mar its whole course: besieged in Rome by the Colonna, threatened by the Duke of Milan, and betrayed by the papal troops, he fled to Florence on May 29th—the eve of Joan's execution. Three months later he was stricken with hemiplegia but, his mental faculties intact, for the next sixteen years he stood up to that extraordinary Council of Basle which has been called "the greatest assembly of indiscipline the world has ever known". It is a curious circumstance that most of Joan's judges were to figure in it, at the head of the faction which wanted to make the pope submit to conciliar authority. Jean Beaupère left Rouen even before Joan's execution, for Rome, to persuade the new pope, if necessary with menaces, that Basle, and not some Italian city as the pope would have preferred, should be the meeting place of the forthcoming council. Among speakers in the debate were Nicolas Loiseleur, Nicolas Midy, Pierre Maurice and Pierre Cauchon himself, while Thomas de Courcelles succeeded in getting a cardinal's hat out of the anti-pope Felix V who had been elected by the council as a move in their struggle with Eugenius IV. In point of fact, the same power was at work in both cases— Joan's trial and the Council of Basle: this power was the University of Paris, which held itself to be the real head of Christendom as, in good faith, it held itself to be the real head of the Kingdom of France. And having come out for the double monarchy in civil government and for the conciliar theses in ecclesiastical government, Joan was the university's enemy as well as the pope himself.

In Paris itself the university did not fail to make known, with great ceremony, the outcome of the trial in which it had played a predominant role. The *Journal d'un bourgeois de Paris*, written by a university man and therefore conveying university feeling exactly, has a long account of how ". . . on the day of Saint-Martin-le-Bouillant (July 4th) a general procession was made to Saint-Martin-des-Champs and a brother of the Order of Saint Dominic, who was an Inquisitor and a Master of Theology, preached a sermon. In this he included a version of Joan the Maid's whole life; she had claimed to be the daughter of very poor folk; she had adopted man's attire when she was only fourteen and her father and mother would willingly have killed her then had they been able to do it without wounding their own conscience; and that was why she left them, accompanied the hellish Enemy. Thereafter her life was one of fire and blood and the murder of Christians until she was burned at the stake."

The *Journal* records, before this, and in all the detail which the writer had been able to obtain, a life and trial of Joan in much the same spirit, adding an account of her execution which no doubt conveys more or less what was known in Paris and echoes the version put about by the university: "When she saw that her punishment was certain she cried for mercy and orally abjured. Her clothes were taken from her and she was attired as a woman, but no sooner did she find herself in this attire than she fell again into error and asked for her man's clothes. She was therefore soon condemned to death by all the judges, and bound to a stake on the scaffold of plaster (cement) on which the fire was built. She perished soon, and her dress was all burned away, then the fire was drawn a little back that the people should doubt not. The people saw her stark naked with all the secrets which a woman can and should have. When this sight had lasted long enough, the executioner replaced great fire under that poor carrion which was soon charred and the bones reduced to ashes. Many people said there and elsewhere that she was a martyr and that she had sacrificed herself for her true prince. Others said that this was not so and that he who had so long protected her had done ill. Thus spake the people, but whether she had done well or ill, she was burned that day." (P.106)

Meanwhile Clement de Fauquembergue, clerk to the Parliament, was noting in his register: "The thirtieth day of May 1431, by trial of the Church, Joan, who called herself the Maid, who had been taken in a sortie from the town of Compiègne by the men of messire John of Luxembourg ... was burned in the Town of Rouen and there was written on the mitre she had on her head the following words: 'heretic, relapsed, apostate, idolater'. And on a placard before the scaffold where the said Joan was, were written these words: 'Joan, self-styled the Maid, liar, pernicious, abuser of the people, soothsayer, superstitious, blasphemer of God; presumptuous, misbeliever in the faith of Jesus-Christ, boaster, idolater, cruel, dissolute, invoker of devils, apostate, schismatic and heretic.' And there pronounced the sentence messire Pierre Cauchon, Bishop of Beauvais, in whose diocese the said Joan had, so they say, been taken. And he summoned to hold the trial many notable Churchmen of the duchy of Normandy, graduates in sciences, and many theologians and jurists of the University of Paris, as they say is contained in the proceedings." He then includes a reference to his first mention of Joan, thus: "See above in our register for the tenth day of May 1429, etc." (Q. iv, 459–460. The original register is in the National Archives.)

Finally, there are various references to the event, notably in the Burgundian chroniclers such as Monstrelet, who gives a copy of the letter addressed by the King of England to the Duke of Burgundy, relating Joan's death: "Most dear and well-beloved uncle, the fervent delectation which we know that you have as a true Catholic prince in our Holy Mother Church and the exaltation of our holy faith exhorts and admonishes us to signify to you and write that to the honour of our Mother the holy Church, . . . has been solemnly accomplished extirpation of errors in our town of Rouen. . . . This woman, who had herself styled Joan the Maid . . . was taken by secular justice to the Old Market within Rouen and there was publicly burned in sight of the whole people." (Q. iv, 403.) The remainder of the letter was simply a translation of the circular mentioned above.

Subsequent events clearly show the English anxiety to wipe out and utterly abolish everything which had been due to Joan's activities.

At the same time as they resumed military operations, they were busy arranging to crown the boy-king Henry VI, King of France. He had been crowned King of England, at Westminster, on November 6, 1429; he received the second crown of his double monarchy at Notre Dame in Paris on December 16, 1431, six months after Joan's death. Paris was chosen in default of Rheims, which was back in French hands. No surprise need be felt at the fact that among the ecclesiastics summoned to assist at this coronation were the Bishops of Beauvais and Noyon. The invaluable Beauchamp Household Book is very interesting at this stage, giving as it does a day-by-day account of the stages in the journey from Rouen to Paris which the countess and her suite entered at night, by way of the river, possibly to avoid attracting too much attention.

The *Bourgeois de Paris* gives copious details of the coronation ceremonies: "Sunday December 16th, early in the morning, King Henry went on foot from the Palais Royal to Notre Dame, accompanied by processions from the town which sang very melodiously. In Notre Dame a long and wide platform, on to which ten men could mount side by side, was erected before the choir, the steps of it were painted azure dotted with fleurs-de-lys in gold. . . ."

There follow some remarks in which, albeit a fervent Burgundian, the diarist expresses his disapproval of English *cuisine*, on the subject of the coronation banquet. "Nobody," he writes, "had reason to boast of the meal. The most part of the meats, especially those destined for the common people, had been cooked on the preceding Thursday, which seemed very strange to the French. . . ." (P. 110)

How was the news of Joan's death received in that part of France which, on a later occasion, was to be known as the *Zone Libre?* The part, in short, which had remained outside the Anglo-Burgundian dominion or had been liberated in the astonishing epic campaign of 1429. The letters circulated by the University of Paris and by the English Government had obviously spread the news widely; it was officially distributed everywhere.

But—and it will suffice those who lived through the more recent Occupation to recall their own memories of 1940–45—many must have received this news with scepticism, convinced that this was a case of false news spread by the enemy to undermine his opponent's morale. And it is probable that in Orleans, even more than elsewhere, eye-witnesses of Joan's exploits, prompt to consider her as an "angel of God", must long have refused to believe that she, the Joan whom they had known in all the glory of an unhoped-for victory, could possibly have suffered the most infamous of all deaths on the scaffold, the death reserved for heretics. The English might do what they would in taking care that nobody could say that she had escaped; many must certainly have believed it and persisted in hoping against hope.

In short, what happened to Joan was what happens to every hero of every age: people refuse to believe in their death, they are endowed with an imaginary post-mortem life. How many times, even in our own epoch, have we not read in our newspapers, concerning a gentleman not precisely beloved by the generality of mankind, that Hitler was still alive, that he was on an island in the Pacific, or in South America, or elsewhere? The same kind of folk legend which brought Frederick Barbarossa back to life after he had died on a crusade in 1190, and did the same for his grandson, Frederick II who died sixty years later, brought Joan of Arc back to life in thousands of imaginations. It was inevitable. National feeling, sharpened in a period of warfare, played its part. An exactly similar fate attended a contemporary of Joan's whose importance was in no way comparable with hers: the astrologer Jean des Builhons, who was said to have predicted to Salisbury the latter's death before Orleans: "King Charles VII had him set at liberty (after the siege) and kept him, giving him a pension and an honourable house, albeit some who are still of the English party say the contrary and that he died in prison." This is from a contemporary treatise on astrology. (See Q. iv, 345, in footnote.)

There was far more reason for such rumours to get about in Joan's case. And we have an echo of them in an anonymous Norman chronicle written after Charles VII's death, which recounts her trial in a few words and adds, referring to the English: "Finally they had her publicly burned or another woman like her, as to which many men were and still are of diverse opinions." (Q. iv, 344)

And as was also to be expected, the situation was exploited by more than one woman, deliberate impostors or under a genuine illusion, who claimed to be Joan the Maid, or thought themselves capable of continuing her exploits. There was, for example, Jeanne la Feronne who, like Catherine de la Rochelle, claimed to have good advice to give the King who certainly wanted none of it.

Among the imitators who claimed actually to be Joan herself, the best known was the famous Claude des Armoises, of whom we shall give some account, since, despite repeated refutations, there have been, even in our own time, diverse writings making use of her history with a view to showing that Joan was never burned at the stake. It was in 1436, five years after Joan's execution and not long after the entry of the royal army into Paris (April 13th), that this good lady made her appearance. The event is thus related in the chronicle which reports it, that of the Dean of Saint-Thiébault of Metz, whose text we give in full:

"Year 1436, sire Philippin Marcoult was chief municipal magistrate of Metz. The same year on the twentieth day of May the Maid Joan, who had been in France, went to La Grande-aux-Ormes, near Saint-Privas. She was led there to talk to some of the lords of Metz and was calling herself Claude. On the same day there came to see her her two brothers, one of whom was a knight and was called messire Pierre, and the other Petit-Jean, esquire. And they thought that she had been burned, but when they saw her they recognized her and she too recognized them. And the Monday one and twentieth day of the said month, they took her with them to Bacquillon and the sire Nicole Louve, knight, gave her a horse whose price was thirty francs and a pair of hose, and the lord Aubert de Boullay a hooded cape, and sire Nicole Grognat a sword. And the said Maid leapt upon the horse very skilfully and told sire Nicole Louve several things by which he understood well that she it was who had been in France. And she was recognized by many signs for the Maid Joan of France who took King Charles to be crowned at Rheims. And there were some who would say that she had been burned at Rouen in Normandy; and she spoke most often in parables, and she told neither the substance nor the appearance of her intentions. She said that she would have no power before Saint-John-the-Baptist's Day. But when her brothers had taken her away, she soon returned for the Feast of Pentecost (May 28th) to the town of Marieulle to the house of Jean Cugnot and there stayed about three weeks. Then she set out on the third for Notre-Dame-de-Liesse. And when she was about to go many from Metz went to see her at Marieulle; they gave her several jewels and they recognized that she was indeed Joan the Maid of France. And then Geoffroy Dex (Desch) gave her a horse and then she went away to Arlon, a town which is in the duchy of Luxembourg. When she was in Arlon she was constantly with Madame de Luxembourg, and she was there until the moment when the son of the Count of Warnembourg took her to Cologne; and the count loved her greatly, so much so that when she wanted to go he had made for her a beautiful cuirass for her armour; and then she returned to Arlon and there was celebrated the wedding of Robert of Armoises, knight, and the said Joan the Maid, and then afterwards departed the said sieur of Armoises with his wife, the Maid, to live at Metz in the house of the said Sir Robert, which he had before Sainte-Segolene. And there they stayed for as long as it pleased them."

Such is the story told by the Dean of Saint-Thiébault of Metz in the oldest MS. of his chronicle. But a second MS. (Bib. Nat. Coll. Dupuy, No. 630), of later date, rectifies in some particulars the terms of the first, thus: "In this year came a young girl who said she was the Maid of France, and playing her part so well that many were deceived by her, and especially all the people of most consequence. She was at La Grande-aux-Ormes and there were the lords of Metz, such as the lord Nicole Louve . . ."

The rest of this MS. recounts, more briefly than the first, how she went to Notre-Dame-de-la-Liesse and to Arlon, and then was married to the lord Robert of Armoises, and it no longer identifies her with Joan the Maid. It is obvious that the Dean of Saint-Thiébault had at first, like many others, been duped, and then changed his mind when the fraud had been exposed.

He was certainly not the only one who was to be fooled by Claude des Armoises, who must surely have had some physical resemblance to the heroine, to pass herself off as Joan; she must also have had that ease in playing her part which has distinguished so many adventurers of the same kind. As we have seen, she put in her first appearance at Metz. The people of Orleans got to hear of her and wanted to know what this was all about; the town's account books give us some information as to what steps they took. On July 31st the municipal council sent a messenger named Coeur-de-Lys to Arlon:

"To Coeur-de-Lys, the twenty-eighth day of October, 1436, for a journey which he made for the town to the Maid who was at Arlon in the duchy of Luxembourg and for carrying the letters which he bore from Joan the Maid to Loches to the King, who was there, in which journey he spent forty and one days, to wit thirty-eight days in the journey to the Maid and seven days to go to the King, and set out the said Coeur-de-Lys to go to the Maid, Tuesday the last day of July and returned the second day of September following. For all this . . . Six pounds *parisis*.

"To Jacquet Lepretre, the second day of September, for bread, wine, pears and green walnuts, dispensed in the chamber of the said town at the coming of the said Coeur-de-Lys who brought letters from Joan the Maid and for drink for the said Coeur-de-Lys who said that he was very thirsty. For this . . . two sous four deniers parisis." (Q. v, 327)

The messenger, then, had been to Arlon and back and had then been sent off again to the King at Loches. But meanwhile Petit-Jean, Joan's brother, had come to Orleans on August 5th, and then had himself gone to the King at Loches. For this fact we are indebted to the Orleans account books: Jean du Lys had been to the procurator of the town to ask for some money, saying that the King had ordered that he be given a hundred francs, but that he had been given only twenty and that he had already spent twelve of them, and that he had not enough left for the return journey. But this exchange of letters does not seem to have made a great impression either on the people of Orleans or on the King: nothing whatever was done to follow it up.

This was the moment of the bogus Joan's journey to Cologne: apart from what the Dean of Saint-Thiébault has to tell us about this, her residence in that city is known to us from a work by the Alsatian Inquisitor, Jean Nidier, prior of the Dominicans at Nuremberg; it is entitled The Formicarium. It tells how the Inquisitor of Cologne summoned the false Joan to appear before him because of the attitude which she had taken in claiming to arbitrate between the two prelates who were, at the time, disputing the archiepiscopal see of Treves, and stating that she had been sent by God to support one of them. The false Joan would appear, on this occasion, to have accomplished such prodigies before the Inquisitor as seem to have made a great impression on Jean Nidier: she is said to have torn up a napkin and reassembled the pieces instantaneously: then to have smashed a glass against the wall and instantly made it whole again under the eyes of those present! What follows in Nidier's account shows the bogus Joan marrying "a certain knight", but without giving the name of Robert des Armoises who was presumably unknown to him. Later he says that she lived in a state of concubinage with a priest. We can hardly take much account of this story, excepting as to the fact of her residence in Cologne which Nidier may have known from the town Inquisitor.

Be that as it may, the adventuress, who thenceforth called herself Joan and no longer Claude, did marry Robert of Armoises on November 7, 1431. The certificate of their marriage was published by Dom Calmet in his History of Lorraine (vol. 3, col. 195). We know of the event only through this publication, which was in 1728, for the author does not give his exact source; the original document has never been found again. However, there is nothing suspect in the form in which Dom Calmet gives it. As for Robert of Armoises, we know very little about him, but it is fairly well established that his family came originally from Champagne; Dom Calmet gives his genealogy but it is not very reliable. It seems clear that Robert's family had settled in Lorraine towards the end of the fourteenth century, and that in the fifteenth Robert of Armoises who had hitherto held the fief of Norroy and the lordship of Tichemont, had had his property confiscated in 1435 by René of Anjou, Duke of Bar. This was probably why he was living in Metz; that town, like the whole duchy of Luxembourg, being hostile to René.

Contrary to what is maintained in certain accounts of Claude des Armoises, notably in that of Anatole France, no document exists to show that she ever went to Vaucouleurs or to Domremy at the time in question. We know, in fact, nothing whatever about her until 1439 when she reappeared in Orleans. It is probable—we will give authority for this hypothesis below—that in the meantime her husband had died. On July 18th she was received by the town, as is proved by the account book; the town entertained her to a *vin d'honneur* and thereafter she was invited "to dine and to sup" on the following July 30th. On August 1st the town made her a present of two hundred and ten pounds *parisis*, "for the good which she did the town during the siege". On September 3rd, again, she was given another *vin d'honneur*; for the same date we find the following item: "For eight pints of wine dispensed at a supper at which were Jean Luillier and Thevenon of Bourges, because it was thought to present it to the said Joan who left before the wine was come." (Q. v, 331–332). It will be recalled that Jean Luillier was the merchant who had formerly provided the cloth for Joan's clothes.

The accounts thereafter do not mention her again. On the other hand, and for the same year 1439, they itemise the expenses for the funeral service which the town celebrates every year for the repose of the real Joan's soul.

Claude des Armoises, then, vanished rather suddenly, for she was expected at a dinner for which she did not turn up on September 4, 1439. It is known from other sources that she then made her way to the famous Gilles de Laval, lord of Rais. Now it happens that the King was expected at Orleans in the month of September

1439 and it may well be that Claude, whose principal object was to get money out of people who believed in her tales, left the town because she was afraid to be seen by him.

As for Gilles de Rais, he was to be arrested at the beginning of the year 1440 and to undergo that famous trial for sorcery at the end of which he was hanged and burned. Claude des Armoises then went to Paris. Touching her residence in that city we have the account of the *Bourgeois de Paris*:

"At the same time (August 1440) came great news of the Maid formerly burned at Rouen for her misdeeds. Many persons, deceived by her, firmly believed that her saintliness had enabled her to escape from the pyre and that another woman had been burned at the stake in error, in her place. But she was really burned and her ashes were really cast into the river to avoid the sorceries which might have followed. Now soldiers brought at this time to Orleans another Maid who was very honourably received, and when she drew near to Paris this great error began again and it was thought that she was the true Maid. But the University and the Parliament brought her to Paris willy-nilly, and she was shown to the people in the great court of the Palace on the marble stone, then preached to and interrogated. She said that she was not a maid and that she had been married to a knight by whom she had two sons." (pp. 146–7)

From this we may deduce, as mentioned above, that Robert des Armoises was dead, and it was probably under the spur of want that Claude went to Orleans and tried her luck, and then to Paris. The next passage in the *Journal* gives an account of the exploits which Claude boasted of having performed: she said that she had enlisted at Rome in the army of Pope Eugenius IV, which is by no means impossible but is attested only by this account.

Thereafter Claude disappears from history. Her fraud is recounted at greater length in Pierre Sala's *Hardiesses des grands rois et empereurs*, a work we have already referred to, when we pointed out that it was written rather late, between 1510 and 1516, but from sources which the author claimed to be first-hand. His story is that Claude des Armoises was unmasked by the King himself who, in greeting her, is made to say: "Maid, sweetheart, be you very welcome again,* in the name of God who knows the secret which is between you and me." Whereupon Claude, frightened, fell upon her knees and cried "mercy" and revealed her fraud.

---

* A play on words: the French is *Vous soyez la tres bien revenue*. Bienvenu, welcome; *bien revenu*, well-come-again; but also a *revenant* is one who returns from the dead, a ghost.—E.H.

At all events, what we can be sure of from the documents is that there was an adventuress gifted enough to pass herself off as Joan, even on Joan's own brothers, at least one of whom, Petit-Jean, the elder, went to the length of undertaking to get her recognized by the people of Orleans in 1436. It has been claimed that Joan's mother, Isabelle Romée, also recognized her. This is quite untrue; it is to be found in no document and, moreover, Isabelle Romée's presence in Orleans is attested only from the month of July 1440, at which time Claude des Armoises was, as we have said, in Paris. The Orleans town account books mention that in July, indeed, Isabelle was in the town, she had fallen ill on the seventh of the month and was nursed at the town's expense until August 31st. A monthly pension of forty-eight sous *parisis* was to be paid her thereafter, and it appears regularly in the accounts until her death in November 1458.

We should likewise note that Joan's other brother, Pierre, is only once mentioned in this connection, and that is in the chronicle by the Dean of Saint-Thiébault which we have quoted, and in the first MS. only. Now it was this brother who had been most devoted to his sister and who was made prisoner with her at Compiègne. It is not certain that he had been released from prison by 1436; he was held by the Bastard of Vergy, Jean, a Burgundian captain in the service of the English. In 1439 Charles VII granted him the farm of the tolls in the bailiwick of Chaumont as a means of livelihood after the payment of his ransom, which had utterly ruined him. Later, in 1443, Charles of Orleans, who had been released from his English prison three years before, made him a gift of the Ile-aux-Boeufs, up-river from Orleans. We shall here quote from the text of the deed of gift, since it has given rise to misleading commentaries:

"Having heard the supplication of messire Pierre du Lys, knight, stating that to acquit himself loyally towards the King our lord and us, he left his country to enter the service of the King our said lord and of ourselves, in company with Joan the Maid his sister, with whom until his absentment and thereafter until the present time, he has exposed his body and his goods in that service and in the matter of the King's wars, both in the resistance to the ancient enemies of the realm who laid siege to our town of Orleans, as in several journeys made and undertaken for the King, our said lord, and his chiefs in war, and otherwise in several and diverse places and by fortune of the said wars was made prisoner by the said enemies and constrained to sell his wife's patrimonies to pay his ransom, requests that we may be pleased to give . . . etc. . . ." (Q. v, 213)

The misleading commentaries in question relate to the words "until *son* (his or her) absentment"*, in which they see an allusion to Joan having supposedly "absented" herself, to reappear with her brother under the form and face of Jeanne des Armoises. But, grammatically speaking, the term absentment (*absentement*) can only be referred to the subject of the sentence, to wit Pierre himself; and, historically, at the date when this deed was drawn, three years had passed since Claude des Armoises had been unmasked and since any document mentions her name.

Claude des Armoises was not the last adventuress to make a name for herself in this field. In 1457 King René, Duke of Anjou, granted a letter of remission to one Jeanne de Sermaize, married to an Angevin named Jean Douillet, who had been detained for three months in the prison of Saumur for having passed herself off as Joan the Maid; she too had succeeded in convincing several people who had formerly seen the real Joan.

The success of such adventuresses may be surprising; it is, however, certainly not exceptional. History swarms with cases of people passing themselves off as somebody else. We may take our choice even in Joan's own epoch. There is the case reported by Maurice Garçon (see his article *Jeanne d'Arc est bien morte sur le bucher de Rouen*, Ecclesia No. 158, May 1962, pp. 59–68). This concerns a woman who, in 1423, turned up in Ghent declaring herself to be own sister to the Duke of Burgundy, Philippe the Good, Marguerite, widow of Louis, Duke of Guyenne, and the elder brother of Charles VII. She was cared for by the people of Ghent for several weeks and so well treated that they refused to believe in the imposture when the duke, having got wind of the business, tried to undeceive them. He had to go to Ghent accompanied by his sister before they would consent to believe that they had been deceived.

Some time before this, in the autumn of 1402, an adventurer had turned up at the Scottish court giving out that he was King Richard II who, imprisoned three years before when Henry IV of Lancaster

* The word "absentment" which I have used for the French *absentement*, in any case archaic, does not exist in good English, but I made it up for obvious reasons. It may be noted that in the translation, above, the misleading commentary has no foundation, for in English we make the pronoun, in this case *son*, agree with the sex of the subject (his, her); whereas in French, since it agrees with the word qualified by it, there is no indication of the sex of the subject. But as Mlle Pernoud says, the commentator had only to parse the sentence in question to see that there was no foundation for his argument. —E.H.

had deposed him, had lived first in the Tower of London, subsequently in Pontefract Castle where he died on February 14, 1401. The bogus Richard was "recognized" under the guise of a beggar, by a lady of his former court, and taken to the Duke of Albany, in Scotland, who entertained him generously. Under the name of Richard Plantagenet he gathered a party of adherents about him. The fraud was carried to such lengths that the King of France sent an emissary to Scotland to investigate. A bastard son of the Black Prince, Roger Clarendon by name, rallied to Richard's cause and there were several uprisings in his favour. People were still talking about it twenty years later. Now the King of England was better known, and had been seen by more people than Joan of Arc had been in a public life which lasted only one year.

Still more remarkable was the famous case of Perkin Warbeck, a native of Tournai, who passed himself off as the eldest son of Edward IV, Richard of York, claiming to have miraculously escaped the Tower of London massacre. He found partisans in the Low Countries with Margaret of York, widow of Charles the Bold, and an invasion of England was organised in support of his claims. In the end he was hanged on Henry VII's orders. Without seeking further examples in the period of the false Louis XVII (of whom there were several), not to mention a certain Grand Duchess of Russia, it is, then, easy enough to find cases of successful historical impersonation which are, on the whole, much more surprising than that of Claude des Armoises.

COMMENTARY

"Joan was not burned at the stake; she was enabled to escape; another woman was burned in her place."

The people who have put forward this hypothesis found their case on the following documents:

The Norman chronicle which we quoted (Q. iv, 344) from a MS. in the British Museum: apparently written in 1439 (see details on this subject in Q. iv, 339), it gives an exact notion of the state of public opinion and of the contradictory rumours about Joan's fate then circulating.

An abridged chronicle composed in Brittany in 1440 and contained in a MS. (No. 1155) now in the Bibliothèque Sainte-Geneviève in Paris (see Q. iv, 344, in a note). The following passage appears in it: "Year 1431, the eve of the Sacrament, was the Maid burned at Rouen or condemned to be."

To these two documents, long well known to historians of Joan of Arc,* is added a work printed in the sixteenth century, Symphorien Champier's *La nef des dames vertueuses*, Lyon, 1503. In this a short passage devoted to Joan is followed by: "... and in the end was by treachery taken and given to the English who, despite the French, burned her in Rouen; they say it nevertheless, but the French deny it."

But this, self-evidently, is a literary work devoid of historic pretensions and which simply sets down the "they say" rumours in circulation about Joan, not the actual circumstances of her life and death. Only the other two documents, then, have any validity for historians. But the doubts which they express only reveal what was thought by many people in circles favourable to the French cause in the years 1439–40. It was natural enough, at that time, that people should refuse to believe in a death which seemed a justification of the English cause. The hope of seeing Joan return would have been strongest in places where faith in her had been strongest: hence we see Claude des Armoises trying her luck in Orleans, where Joan had spent only a short time in all (certainly from April 29th to May 9th, also January 19th 1430, when there was a banquet in her honour; and perhaps—but this is purely conjectural—on other occasions of which no record remains), but where the people would certainly all be fervently hoping that the news of her execution was false.

The two chronicles in question date from the time when Claude des Armoises was creating a stir, the consequent rumours in circulation giving some foundation to the hope that Joan might have escaped from the English.

Apart from those people who had actually seen her burned at the stake in Rouen, what, indeed, could be exactly known in a France divided by occupation and torn by war? All the people had to go on were the letters circulated by the English government and the University of Paris, both sources highly suspect among partisans of the French cause. For the French, no real light was to be shed on the case of Joan of Arc until they had reconquered Rouen in 1449 and were in possession of the trial papers and able to gather evidence from eye-witnesses (see Chapter 9).

---

* First published by Vallet de Viriville, who was one of those who refuted the errors of Caze touching the alleged bastardy (see *Bib. de l'Ecole des Chartes*, 2nd S., Vol. 11), they were republished by Quicherat himself.

Thus, for the historian, the two chronicles throw light on the state of mind during the period of doubt between Joan's death and the reconquest of the realm; they can throw no light on *facts*, nor, moreover, does either of them claim to do so. But on the other hand, the facts are established very clearly indeed by the documents which we have quoted in this chapter:

1. Official documents: Letter from the University of Paris to the pope notifying him of Joan's trial, condemnation and execution. It is definitely and expressly stated that she is dead—*migravit a seculo*. (C.435)

The same notification made to the College of Cardinals. (C.435)

Letter from the King of England to the emperor, kings, dukes and princes of all Christendom, dated from Rouen, June 8, 1431. (C.423)

Letter from the same notifying likewise "the prelates of the Church, dukes, counts and other nobles, and to the cities of our realm of France". Also from Rouen, June 28th. (C.426)

2. Chronicles: That of the *Bourgeois de Paris* which we quoted and which relates a public act in which the Inquisitor of France in person officially announces to the people of Paris the condemnation and death of a heretic. Also Monstrelet's.

To the above may be added the diverse deeds and documents which imply Joan's execution, for example the condemnation of Jean Bosquier accused in the official proceedings of saying that "it had been ill done . . . to abandon Joan to secular justice", the conventional term used to indicate the execution of heretics (C.432); and, again, the letters of warranty given to those who had taken part in the trial and condemnation.

Surprise has sometimes been expressed that no record of the execution is to be found in the file of the proceedings; but this is to demonstrate a singular ignorance, for in fact, of course, all Inquisitorial trials closed at the very point where Joan's was closed: at the point where the culprit is handed over by the court to the "secular arm". It was always the secular arm, lay justice, which carried out conviction and sentence. Thus the record, if one existed, should be sought in the archives of the bailiwick; but custom varied in this respect from place to place, and it is by no means certain that any such record was ever written.

3. Finally, we have the evidence of a whole series of eye-witnesses bearing every sign of veracity and all agreeing in the main particular:

Joan's execution. The evidence in question is to be found in the depositions made at the Trial of Rehabilitation and given by a very varied set of people, for it includes not only some who were actively involved in the matter, such as the Bishop of Noyon, the notaries, the usher and the two Dominicans who supported Joan to the scaffold, but also people who were simply there as sight-seers like Jean Riquier, or who, like Pierre Cusquel, refused to be present because they could not have borne the sight.

But, curiously enough, the amateurs of fancy hypotheses, instead of taking note of eye-witness accounts, turn to the Chronicle of Perceval de Cagny—who could not have been present at the scene and for good reason!—from which they extract a single detail which they flourish as decisive.

We may, indeed, read in this Chronicle, which as we know was written by an esquire in the Duke of Alençon's service and gives the most vivid details of other points in the story, notably on the Loire campaign—the following lines:

"The people of the King of England's justice in the town of Rouen made ready fitting places and made preparations to execute justice in a place which could be seen by a great concourse of people; and the said 24th day of May . . ." (here he is confusing the date with that of the Saint-Ouen business) ". . . at about the hour of noon Joan was brought from the castle, her face veiled (*embronché*) to the place where the fire was ready, and after certain things (having been) read in that place, was bound to the stake and burned, by the report of those who say they saw it." (Q. iv, 36)

The word *embronché* has given rise to innumerable arguments. In point of fact, in old French it signifies either veiled or *penché* . . . stooped, bent forward. It is probable, as Maurice Garçon has pointed out (in Ecclesia *op. cit.*), that all it meant in this context was that the mitre which was usually placed on the heads of condemned persons had, derisively, been put on crooked.

At all events it is clear enough that the real historian is bound to prefer direct evidence to this single, and second-hand, account by Perceval de Cagny, who was not present and clearly says so. Brother Isambart and the others quoted above were present; and they do not tell us that Joan's face was veiled.*

* *Embroncher* in current French is a building term, meaning to lay tiles with an overlap. De Cagny's words may mean that her face was overlapped, i.e., shadowed by, as M. Garçon suggests, the mitre of the condemned. But is it not possible that the word was used, by extension, to describe facial expression? Her face was darkened, overshadowed—i.e., by fear or grief?—E.H.

There is another point: who is supposed to have been burned in Joan's place? This causes our fancy theorists no trouble at all: the prisons, it seems, "were overflowing with witches for burning". At this point their argument becomes merely ludicrous. As we have said, whereas heresy trials were fairly numerous in the fifteenth century, trials for witchcraft were extremely rare. Joan, herself, as we have seen, was not condemned as a witch, although in the Instruction phase of the trial attempts were made to convict her of having practised some witchcraft. And the supposition of our theorists become merely fantastic when they claim that in 1432 four hundred witches were burned in Rouen alone. In point of fact, a trial for witchcraft held in Lorraine in 1456, at which eight people were victimised, raised a great deal of strong feeling. Readers interested in this aspect of the question and wishing to know more about it cannot do better than refer to Maurice Garçon's *Les Proces en Sorcellerie* and a little work by Jean Palou which was published in the *Que-sais-je?* collection, *La sorcellerie*.

We may perhaps conclude with a piece of free entertainment provided by the same amateurs of fancy theories. They declare that they have found details of the four hundred executions of witches in the *Archives des domaines de la cité de Rouen*, in which, they further declare with astonishment, they can find "no trace of the execution of Joan of Arc"

The *Archives des domaines* anterior to 1789 were removed to the *Archives départementales de la Seine-Maritime*, where they occupy the following series: C.632-641, C.2329, 2348-2349, 2353-2355, 2554 and 2602. And we have no hesitation in offering a large reward to anyone who can find therein any reference to witch-burning in the fifteenth century.

As for the des Armoises lady, her history is well established (see Grosdidier de Mattons' *Le Mystère de Jeanne d'Arc*). As we have seen, her assimilation to the real Joan of Arc is founded solely on misconceived interpretation of facts, e.g., the term *absentement*; or upon more glaring mistakes, e.g., the "proof" which is found in the fact that she was received by "la dame de Luxembourg", who is confused with the one who had received Joan herself but who had died before Joan was executed.

Furthermore, all who have tried to maintain her cause in the face of history, show clear evidence of serious gaps in their historical education and information. To begin with the all too famous Father Jerome Vignier, from whom Dom Calmet borrowed most of the material which he published about Claude des Armoises. This Oratoire priest was a forger of remarkable nerve, who applied himself to the fabrication of letters supposed to have been written by popes of the fourth and fifth centuries, and who composed, with a talent which cannot be denied, a so-called "colloquy between Christians and Arians" supposed to have taken place at Lyon in 499, and which for a long time fooled historians. (See the article on this subject by Julien Havet in the *Bibliothèque de l'Ecole des Chartes*, 1885.)

As for those "recently discovered portraits" of the Maid and her husband, Robert des Armoises, which were published in a work advocating that well-worn theory, they are, alas, quite incapable of convincing the reader: the only photograph of them shows that they are in a manner somewhere between the troubadour style and that of the illustrator "Bibliophile Jacob"; one does not have to be an expert to refuse to accept them as fifteenth-century portraits. The only people who are likely to be taken in are those with a penchant for mystification!

9

REHABILITATION

On October 24, 1430, while Joan was still a prisoner at Beaurevoir, the Duke of Burgundy had been forced to raise the siege of Compiègne, that town having been relieved by a French army commanded by the Comte de Vendome and the Marshal de Boussac. The offensive operations which the duke had been able to prepare, thanks to the imprudent truces signed by Charles VII, had not been as profitable as he had hoped. In 1431 there were more French successes, chiefly owing to the energy of La Hire, who had been appointed captain-general in Normandy immediately after the taking of Louviers in December 1429, and of the sire de Barbazan in Champagne. The Bastard of Orleans was sent to Louviers in March 1431. But this military effort was not maintained: on October 28th Louviers was forced to capitulate to the English, a fresh body of English troops having disembarked at Calais in June. And on July 2nd the sire de Barbazan—"heart of fine silver, flower of chivalry" says his epitaph—was killed at the battle of Bulgneville during which René of Anjou was taken prisoner. By a curious coincidence, on May 30, 1431, the day of Joan's death, news of which cannot therefore have reached the king, Charles sent a letter to the inhabitants of Rheims asking them to make the sire de Barbazan welcome.

However, after a compaign which had been fruitless from his point of view, the Duke of Burgundy seems to have decided to seek peace with the King of France. He kept away from Henry VI's coronation ceremony in Paris in December 1431, and this alone was a gesture of independence of the English: and in the course of the same month he signed another truce with Charles VII's ambassadors, at Lille. Much more advantageous for the French King than its predecessors, the truce in question was for a period of six years and has the appearance of being preliminary to a definitive peace treaty. In Rouen itself the French sentiments of the population must have been roused by Joan's death: on February 3, 1432, a free-lance called Ricarville, with one hundred and three followers, succeeded by a *coup de main* of astonishing boldness, in making himself master of the castle. Unfortunately the reinforcement which was necessary if he was to hold the place was not forthcoming, and a few days later the one hundred and four soldiers were decapitated in the same Old Market Place which had witnessed the conflagration of that sinister pyre in the previous year, at the order of Bedford and the Earl of Arundel, captain of Rouen.

Meanwhile the King's attention was more than ever absorbed by his unworthy favourite, Georges de la Trémoille who, as always opposed to military action, fostered the King's natural apathy. One fine day he received a sword-stroke through the stomach; this attempt at assassination had been organised by the Constable Arthur de Richemont and the Angevin family, Queen Marie of Anjou, Charles du Maine and their mother Yolande of Sicily, who had made up their minds that the King of France should prosper even despite himself. His life saved by the thickness of his own fat, La Trémoille left the court never to return, and from that moment French military activity was more energetic and better sustained. On January 16, 1435, there began, between France and Burgundy, the conferences of Nevers in which René of Anjou played the part of honest broker. They concluded with an adjournment to Arras where, despite protests from England, peace was concluded between France and Burgundy on September 20, 1435. The Regent Bedford had seen the beginning of the negotiations, but was not to see the end of them, for he died on September 14th in the castle of Rouen where he had held Joan prisoner. One of the principal French negotiators had been Cauchon's successor in the see of Beauvais, appointed by the King of France after the town had been retaken in 1429, Jean Jouvenel des Ursins.

At the same time and throughout the country the people were quivering with impatience: there were uprisings in Lower Normandy in 1434; at the time of the treaty of Arras the English were virtually helpless in that region, and the town of Dieppe went over to the King of France. At last, on April 13, 1436, Arthur de Richemont, taking advantage of the insurrection which had been seething in Paris for four months, made his way into the city by the Saint-Jacques gate, while the "foresworn Frenchmen", among them Pierre Cauchon himself, fled hastily, pursued by the shouts of the mob, "After the fox! Have his tail!" (There was a curious popular superstition that all Englishmen had tails.) "Before seven years,"

Joan had said in 1431, "the English will lose a greater gage than they have ever lost in France."

But the Parisians had to wait a year before the King came to their town: he did not make his entry until November 12, 1437. Even the *Bourgeois de Paris* was obliged to admit that "he was fêted like God himself". (P.136) The King was accompanied by the Dauphin Louis, heir to the throne.

Several years passed thereafter during which neither England nor France seemed to be in a state to continue the strife. In both countries finances were in a parlous state, as we may judge from the monetary measures of the time: the coming and going of free-lance bands paralysed agriculture by terrorising the peasantry; disorder reigned throughout France and, as a last straw, plague broke out in the kingdom, and in Paris raged throughout 1438 and 1439, killing fifty thousand people in that city alone; among the victims was Marie de Poissy, the King's sister and prioress of the convent of Poissy.

Military action was resumed in 1441 with the taking of Pontoise and, in the following year, with a raid into Guyenne: the King recovered Saint-Sever and Dax, but failed to take La Réole. Discouraged by this failure he hurried back to the banks of the Loire and was again overtaken by inertia, the more so in that his mistress, Agnes Sorel, who first appeared at the court in 1444, roused in him a belated appetite for pleasure: banquets and tournaments followed one upon another, in which the taste for luxury, which had distinguished the Valois line since the first of them became King, reappeared. The Archbishop of Rheims, Jean Jouvenel des Ursins, raised an indignant voice in an effort to recall the King to a sense of his duty and to the misery of the people confronted with this extravagance of luxury paid for with "aids (taxes) raised for the war". But, also in 1444, a truce was signed with England and reinforced by the marriage of Henry VI to Margaret of Anjou, King René's daughter: this truce was renewed periodically until 1449.

In that year an English raid against Fougères caused the resumption of military operations, centred in Normandy where the population rose. In the month of May the French took three small towns in succession, Pont-de-l'Arche, Conches and Gerberoy; next, Dunois seized Verneuil, and at last, on August 6th, Charles VII set siege to Louviers. Towns rose in his support on all sides. In Rouen an insurrection forced the governor, Somerset, to quit the castle in haste and take refuge in Caen on October 29th: a few days later Charles made his entry into the capital of Normandy, reconquered after thirty years of occupation.

Then, and not till then, did it become possible to determine in what manner the trial and execution of Joan of Arc had taken place. All the documents in the case had been preserved at the archbishopric; and it was also in Rouen that eye-witnesses of her last moments were to be found. It had, therefore, been impossible until then to undertake any kind of action with a view to her rehabilitation. It is, of course, self-evident, but historians have not always made the point clearly enough. For a long time, indeed, the rehabilitation proceedings were misunderstood because they were so little known. The rehabilitation was seen as an act of mere opportunism: Joan is condemned by the Church when the English are victorious, rehabilitated as soon as they are vanquished. This is to forget the actual circumstances in which the events took place. So long as the English were masters of Rouen, the mere fact that they held the papers in the case, a case which they had managed themselves, maintained their version of what the trial had been—a trial by the Church carried on in the ordinary and regular manner, by which it had been established that Joan was a heretic. In the event, to reproach the King or the Church with having done nothing until that time is tantamount to reproaching the French government with having done nothing to bring the Oradour war criminals to justice before 1945.

Perhaps the only deed which can be placed on the credit side of Charles VII's account is this: that he did, shortly after his entry into Rouen, undertake to find out what had really happened in the matter of Joan. On February 15, 1450, a letter in the following terms was sent to one of his councillors, Master Guillaume Bouillé, canon of Noyon cathedral:

"Whereas formerly Joan the Maid was taken and apprehended by our ancient enemies and adversaries the English, and brought to this town of Rouen, against whom they caused to be brought proceedings by certain persons to that end committed and deputed by them, in which proceedings they did and committed many faults and abuses, to such point that, by means of that trial and the great hatred which our enemies had against her, they brought about her death iniquitously and against right reason, very cruelly; therefore we would know the truth of the said trial proceedings and the manner according to which it was carried on and proceeded with. We

authorise, command and expressly enjoin that you enquire into and
inform yourself diligently on that which is said about it; and the
information (gathered) by you on this matter, bring it close and
sealed before us and people of our council. . . ." (R.11–12)

The terms of this letter are significant: *we would know the truth
of the said trial*; until then, in fact, they knew nothing, excepting
what their enemies had been willing to tell them. But now, and only
now, might the truth be discovered.

Guillaume Bouillé was to bring to this business a punctuality
and energy which clearly reveal his own feelings; having always
been loyal to the royal cause, he was designated Rector of the purged
University of Paris in 1439. Less then three weeks after the date
of the above letter, the first witness called by him appeared before
him: Guillaume Manchon, the notary in the other trial. As we know,
he had been present throughout that trial from beginning to end;
he had signed every page of the proceedings and set his seal on the
completed document and kept his notes in French, where Joan's
own words were set down together with a translation into Latin.
The whole of March 4th was necessary for hearing his evidence.

On the following day six more witnesses were heard, four of
whom belonged to the convent of Saint-Jacques in Rouen in which
Joan's execution had caused a stir of anger, since it was there, on
the day after the burning, that Pierre Bosquier was arrested. The
two Brothers who had supported Joan to the stake were there,
Isambart de la Pierre and Martin Ladvenu: their interrogation took
a long time. Two others, whose role had been more obscure, were
also examined, Guillaume Duval and Jean Toutmouillé. The usher,
Jean Massieu, was called. And by a lucky chance a man who had
played one of the leading parts, Master Jean Beaupère himself, was
in Rouen, having come to take possession of a canon's prebend to
add to the large number of others he had accumulated: as a rule he
lived in retirement in the diocese of Besançon.

The evidence given by these seven men was amply sufficient
to establish what Joan's trial had really been: a political trial in
which, by convicting Joan of heresy, the English had successfully
sought to destroy the woman in whom they saw, not without
reason, the instrument of Charles VII's victories and coronation.

This interrogation of seven witnesses was staged against a
dramatic backcloth. Normandy was seething with excitement, town
after town was opening its gates to the King of France—Lisieux,
Coutances, Saint-Lo—and meanwhile, on the other side of the

Channel, Henry VI was making a supreme effort, going even to the length of pledging the Crown Jewels, in order to raise another army for service in France.

That army landed at Cherbourg on March 15th under the command of Thomas Kyriel, who was to make a junction with Somerset's forces entrenched at Caen. But Richemont's army, arriving unexpectedly, was too quick for him, and on April 15, 1450, Formigny avenged the shame of Agincourt. Normandy was virtually recovered; and completely so after Caen had been taken on June 24th and Cherbourg on August 12th. All northern France was in the King's hands.

Now in the following year Pope Nicholas V, who had succeeded Eugenius IV after the latter's victory over the fathers at the Council of Constance and the resignation of the anti-Pope Felix V, sent a legate to France, Guillaume d'Estouteville by name, whose primary mission was to restore peace between all Christian princes. Not without anxiety did the Pope see the Turks threatening Constantinople, and his object was to bring about a closing of ranks in Christendom so that some new enterprise might be attempted in the East.

Guillaume d'Estouteville was the brother of that Louis d'Estouteville who had successfully defended Mont Saint-Michel from 1425 until the liberation of Normandy. There can be no doubt as to what his personal feelings were. He was the first legate sent to France after the long series of disturbances and quarrels which had enfeebled the papacy, and he was coming into a realm which was itself in the process of being re-established. Shortly after his arrival (August 13, 1451) Dunois, conducting operations in Guyenne, the last English bastion in France, entered Bordeaux on June 30th and by August 25th had taken Bayonne. Not the least important for him of the matters which were pending between France and the papacy was that of Joan of Arc's trial.

For the business stood thus: the enquiry initiated by the King the year before had established, indeed, that she had been destroyed by the hatred of her political enemies. But since they had been clever enough to make the Church try her, her cause remained a matter for the Church and, officially, she was still a heretic condemned as such. Her trial had been conducted by an Inquisition Court; only the Inquisition could annul it.

Guillaume d'Estouteville had an interview with the King at Tours in February 1452. Two months later he made his way to

Rouen, and it is probable that he was already in possession of the facts which had emerged from Guillaume Bouillé's enquiry.

In Rouen, struggling to rise out of the decline in which the horrors it had had to endure had left it (the population had fallen during the Occupation from 14,992 to 5,976), he must himself have heard memories of *la bonne Lorraine* as they called Joan, recalled by eye-witnesses of her trials and death. He put himself in touch with the Inquisitor-General of France, the recently appointed Dominican Jean Bréhal, a Norman like himself. And Bréhal took Joan's cause in hand and carried it through to a satisfactory conclusion.

The impetus given to the business by d'Estouteville and Bréhal resulted in the opening of the first official enquiry into the matter of Joan the Maid on May 2nd. The earlier enquiry, although it was carried out under the orders of the King of France, had no official standing in the eyes of the Church and the Inquisition courts; but its results were studied and they were embodied in the file of the Rehabilitation proceedings. The record of the Trial of Condemnation was carefully studied by the two prelates, who called to their aid two jurists who were members of the legate's suite, Paul Pontanus and Theodore de Leliis. On the foundation of that study they drew up an interrogatory designed to be used in examining the witnesses who would appear before the commissioners in charge of the official enquiry.

The first witnesses were called for May 2nd: but within two days their answers had raised such a host of new questions, that a second questionnaire, much more thorough than the first and comprising twenty-seven questions, was drawn up. This was used as the basis for the whole of the rehabilitation proceedings, which were resumed on May 8th. (The text of both lists of questions is to be found in R.277–282.) On the whole, the questions asked bore chiefly on the fundamental flaws of the first trial: the partiality of the judges; the hatred which the English seemed to have had for Joan; the want of liberty which this entailed on the judges and assessors; what pressures had been applied. Also examined were errors of form: the fact that Joan had been held in a lay prison while under trial by an ecclesiastical court; the want of an advocate, which was contrary to the law; the methods employed to embarrass her in the capital matter of rebellion against the Church; the way in which the interrogations were conducted. Finally, the proceedings tried to throw light on the question of Joan's innocence and piety or otherwise, on the causes of her relapse, her attitude in her last moments, and so forth.

Some of the witnesses who appeared in this new ecclesiastical enquiry had already been questioned by order of the King, such as Manchon, Ladvenu and Isambart de la Pierre; others were being questioned for the first time, such as Pierre Miget, one of the assessors in her first trial, and Pierre Cusquel who, as a mason in the public works department of Rouen Castle, had the *entrée* to Joan's prison. After May 8th most of the old assessors who were still alive were examined, among them being Nicolas Caval, who had been the executor of Pierre Cauchon's last will and testament, Andre Marguerie, Richard du Grouchet, Jean Fabri, Guillaume du Desert, and some others who had expressed a wish to testify although they had taken no effective part in the trial, such as Jean Fave, Jean Riquier, Thomas Marie and above all the famous "resistance leader" Nicholas de Houppeville. Most of the other participants in the Trial of Condemnation were dead; both Couchon and Loiseleur had died suddenly in 1442, the latter in Basle. The promoter, Jean d'Estivet, had been found drowned in a drain. As for the vice-Inquisitor, Jean Lemaitre, was he dead or alive? We have no means of knowing, but there exists no further trace of his existence after 1452. Nicolas Midy, who had preached the last sermon to Joan in the Old Market, had died of leprosy ten years ago.

On May 22nd Guillaume d'Estouteville officially notified the King that the enquiry was finished. A few days later, acting in his capacity as legate of the Holy See, he granted indulgences to all who should walk in the procession and be present at the ceremonies of May 8th; which can only mean that already, in June 1452, he was fully convinced of Joan's innocence and the injustice of her condemnation.

At about the same time Jean Bréhal and Guillaume Bouillé were passing through Orleans. They were received with eager respect by the municipality and entertained to a *vin d'honneur*. Finally, during the first days of July, d'Estouteville was received by the King at his castle of Mehun-sur-Yevre, and communicated to him the conclusions he had reached during the ecclesiastical enquiry. The rehabilitation cause thereafter entered upon a new phase, juridical and theological in character; it was a question of collecting opinions from specialists in canon law on the whole business. For their convenience Jean Bréhal drew up a *résumé*, known as the *Summarium*, which, taking each principal charge in turn, grouped the answers from the trial record each under its appropriate head. Each doctor then had to answer the following question: given these answers, would you have reached the same conclusion as did the judges at Rouen? These consultations alone compose a stout volume, which bears witness to the fact that every canonist and theologian of importance in the realm, and one or two outside the kingdom (e.g., Leonard von Brixenthal of Vienna University), had been asked to give an opinion. Among them, and apart from the two Roman jurisconsults already mentioned, were Robert Ciboule, former rector of the University and chancellor of Notre-Dame of Paris; Elie de Bourdelles, Bishop of Périgueux; Thomas Basin, the famous Bishop of Lisieux who was later to write the life of Charles VII; Martin Berruyer, Bishop of Le Mans, and Jean Bochard, Bishop of Avranches.

D'Estouteville returned to Rome at the end of 1452; in April of the following year he was made Archbishop of Rouen, an appointment which seemed likely to quicken the rehabilitation proceedings again.

The year 1453 was to be rich in military events; for much amazement was caused when, in October 1452, Talbot, the aged Talbot whom Joan had once taken prisoner at Patay, disembarked in Guyenne—he was then 81 years of age—and was received with eager respect by the inhabitants of Bordeaux while the French seneschal, Olivier de Coetivy, was seized and imprisoned by them. This was the outcome of a plot hatched by the burgesses of Bordeaux and its neighbourhood whose income was chiefly derived from the large sale of wines of Guyenne in England; the restoration of French government had impoverished them. And during the first months of 1453 it looked very much as if Guyenne and Gascony, detaching themselves from France, were returning under the aegis of England. However on July 17th the battle of Castillon decided matters otherwise: Talbot was killed and Bordeaux forced to submit.

Meanwhile things were happening in the East; on the morning of May 29, 1453, Constantinople fell to the Turks. The last of the Byzantine emperors, Constantine Paleologus, was found among the dead and his embalmed head was to be sent to all the principal towns of the Ottoman empire as a sign of the victory of their sultan, Mahomet II who, standing on the altar in Saint Sophia, himself transformed that venerable Christian basilica into a mosque. The pope was more than ever anxious to urge upon the Christian princes the necessity of uniting to take some action in the East. The answers he received were evasive, or even fantastic, like the promise made by Philippe the Good in the middle of a luxurious banquet— to go on a Crusade. In the event the advance of the Turks was not

to be checked until they were at the walls of Vienna, and after they
had committed appalling ravages in Hungary.

Was it because of these events that the rehabilitation proceedings
seemed to be suspended? At all events, it does not appear that
Charles VII's victory in Guyenne did anything to hurry things up;
on the contrary, a whole year passed without providing us with
anything new in the matter.

In 1454 we note that Jean Bréhal made a journey to Rome "to
go to our Holy Father the Pope touching the trial of the late Joan
the Maid". It was doubtless on this occasion that there was delivered
to the pope a supplication from Joan's family that a Trial of
Rehabilitation be initiated. Only the pope could authorise the
opening of such a trial, since there was no appeal from decisions of
the Inquisition. One of the canonists consulted, Jean de Montigny
of the University of Paris, had given it as his opinion that Joan's
family were best qualified to act as plaintiffs or appellants (*se porter
partie civile*):

"Although many persons could be the plaintiffs, as all those
whom the thing concerns could be so considered (or 'must be
included'), and the thing concerns many persons in general and in
particular . . . it seems to us that the near relatives of the deceased
Maid must have an advantage over the others and ought to be
admitted to this trial (ought to be granted the right to proceed)
as prosecuting (bring suit) for the injury done to one of their
family in the murder (killing) and lamentable smothering (stifling)
of the said Maid."

Of Joan's family the only survivors were her mother, Isabelle
Romée, who lived as a pensioner of the city of Orleans; and her
two brothers, Pierre and Jean. It was therefore in their name that
the proceedings were to be initiated. Meanwhile the pope, Nicolas
V, died. His successor, Calixtus III, had not been two months on
the papal throne when he delivered a rescript which, dated June 11,
1455, authorised Isabelle Romée and her sons to demand the rehabilitation of Joan the Maid. This rescript designated three commissioners who were to "cause to be delivered a just sentence
without appeal" (lit. "in last resort"). They were Jean Jouvenel
des Ursins, Archbishop of Rheims; Guillaume Chartier, Bishop of
Paris, and Richard Olivier, Bishop of Coutances.

On November 7th Isabelle Romée, assisted by her sons (but the
final record mentions only Pierre), went in person to present the
papal rescript to the commissioners, in the nave of Notre-Dame of

Paris, Jean Bréhal, the Inquisitor, being also present. It was a very moving audience, for the old countrywoman was escorted by a whole group of people from Orleans who joined their plaint to hers, and soon the nave of the cathedral was so crammed with people, and there was such a tumult, that the commissioners were obliged to take refuge in the sacristy, taking Isabelle and her immediate escort with them. And we may share the feeling of the crowd at the reading of the old woman's request, as it is set down in the record:

"I had a daughter born in lawful wedlock, whom I had furnished worthily with the sacraments of baptism and confirmation and had reared in the fear of God and respect for the tradition of the Church, as far as her age and the simplicity of her condition allowed, in such sort that having grown up amid fields and pastures she was much in the church and received every month, after due confession, the sacrament of the Eucharist, despite her youth, and gave herself up to fasts and orisons with great devotion and fervour, for the wants at that time were so great which the people suffered and which she compassionated with all her heart; yet although she did never think, conceive or do anything whatever which set her out of the path of the faith, or spoke against it, certain enemies . . . had her arraigned in religious trial . . . and . . . despite her disclaimers and appeals, both tacit and expressed, and without any succour given to her innocence, in a trial perfidious, violent, iniquitous and without shadow of right . . . did they condemn her in a fashion damnable and criminal, and put her to death very cruelly by fire . . . for the damnation of their souls and in notorious, infamous and irreparable damage done to me, Isabelle, and mine. . . ." (Q. ii, 82)

It was the real trial of Joan of Arc which was beginning there in the sanctuary of Notre-Dame, more charged with history than any other on the soil of France. In it were to appear the majority of those who had known her, peasants of Domremy, comrades in arms, princes of the blood royal, prelates of the Church, each with his own particular emphasis and personal memories. It is true that, after a lapse of twenty-five years, those memories must often be faded or defaced; certain, too, that failures of the memory would be numerous among the former assessors at the Trial of Condemnation who, obviously, while they were being questioned at the Trial of Rehabilitation must wish themselves elsewhere. Such, for example, was to be the case of André Marguerie, Nicolas Caval, Thomas de Courcelles, declaring that they could not remember and besides had taken but a very minor part in the proceedings, and so forth. It remains nevertheless true that, from the whole body of the evidence, emerges a portrait of Joan which bears comparison with the Joan we know from her own words, words which the Trial of Condemnation at least has the merit of having handed down to us. And the rehabilitation was carried on in an atmosphere of peace restored; of unquestionable freedom, too—Charles VII had granted "letters of abolition" thereby deserving credit for showing himself clement in victory. Thus we may almost feel surprise when, in the course of the preliminary royal enquiry, we see certain witnesses, and among them the most thoroughly compromised, for example Jean Beaupère, persisting in their original attitude, and being thereafter permitted to withdraw with impunity. No doubt there were, especially among the witnesses from Rouen, a certain number of opportunists—men like Jean Marcel, a merchant of that town and a notorious "collaborator", whose sole purpose in volunteering to bear witness seems to have been to whitewash himself. But overall there is, in the depositions, both a general agreement in essentials and enough individual differences due to age, condition and personal character, to carry conviction.

To represent them at the trial Joan's family chose as advocate Pierre Maugier, and various procurators, the chief of these being Guillaume Prevosteau, councillor of the Exchequer. One reason for this was that the court was to move from place to place, so as to carry on its work in every place where important information about Joan was to be had; and obviously the family could not follow it about everywhere. The first session was held in Paris, at the bishopric, on November 17th, a solemn session attended by the three pontifical commissioners, the Inquisitor, and numerous prelates. The two clerks designated to keep the record, Denis Lecomte and François Ferrebouc, began their duties on this occasion.

From Paris the court moved to Rouen where everybody involved was required to appear between December 12th and 20th. As was usual in the case of Inquisition or Officiality causes, proclamations were made by means of publicly displayed notices, and by their being "cried" in the streets. It was during the most important of these sessions, December 12th, held in the great hall of the archiepiscopal palace, that Guillaume Manchon delivered over to the court all the documents which he still retained, including the famous notula, the French Minute, of which it is possible that the MS. now preserved at Orleans may be a copy, as likewise the so-called "Urfé" MS. in the Bibliothèque Nationale. It was also in the course of this session that a promoter* was appointed—Master Simon Chapitault. Most of the witnesses who had already appeared in the preliminary enquiries were called, and in the course of these sessions, notably that of December 17th, which was almost wholly devoted to the examination of Guillaume Manchon, it was the Trial of Condemnation which was on trial and the flaws in it revealed. The fact that the twelve articles of accusation, the effective indictment, were never read to Joan, and the substitution of the *cédule* of abjuration for another, were what particularly impressed the court. And at the conclusion of this session Simon Chapitault was able to deliver an indictment (*réquisitoire*) in which he declared that the Trial of Condemnation had been "vitiated" in both substance and form.

A series of particularly moving interrogatories was that which took place at Domremy and Vaucouleurs. The sessions began on January 28, 1456, in the presbytery of the little church at Domremy. As is still the custom of Officiality courts to-day, local worthies had been designated to compose the court, and given the list of questions to be asked. In this case the substitute pontifical commissioners were the dean of the church of Notre Dame of Vaucouleurs, Master Reginald Chichery; and a canon of Toul cathedral, Wautrin Thierry. But, of course, the promoter Simon Chapitault had come from Paris to be present. The sessions ended on February 11th after, in default of Baudricourt who was dead, Jean de Metz and Bertrand de Poulengy, the knights who had escorted Joan, had been heard. On February 16th sessions were resumed in Rouen and two inquiries were ordered, one at Orleans and the other in Paris where depositions had already been taken between January 10th and 15th: these included those of Thomas de Courcelles and of Cauchon's devoted friend Jean de Mailly, Bishop of Noyon.

In Orleans as in Domremy, popular feeling was manifest: numerous were the ordinary, the "little" people who passed before the commissioners between February 22nd and March 16th, 1456; and in their evidence is apparent that enthusiasm for the heroine which also marks the depositions, taken in Paris on May 12th, of great noblemen like Dunois and Alençon.

One witness of the first importance, Jean d'Aulon, Joan's faithful intendant, would have been left out if the archbishop of Rheims had not written to ask him at least to send his deposition in writing. Jean d'Aulon had become seneschal of Beaucaire; rather than fetch him to Paris he was invited to say what he knew before the Lyon

---

* He fulfilled the functions of Public Prosecutor (*Ministère public*).

Officiality. His deposition was forwarded in French whereas all the others were translated into Latin by the clerks as they wrote. It was the last in date, May 20, 1456, and meanwhile hearings had been resumed in Rouen on May 10th to finish on the 14th.

On May 30th a new hearing opened, but this was simply a formality: contradictors—people who might wish to speak against the rehabilitation—were called upon to appear. None did; and on June 2nd the evidence collected in the course of the enquiries was declared officially accepted by the court. At last, on June 10th, after a final assignation, all the documents in the case were placed in the hands of the Inquisitor Jean Bréhal, who, having returned to Paris, drew up that over-all summary of the case which is known as the *Recollectio*. Point by point the charges brought against Joan twenty-five years before were refuted from the evidence in hand, by a detailed and careful comparison between the answers Joan had given in the first trial, and the material obtained during the enquiries connected with the new trial. The work was very thoroughly done and thereafter nothing was left of the heresy charge.

During the month of June the Commissioners devoted themselves to a study of all the documents and of the *Recollectio*. Once again, on the 24th of the month, notices were fixed to the doors of all the churches in Rouen calling upon objectors to the rehabilitation to come forward and say what they knew; but nobody came forward. On July 2nd, in solemn session, the promoter, Simon Chapitault, then Guillaume Prevosteau on behalf of Joan's family, appeared to implore the judges to pronounce, in the name of the Holy See, Joan's rehabilitation.

On July 7, 1456, at nine o'clock in the morning, the three pontifical commissioners took their places in the great hall of the archiepiscopal palace of Rouen; with them were the Archbishop of Rheims, the Bishop of Paris, the Bishop of Coutances, and the Inquisitor Jean Bréhal. Prominent among the crowd in the body of the court, seated on the front bench, was the promoter Simon Chapitault; and, standing at the bar of the court, Jean d'Arc, who was called Petit-Jean and also Jean du Lys, beside him being his advocate Pierre Maugier and the procurator Guillaume Prevosteau. Among those present was one who had supported Joan in her last moments, Martin Ladvenu; but Isambart de la Pierre was not there, he had died.

A solemn ceremony; but, as has been pointed out, a wholly juridical one. After the customary preliminaries and formalities,

the Archbishop of Rheims, acting as president of the court, read
aloud the following document:

"In consideration of the request of the d'Arc family against the
Bishop of Beauvais, the promoter of criminal proceedings, and
the inquisitor of Rouen . . . in consideration of the informations
. . . and juridical consultations . . . in consideration of the facts, in
consideration of the defamatory (or dishonourable) articles. . . .
We, in session of our court and having God only before our eyes,
say, pronounce, decree and declare that the said trial and sentence
(of condemnation) being tainted with fraud (*dolus malus*), calumny,
iniquity, contradiction and manifest errors of fact and of law,
including the abjuration, execution and all their consequences, to
have been and to be null, invalid, worthless, without effect and
annihilated. . . . We break and annul them and declare that they must
be destroyed (lit. *lacerated*). . . . In consideration of Joan's appeal
to the Holy See . . . in consideration of the threats of torture . . .
We proclaim that Joan did not contract any taint of infamy and that
she shall be and is washed clean of such and, if need be, we wash
her clean of such absolutely. . . ."

One of the original copies of the articles of accusation was then
symbolically torn-up ("*lacerated*"); the whole court and assembly
then moved to the cemetery of Saint-Ouen where the "abjuration"
had taken place, and the verdict just given was repeated. On the
following day this was done yet again, this time at the Old Market,
where there also took place a solemn preaching and the erection
of a cross "in perpetual memory and that prayer for the salvation
of her soul and those of the other dead be here offered up".

The Rehabilitation of Joan of Arc was celebrated in many towns
throughout France, among them being, needless to say, Orleans,
where, on July 27th, celebrations were presided over by Jean
Bréhal and Guillaume Bouillé. The municipality spread itself and
gave them a grand banquet for which were purchased "ten pints
and chopines of wine . . . twelve chickens, two rabbits, twelve
pigeons, two leverets . . . etc." And it is pleasant to imagine Isabelle
Romée in the midst of that friendly crowd: long dishonoured by
the taint of infamy which the enemy had succeeded in inflicting
upon her, the true countenance of her daughter had at last
been restored to her: she was free to die now. And tradition has it
that she died in the little village of Sandillon, near Orleans, on
November 28, 1458.

COMMENTARY

It has often been regretted that Joan, a girl full of life and sap, should be known to us only and paradoxically in lawyer's jargon. We confess that we do not share this regret. In a case which is so very out of the ordinary—for everything from herself to the least detail of her history is exceptional—it is well, on the contrary, that the documents which are our sources should be as strictly factual as possible; that is why it seems to us that even contemporary chronicles should give way to the records of the trials; and why we hope against hope that one day the first "trial"—her examination at Poitiers—will turn up. The dryness of juridical forms and the bareness of the direct evidence unadorned by literary graces, all recorded on the pages of a register, each page authenticated by the notary's signature—all this is, for the historian and his reader, a sort of retrospective guarantee. No historian could possibly have the same measure of confidence in a chronicle—in which the facts are invariably seen through the deforming prism of the author's ideas, temperament and point of view—as he can have in a sworn affidavit.

And this point is brought out in all its importance in the actual scene of the Rehabilitation: it was Father Doncoeur who first drew attention to absence of feeling, the true legal dryness, of that ceremony. Not one act or word but was a juridical act or a juridical word. You may study the judgment in vain for a single term which even suggests praise. Certain commissioners were appointed to answer a question: Was Joan, or was she not, a heretic? They answer: No. And that is all. The verdict is negative: the Church confines itself to disavowing a judgment formerly handed down by an ecclesiastical court of judges who judged ill. Certain historians have tried to see in this rehabilitation scene the beginning of the Joan of Arc "legend", by which she is supposed to have been artificially aggrandized and prepared for the admiration of the mob. All this proves is that they never bothered to read the documents. Whereas, if one does go to the actual documents, being in the habit of hearing Joan made the subject of extravagant panygyric pronounced by politicians as well as prelates, one is curiously disappointed. One seeks for the moment of feeling and fails to discover it. Only at the very beginning of the proceedings do we find a moment of feeling in the record, on the day when Isabelle

Romée made her petition in Notre-Dame; but that derived from the drama inherent in the old countrywoman's cry for justice, and had no place in the trial itself.

We thought it as well to report one by one the stages of Joan's rehabilitation because, dry though the reading must be, it is necessary to an understanding of the care and earnestness with, which the business was conducted. Too often, as we have said, even historians have failed to recognize this. It is well worth while taking the trouble to realise that, taking account of the first royal enquiry set on foot to "learn the truth" about Joan's condemnation, the proceedings were spread over seven years, that they involved the setting up of a royal commission and an ecclesiastical court, that two popes took a hand in it, that one hundred and fifteen witnesses were called to give evidence, some of them as many as four times. A bogus trial on that scale is simply not conceivable.

We have seen how the court of rehabilitation heard evidence in most of the towns where Joan had lived, including the places where she had spent her childhood, those where her prowess were performed, and the places of her agony and death. The procedure on these occasions was exactly the same as for any other trial: there was a clerk who kept a minute of what was said and done as the evidence was heard, his notes were put into Latin, and the record of each session drawn up. Three copies of all these notes were re-copied into registers—three copies of the whole *dossier* in fact—each page bearing the signature of both the notaries present at all the hearings, Denis Lecomte and François Ferrebouc. These registers were enormous, for apart from the record of the trial itself which was held in 1455–56, comprising records of sessions, questions asked of witnesses and their depositions, the notaries also copied all procedural papers into these files, for example counsels' opinions from jurists and all the canonical enquiry conducted by Cardinal d'Estouteville in 1452. Some idea of the sheer bulk of the whole can be gathered from the fact that the two volumes of Quicherat's edition comprise 855 pages of small, close print; but he did not include all the counsels' opinions (*consultations juridiques*) and theological opinions which make another two fat volumes in Lanéry d'Arc's edition of 1889; and he also left out all Bréhal's work, the *Summarium* and the *Recollectio*, which were published in 1893 by Fathers Belon and Balme. To all this must be added the fact that the MSS. of the rehabilitation proceedings do not include the first, royal enquiry, nor the memorandum drawn up by

Guillaume Bouillé, which was recopied separately. (The so-called De Soubise MS., No. 1613 in the Bibliothèque of the town of Orleans; and the Urfé MSS. in Bib. Nat. *fonds latin* 8838.)

The three authenticated copies of the rehabilitation proceedings have been preserved intact. Two are in the Bibliothèque Nationale, *fonds latin* in 17013 and 5970. The third copy is, oddly enough, in England, at the *British Museum*, MS. Stowe 84.

For a more complete description of the different MSS. and their contents the reader should consult Pierre Champion's *Notice de Manuscrits des procès de rehabilitation*, Paris, 1930. In order to read the original Latin text we still have nothing better than Quicherat's edition and the two works, Lanéry d'Arc's and that of Belon and Balme, already mentioned. But a new edition is in hand. And we already have a recent edition of the royal enquiry (*enquête civile*), published on the occasion of the fifth centenary of the rehabilitation. This is *L'enquête ordonnée par Charles VII en 1450 et le codicille de Guillaume Bouillé* (Paris, 1956, Librairie d' Argences), by P. Doncoeur and Y. Lanhers. It is in a series entitled *Documents et recherches relatifs à Jeanne la Pucelle* which already comprised an edition of the *Minute française des interrogatoires de Jeanne* and an edition of *L'instrument des sentences portés par Pierre Cauchon et Jean Lemaitre contre Jeanne la Pucelle.*

The methodical work of the Société de l'Histoire de France will soon provide us with a new edition of the rehabilitation proceedings. This will be of the original Latin text as explained above. But several French translations are available: Eugene O'Reilly, *Les deux procès de condamnation, les enquêtes, et la sentence de réhabilitation de Jeanne d'Arc*. Paris 1868, 2 vols.

Joseph Fabre, *Procès de réhabilitation de Jeanne d'Arc raconté et écrit d'après les textes officiels latins*. Paris 1888. A second edition in 1912.

Régine Pernoud, *Vie et mort de Jeanne d'Arc, les témoignages du procès de réhabilitation, 1450–56*. Paris, Hachette, 1953. This is a translation into French of depositions in the rehabilitation proceedings.

Finally, an analysis of the trial with extracts from the evidence is to be found in a work published by the *Club du meilleur livre* in 1954. And a very complete study of the circumstances of the rehabilitation and the drafting of the record of the proceedings is available in a work published in 1956 under the auspices of the *Comité national de Jeanne d'Arc, Mémorial du Ve centenaire de la réhabilitation de Jeanne d'Arc, 1456–1956.*

Readers may like to be reminded here, by way of rounding off the story, that Joan was beatified on April 18, 1909, and canonised on May 9, 1920. July 10th, Joan's Feast day, was declared a national holiday.

A final word should be said touching the mistakes persisted in by the partisans of the theory that Joan was a bastard of the house of Orleans. Their method consists in setting aside the mass of the documents which destroy their theory while extracting from the same texts here a line and there a detail to which they give importance to the exclusion of everything else. Thus, for example, in the case of the rehabilitation proceedings they ignore all the depositions with a single exception. This, to put it mildly, is very curious, for it is difficult to see how, if the totality be false, one element in it could be more exact and truthful than all the rest.

In this case the choice of detail upon which to make their case is doubly unfortunate, for it is only by retaining a mistranslation that this detail can be made to mean what they want it to mean. The point in question is from the deposition of the notary Guillaume Colles, called Boisguillaume, who, speaking of the examination into Joan's virginity carried out at Rouen under the direction of the Duchess of Bedford, adds:

". . . et quod dux Bedfordie erat in quodam loco secreto ubi videbat eandem Johannem visitari."

The meaning of this is perfectly clear: "And that the Duke of Bedford was in a secret place where he saw Joan examined (more literally: "Joan to be examined (or visited)"). From this partisans of the bastardy theory contrive to deduce that the Duke of Bedford was in the habit of paying visits to Joan by means of an underground passage from his dwelling to the prison. In this connection we will quote from the article by Maitre Maurice Garçon to which we have already referred: "One stands astounded: *loco secreto* has never meant an underground passage; *ubi* is an adverb of place exclusive of movement which has not the meaning of either *quo* nor of *unde*; *videbat* is not *solebat* and *visitari* is a passive infinitive."

As it happens archaeology confirms the correct translation. For—the contrary has been maintained but without the production of a scintilla of evidence—Rouen Castle has twice been the object of very thorough archaeological investigation, diggings which have not revealed the existence of any such passage. An account of the results of these digs, which were carried out by F. Bouquet and subsequently by Commandant Quenedey, is in the latter's book, *La prison de Jeanne d'Arc à Rouen*, Paris, 1923. (See also the proceedings of the *Congrès archaeologique de Rouen*, 1926.)

One writer on the subject refers us to the *Journal de Pierre Cusquel*, according to which, he tells us, Joan escaped from Rouen Castle. He will have to try again, for there is no such *Journal*. All we have of Cusquel are his depositions in the Trial of Rehabilitation; and in these he does not say that Joan escaped; he tells, three times, how she was burned.

CONCLUSION*

We have tried in this work to lay before the reader, as faithfully as possible, the case of Joan of Arc, letting the contemporary records speak for themselves after they had been duly checked and passed through the sieve of historical criticism, and to the actual words of which anyone is, nowadays, at liberty to refer, since translations are accessible and reliable. And we urge the interested reader to read those documents for himself because, limited by the dimensions of the present work, we have given only extracts from them. And while these suffice perhaps to enable the reader to follow Joan's history, they are inadequate when it comes to the question of really getting to know her as she was. Everyone should at least have read the Trial of Condemnation, one of the most beautiful texts in the French language. It is shocking to reflect that at the present time nothing of this text is to be found in those "selected passages" of our literature which are offered to school-children.

Does this mean to say that henceforth everything is clear in the case of Joan of Arc? No: everything is not clear, and the historian owes it to himself to be the first to recognize the fact. Among the events which he expounds are some for which no rational explanation is forthcoming, and the conscientious historian stops short at that point. His part consists in recounting the facts, in sorting the true from the false in the material set before him, in retracing the course of events and the careers of the people concerned in so far as reliable documents enable him to do so; the rest is conjecture, and in

---

* This is addressed to the French reader but may be of interest to English students of the period and of language.

that field the historian is no better qualified, on the whole, than his readers.

In the case of Joan of Arc, particularly, there has too often been a singular confusion between the expounding of the facts and explaining them. We are confronted by facts whose extraordinary character is self-evident. The desire to explain them is all the keener and everyone proceeds to do so, each putting forward his own explanation. Nothing, one might think, could be fairer than that. Joan herself had her own explanation of the events in which she was the protagonist: "All that I have done I have done at the Lord's commandment . . . I am come from God . . . But for the grace of God I could do nothing. . . . I have told you often enough that I have done nothing but by God's commandment . . . etc." But it must be obvious that from the point of view of historical criticism, an affirmation which emanates from a single witness and cannot be checked by reference to any other source, is not tantamount to a certainty. The believer can no doubt be satisfied with Joan's explanation; the unbeliever cannot.

So that we cannot but consider the attempts at an explanation which have been offered down the centuries, concerning Joan's history, to be perfectly in order. These explanations are of all sorts, and every reader is at liberty to add his own or to choose among those offered to him.

There are some, however, which appear a little too simple for our taste: when, for example, Mr. and Mrs. Butterfield tell us without a smile that Joan had tuberculosis of the brain from drinking cow's milk, and that that explains everything, the only conclusion we can possibly come to is that measures should promptly be taken to prohibit pasteurisation of milk: for clearly the risk of tuberculosis of the brain, since it is capable of producing such beneficent results for the nation, would be well worth running.

Happily, there are some explanations which are at least more logical; when the American historian Francis Leary (see *The Golden Longing*, New York, 1959) proposes to explain Joan's history by reference to spiritualism, his explanation must, no doubt, be perfectly convincing to those who share his belief in spiritualism, especially since the author gives first of all a perfectly fair account of the facts in Joan's life.

For that is the important point, and the one where too many writers on the subject fall down: in their anxiety to present an explanation of the events which constitute Joan's history, they

manipulate history. This is an inadmissible proceeding. The interpretation of events and personalities is a matter of personal conscience; but the facts, the historical facts, are a matter of documents,
of proofs received and checked by the historical method; individual
fancies have nothing whatever to do with the matter. And that is
why we consider that some of the explanations offered must be
set aside to start with; they are based on ignorance of the historical
facts. The Burgundian chronicler who makes Joan a serving wench
at an inn, was in error: it is proved that she was nothing of the sort.
When, in the sixteenth century, Girard du Haillan makes her a
prostitute, he was in error. And so are they in error who imagine
that Joan was able to escape from the stake and reappear in the
guise of the adventuress Claude des Armoises. As for the hypothesis of bastardy, it is proved that this is without foundation;
moreover, one cannot help wondering how it is supposed to "explain" her career; for, after all, the fact of being a bastard does not
necessarily enable one to win battles. By and large, it has been
this desire to explain that has muddled the data and complicated
the story. Yet that story is one of the best-established in history.
The text of the two trials, and the public and private papers which
confirm the conclusions from those texts, make Joan one of the
best-documented people in history, one of those about whom we
are really well-informed. And to reject a conclusion established
by historical method is about as sensible as casting doubt on an
algebraical formula: it cannot be done without arguments, that is to
say without documents duly established and unquestionable.

But, we repeat, the question becomes one of distinguishing
between the fact and its explanation. To establish the progression
of factual events is the historian's work; and one can no more
improvise oneself as an historian than as a nuclear scientist. But
as to the interpretation of the fact, once properly established, that
is a personal matter and each of us, historian or not, is at liberty
to draw his own conclusion.

Once this distinction has been made, it is much easier to understand why historians of every persuasion, clerical or anti-clerical,
communist or monarchist, are in complete agreement as to the actual
events of Joan's history: those events have been recounted in the
same way by Michelet, anti-clerical; by Quicherat, scholar and likewise anti-clerical; by the Catholic canon, P. H. Dunand; by Charles
Peguy, socialist both before and after his conversion; and in our
own time by Edith Thomas, communist; and by P. Doncoeur,

Jesuit. There is, in fact, one trait in common among all these writers: they are professional historians. And it would not even have occurred to any of them to deny the historical facts.

On the other hand, the very numerous works which, in our own time and in the past, have maintained the theory of bastardy, also have one trait in common: not one of their authors is an historian. And one cannot prevent oneself from finding their way of reading and understanding history somewhat suspect when one notices that all of them claim to found their case on "new" or "newly discovered" documents, and that the said documents turn out to be invariably and eternally the same old ones. The marriage contract of Robert des Armoises, for example; or, worse if anything, "documents" which turn out to be non-existent, like the one which lists the four hundred witches to be burned at the time of Joan's execution.

History has nothing in common with such fancies, and Joan of Arc's history less than nothing. How very much we prefer to these clumsy fumblings the remark made by Robert Bresson, the first French film-producer to devote a film to the history of Joan of Arc: asked whether his work would offer an "explanation" of the heroine, he replied: "One does not explain greatness, one tries to attune oneself to it." One might easily pour out torrents of ink in trying to explain Joan, futilely, and without having understood in the least what kind of person she was. Quite otherwise has been the attitude of the people of France since the fifteenth century: the people, feeling that, confronted with Joan, the wisest plan was to admire her, in admiring have understood her. They canonised Joan and made her their heroine, while Church and State were taking five hundred years to reach the same conclusion.

It remains true that, for us, Joan is above all the saint of reconciliation—the one whom, whatever be our personal convictions, we admire and love because, over-riding all partisan points of view, each one of us can find in himself a reason to love her.

INDEX